Leisure, Voluntary Action and Social Change in Britain, 1880–1939

Leisure, Voluntary Action and Social Change in Britain, 1880–1939

Robert Snape

BLOOMSBURY ACADEMIC
LONDON • NEW YORK • OXFORD • NEW DELHI • SYDNEY

BLOOMSBURY ACADEMIC
Bloomsbury Publishing Plc
50 Bedford Square, London, WC1B 3DP, UK

BLOOMSBURY, BLOOMSBURY ACADEMIC and the Diana logo
are trademarks of Bloomsbury Publishing Plc

First published in Great Britain 2018
This paperback edition published 2020

A catalogue record for this book is available from the British Library.

Library of Congress Cataloging-in-Publication Data.
Names: Snape, Robert, author.
Title: Leisure, voluntary action and social change inBritain, 1880-1939 /
Robert Snape.
Description: New York : Bloomsbury Academic, [2018] |Includes
bibliographicalreferences and index.
Identifiers: LCCN 2017061320| ISBN 9781350003019(hardback) | ISBN
9781350003026(epub ebook) | ISBN 9781350003033 (PDF eBook)
Subjects: LCSH: Social change–GreatBritain–History–19th century. | Social
change–GreatBritain–History–20th century. | Leisure–Great
Britain–History. | Voluntarism–Great Britain–History.
Classification: LCC HN385 .S625 2018 | DDC 306.0941–dc23LC record available at
https://lccn.loc.gov/2017061320

ISBN: HB: 978-1-3500-0301-9
PB: 978-1-3501-3608-3
ePDF: 978-1-3500-0303-3
eBook: 978-1-3500-0302-6

Typeset by RefineCatch Limited, Bungay, Suffolk

To find out more about our authors and books visit
www.bloomsbury.com and sign up for our newsletters.

To Mary, James and Anna

Contents

List of Figures

Acknowledgements

Several individuals and institutions supported the research for this book and my thanks are owed to numerous librarians and archivists. In addition to the staff of the University of Bolton Library, those at the following institutions have helped retrieve materials over several visits: Bolton Public Library, Bolton Museum, Borthwick Institute, British Library, Co-operative Wholesale Society Archive, Greater Manchester County Record Office, Lancashire County Library, Liverpool City Libraries and Archives, Liverpool University Archive, London Metropolitan Archive, Manchester Public Library, Manchester University John Rylands Special Collections and the Working Class Movement Library in Salford.

I would like to express particular thanks to Bolton Museum for kind permission to reproduce photographs from the Humphrey Spender Worktown Collection and to Matthew Watson and Perry Bonewell for their assistance with these, and also to Liz Perry, Lisa Croft and Adrian Greenhalgh for permission and help in taking photographs of Bolton Socialist Club. Thanks also to Beatriz Lopez at Bloomsbury Publishing and to Sarah Webb and Merv Honeywood who helped with the proof-reading and production of this book.

I also wish to thank my colleagues Dr Peter Swain and Bill Luckin, Emeritus Professor of History at the University of Bolton, for their support and for comments on a draft manuscript. Thanks are also due to Professor Jeffrey Hill, Gwyndon Boardman and the Nelson Independent Labour Party and Land Society for help with information on 'Red' Nelson and the Clarion movement. Needless to say, any errors are my own.

Finally, thanks to my family for their continuing interest, patience and support.

Abbreviations

BWSF	British Workers' Sport Federation
CHA	Co-operative Holidays Association
COPEC	Conference on Christian Politics, Economy, and Citizenship
COS	Charity Organisation Society
CUKT	Carnegie United Kingdom Trust
NCSS	National Council of Social Service
NHRU	National Home Reading Union
YMCA	Young Men's Christian Association
YWCA	Young Women's Christian Association

1

Introduction

1.1 Historicizing leisure, voluntary action and social change

This book is concerned with the idea of leisure as a field of voluntary association in Great Britain between 1880 and 1939. It focuses on the historical theorization of leisure as an agent for social change in a period of rapid technological advancement, strident demand for greater democracy and the social and cultural upheaval of the First World War. Although popular leisure was largely shaped by commercial entrepreneurship throughout the period, there is an alternative and synchronous history of leisure not as an economic commodity but as a primary or social good, essential to individual and community well-being in a modernizing industrial society. It is an aim of this book to explain how and why, in this period, leisure became associated with the idea of the common good, valued for its potential capacity to realize the good society and adopted as a field for experimentation in the advocacy of social, cultural and political values. In the later nineteenth century social and philosophical interpretations of leisure became of interest to social policy makers and cultural commentators, producing a discourse of leisure and voluntarism that flourished until the Second World War but that remains largely overlooked in the historiography of both leisure and voluntary action. Although acknowledging that some aspects of leisure were socially problematic, the general tenor of this discourse was optimistic, articulating leisure as beneficial and desirable to a more harmonious and democratic society. Leisure became a feature of wider social debates on work, democracy, community, civic life and post-First World War social reconstruction, with notable contributions from figures as diverse as John Ruskin, William Morris, Samuel and Henrietta Barnett, John Brown Paton, Ebenezer Howard, Bernard Bosanquet, Robert Blatchford, John Atkinson Hobson, Bertrand Russell, William Lever, Clive Bell, R. H. Tawney and Storm Jameson. These writers were concerned not only to expose faults and fractures in contemporary society but also to propose new social and cultural frameworks in which leisure could help bring about social improvement and community well-being. Their work was influential on social theory and policy, diffused through a multiplicity of channels which included monographs and journal articles, particularly those published in the *International Journal of Ethics*, and seminars and discussion circles concerned with the social sciences. In practical terms they were of little immediate influence on state provision for leisure, which, apart from public parks, municipal libraries and museums, remained minimal for much of the period, but their ideas influenced numerous voluntary organizations and policy interventions committed to social change and an improved quality of life. Examples include the university and social settlements, the Clarion movement, Guilds of Help, Councils of Voluntary Aid and, after 1919, the National Council of Social Service.

Both leisure and voluntary action are anachronistic terms in the context of the earlier decades covered here and modern meanings of leisure and voluntary action cannot be read back into the nineteenth century.[1] The meanings and practice of social work have been noted to be historically fluid[2] and this is equally true of leisure. Consequently, one of the objects of this book is to explain how modern social meanings of leisure and voluntary action evolved in response to cultural change and social need. The term voluntary action is used in the broad sense described by Colin Rochester as volunteering by individuals and also the collective organized actions of voluntary bodies.[3] It therefore accommodates the historical constructs of charitable philanthropy, social work, voluntary aid and social service. Leisure, it will be argued, is a more complex concept, but for ease of reference to its historiography it is generally used to mean both the non-work time available for relaxation, entertainment or self-improvement and the activities people chose to undertake in it. However, it will be argued that the deconstruction of this normative and all-embracing understanding of leisure was crucial to the philosophical justification for its inclusion in social policy.

Since Keith Thomas' seminal work on leisure[4] in the 1960s, an extensive historiography of leisure has come into being, much of which deals with the provision and consumption of leisure since the industrial revolution. Common themes have been the regulation of working-class leisure in terms of time and activity, the reproduction of societal divisions of class and gender in leisure and the emergence of new mass forms of popular culture after the First World War.[5] All these are relevant to the current project. However, the questions this book aims to address are not primarily concerned with the socially problematic aspects of leisure, though these will not be ignored, but the ways in which leisure, as a field for voluntary association, was articulated in terms of social change in the broad sense of leading to the improvement of society according to a particular set of social, religious, political or cultural ideas and values. This change was not expected by its protagonists to be revolutionary but rather to be progressively transformative in the sense, outlined by Maeve Cooke, in which obstacles to social improvement are seen to be contingent and thus replaceable by enabling conditions.[6] In modern terms this implies critical social theory but, as Cooke notes, it applies to any ethical reflection leading to a critique of social arrangements in terms of their preventing human flourishing. In identifying social, cultural, economic and political barriers to the common good, critics, social policy theorists and voluntary movements were engaged in such a process of ethical evaluation and discussion. Considered in terms of the theoretical processes of gradual transformation outlined by Jennifer Todd, public debate and voluntary action through leisure contested cultural values and social practices seen as obstacles to individual and community well-being through an articulation of and experimentation in alternative forms of leisure and new values.[7] Although not all hoped-for change was achieved, neither were all interventions meaningless. It was in terms of this transformative process that leisure and voluntary action were theorized in progressive social thinking and acquired modern understandings.

Voluntary association for leisure and conviviality has been under-explored in the historiography of voluntary action in comparison with efforts to provide social relief or health care.[8] Nevertheless, it is not historically insignificant. Voluntary association and voluntary action were not mutually exclusive terms as conviviality and sociability by themselves served as vehicles for the expression of values, as for example in the temperance movement and the Clarion cycling clubs. As G.D.H. Cole noted, although friendly societies, trade unions and co-operative organizations were animated by motives different from those that informed voluntary social service they were nevertheless part of a wider understanding of service and not distinct from it.[9] The importance of voluntary association to a sustainable community has gained a high profile over recent decades through Robert Putnam's work on social capital and community vitality.[10] In historical terms Jeffrey Hill has shown how voluntary leisure associations, for example musical and dramatic societies, working men's clubs and sports teams, were crucial to the formation of an urban civic culture in the late nineteenth and early twentieth century.[11] Of particular importance to the current study are Helen Meller's seminal study of leisure as an engine of social and civic reform in Bristol between 1870 and 1914[12] and Jose Harris' analytical account of voluntarism, social welfare and social thought in the same period.[13]

Both demonstrated the importance of voluntary leisure association to civic culture and the formation of a social community. More recently Helen McCarthy has illustrated how in the inter-war period associational life was shaped by leisure through membership-based clubs and societies, which increased opportunities for social citizenship.[14] A related strand of research has focused on women's leisure as a sphere of emancipation and political empowerment; Caitriona Beaumont, for example, has explained how the Young Women's Christian Association and Women's Institutes not only provided opportunities for sociability and conviviality but also enabled women to take a greater part in public life;[15] McCarthy too has noted the importance of Women's Institutes to women's active participation in civic work.[16] Narratives of a decline in voluntarism after the First World War have thus been challenged by historical accounts of a dynamic and changing field of associational life of increasing importance to civic identity and one to which leisure was crucial.[17]

This study goes beyond the period covered by Harris and Meller to explore how, through differing phases of social reform between 1880 and 1939, voluntary leisure associations expressed values and behaviours that reflected the social and cultural characteristics of ideal social communities imagined by reformers. Although leisure activities are chosen and enjoyed individually, there are few forms of leisure that are not in some ways collective undertakings in which voluntary association and social intercourse are important and desirable. Much voluntary leisure association lies outside the field of organized voluntary action while nevertheless fulfilling social objectives. It is possible therefore to distinguish between leisure associations formed solely for the benefit of their members and those with ulterior social objects. Hobby societies, gardening clubs and sports clubs, for example, are collective groups formed around a particular leisure interest to enable shared enjoyment, increased knowledge and expertise and social intercourse. As expressive associations, they have no consciously adopted instrumental objects but have served historically important sociological functions in enabling social integration and a sense of community.[18] Instrumental voluntary associations, in contrast, aim to produce something of value to others rather than for the specific benefit of their members. In many cases the intended benefit has been societal; historical examples include the National Anti-Gambling League, formed in 1890 to reduce poverty by preventing people falling into debt through betting and the Young Women's Christian Association's promotion of Christian values in everyday life through leisure activity.

Instrumental voluntary associations are central to this study. Between the middle of the nineteenth century and the Second World War leisure was adopted by a range of secular and religious voluntary organizations as a core around which to form inter-connected social, spatial, political, cultural and work-place communities embodying and promoting values associated with an imagined society. While these leisure-based associations were often formed in response to perceived misuses of leisure, they were not simply a means of containing leisure behaviours within normative bounds but were concerned to promote alternative and sometimes contested social values and moral principles, and were thus implicitly engaged in the processes of social reform. The extent of this involvement is impossible to quantify as it often lay below the surface. For example, despite their heterogeneous aims, the National Federation of Women's Institutes, British Legion, Boy Scouts and Girl Guides all gave support to the League of Nations Union in the inter-war years.[19] Much instrumental voluntary intervention in leisure has been grounded in a deficit model; in the early nineteenth century, for example, paternalistic interventions in leisure were concerned to address the social problems of industrialization and maintain the established social order rather than to effect social change. However, from the mid-century, Christian socialism and the embryonic social sciences opened new perspectives on political, economic and social questions. As Robert Tombs observes, the period between 1880 and the First World War produced a calmer and more stable society, which enabled reforming movements and voluntary bodies to think in terms of social change and reform.[20] Reformers and social philosophers articulated imaginations of a new society defined not by materialism and social class but by ideas of democracy, equality and well-being. Several offered alternative and utopian models of society representing, as Bauman terms it, a kind of world preferable but not necessarily available.[21] A familiar example is William Morris' *News from Nowhere*[22] but more practicable alternatives included the experimental societies of garden cities, model villages and inter-war housing estates in which leisure was adopted as a field in which an associational culture and sense of community could be nurtured.

1.2 Leisure and community

The theme of community runs throughout this study. Throughout the period there was a concern that society was increasingly divided in terms of class, culture and space. Leisure was a field in which boundaries of class could be dissolved by enabling working-class people to experience middle-class culture through intermingling in public spaces, typically municipal libraries, galleries and parks. In the second half of the nineteenth century missions and church societies deployed leisure as a means of reaching into working-class communities, a technique further developed in the settlement movement's extension of middle-class friendship, through a shared leisure, to the poor of the community in which they were located. In the inter-war period the idea of community, by then conceptualized in terms of social science, formed a major policy area of the National Council of Social Service in terms of community well-being and of the village hall and new estate community centre movements.

Community is a complex concept and has been described as elusive and without specific meaning.[23] However this has not prevented its wide usage in historical discourses of leisure and voluntary action. The core meaning of community is of a group of people sharing common interests and an identity formed through social relationships and interaction.[24] Hobby groups, dramatic societies, sports clubs and similar voluntary leisure associations can thus be conceptualized as communities of leisure, bringing people together through a shared interest and enabling social networks and mutual interests to develop.[25] Leisure communities are also spatial, forming around neighbourhoods, pubs, churches, and workplaces.[26] Neither of these interpretations implies that community, as an historical concept, was synonymous with neighbourliness or that those living in a community necessarily shared a sense of belonging to it.[27] Rather, through the growth of the social sciences, the idea of community became an object of social reform and an informing principle in the historical development of voluntary action through leisure.

The work of Robert MacIver and Amitai Etzioni offers useful perspectives on the historical relationships between community, leisure association and voluntary action. MacIver, a sociologist and political theorist, published his monograph *Community*[28] in 1917 as First World War reconstruction raised questions about post-war social renewal, bringing community well-being into social policy debate. To MacIver social progress depended on a functional community and in the opinion of a contemporary reviewer *Community* was one of the most important sociology books of the decade.[29] Community, as MacIver stated, was the object rather than the subject of social science. Sub-titled as a sociological study, the book marked a shift from the quantitative methods of natural science to a discursive interpretation of social relationships and social institutions; the former being activities or the 'threads of life' and the latter the loom on which these threads were woven into a cloth.[30] A community was any area of common life within which there existed associations, not simply aggregations but purposeful organizations of men and women formed for the pursuit of some common interest. Associations were essential to the development of community, having interests and objectives that determined the nature and range of their activity. In this sense a leisure association was not a casual gathering or a crowd but a social collective with a sense of itself as an association and a shared purpose, or interest. It is of note that MacIver identified associations of conviviality and camaraderie such as clubs and societies formed around art, music, literature and drama, to be important to the socialization of individuals into the community.[31] Associations could however have competing or conflicting interests. Working men's clubs and gentlemen's clubs, for example, were leisure associations that catered for a shared interest of male sociability and conviviality but served different interests in terms of social class solidarity. The final point to note from MacIver is his emphasis on the ethical nature of the good society and its values.[32] Through MacIver, associational leisure can be interpreted in terms of community and the interests of a leisure association theorized as harmonizing or conflicting with those of other associations and the dominant interests and values of wider society.

Much voluntary action was geared to social improvement; as William Beveridge commented, whether conducted through charitable philanthropy, social work or social service, its unifying feature was private action for social advance that was not subject to the authority of the state.[33] Social advance implies the idea of social change and the good community. It was noted above that social change is gradual rather than immediate. Amitai Etzioni, an authority on the social theory of community, argues a useful model through which to evaluate voluntary action through leisure, noting that a community is not just a social entity formed by affective bonds but one in which members share a set of shared values, or a moral culture.[34] Etzioni sees society itself as a form of community, a good society being one committed to ethical values, norms and identities acquired through cultural practice. These values are derived and accepted through what he terms as a process of moral dialogue. For new or changed values to gain social recognition they must be widely embraced and, as Etzioni notes, a good society requires moral dialogues to determine the values that constitute the shared cultures of its communities. His emphasis on the role of cultural practice links his model directly to leisure and voluntarism. As Nick Stevenson has noted, ideas of the good society have emerged through cultural citizenship and democratic debate and deliberation,[35] a process that seems close to that of a moral dialogue. Following Gerard Delanty's interpretation of modernity as an encounter between the cultural and institutional models of society, cultural practice – including leisure – becomes a process of reflection and cognitive self-interpretation that can lead to the transformation of the institutional order of social, economic and political structures.[36] Voluntary action through leisure can thus be read as one element of an historical moral dialogue through which cultural values and practices were promoted and debated in terms of a better society. The critical question was of course what was meant by a better society, a concept always contested and historically evolving in response to a continuously changing contemporary social order and dominant culture.

Moral and ethical considerations have been important to historical concepts of the right use of leisure, reflecting contemporaneous social ideals and values and influencing socially instrumental interventions in leisure. The nineteenth century saw a sustained evangelical effort to replace perceived immoral forms of leisure with alternative practices as middle-class reformers sought to substitute drinking and gambling with improving forms of recreation.[37] Although concepts of the right use of leisure never became fully detached from moral concerns, they were, from the final third of the century, increasingly articulated in terms of social change and citizenship. In this process leisure acquired sociological meanings. A similar turn to the social was the challenge to the personal case-work approach of the Charity Organisation Society by a model of social work that focused instead on the social community.[38] Morality remained important but increasingly in the guise of social ethics. The ethical society was a central concern of British social idealism in the late nineteenth and early twentieth centuries. Social idealist philosophy borrowed from the Greek political community of the *polis* and its emphasis on participatory citizenship.[39] Drawing from Aristotle's politics and ethics in its articulation of the good society, social idealism brought Athenian ideas of leisure and voluntarism into social policy discourse. It exercised a direct influence on the new liberalism, voluntary action and the notion of the ethical community. In the inter-war period it was a prime motivating force in the theorization of social service and leisure. Social service adopted community well-being as the primary focus of its work, building village halls and new housing estate community centres as spaces for an associational community life in which an active use of leisure would be a catalyst for the formation of a social community and social citizenship.

From the late nineteenth century socialism became a further voice in the moral dialogue of charitable philanthropy and leisure. Through Marx, and especially William Morris, leisure entered political discourse as inequalities in its distribution and its undemocratic regulation by a leisure class were interpreted as products of industrial capitalism. After the First World War labour demands for more leisure led to a gradual shortening of the working week but increased automation raised concerns about boredom and its perceived tendency to passive uses of leisure. In its religious and cultural forms, ethical socialism was a guiding principle for the Clarion and worker sport movements and also the less politically radical but equally influential Co-operative Holidays Association and rambling movement.

1.3 Leisure, voluntary action and civil society

John Garrard's observation that civil organization in Britain was not a resistance to the state but a response to its lack of ambition[40] is particularly appropriate to voluntary action and leisure. Leisure was not a major concern of the state until the later twentieth century. Prior to the First World War, government interest was largely confined to the maintenance of public order through permissive Acts; only with the Holidays with Pay Act (1938) did it recognize the validity of a need for leisure amongst the working classes.[41] The theorization and practice of voluntary action through leisure were accordingly conducted primarily within civil society rather than government. Civil society is a further contested idea.[42] Nevertheless, as Jose Harris has argued, it is a useful conceptual framework in which social institutions and practices can be appraised.[43] Discussing the structural transformation of welfare provision between 1870 and 1940 Harris drew attention to the 'mass of voluntary and local institutions' that helped form British civic culture and civil society, shaping policy and provision through dialogue and practice.[44]

Michael Edwards has identified three theoretical models of civil society as associational life, a desirable order, and a public sphere for debate on the common good.[45] These are not mutually exclusive categories but broad perspectives through which leisure and voluntary action can be evaluated in relation to social change. As a field of associational life leisure was an enabling sphere of voluntary association, distinct from the state, in which shared interests led to the formation of hobby societies, sports clubs and cultural associations. Religious and political groups formed around leisure interests also belong within this category. This type of voluntary associational culture has historically been associated with the growth of civil society and participatory democracy, enabling both the middle and the working classes to construct a civil society that, as Rodger and Colls argue, reflected their own needs and interests.[46] The urban civil society of the Victorian town, for example, involved voluntary institutions and organizations, typically temperance societies, literary and philosophical societies and church-based social organizations, in the civilizing processes of industrial society.[47] In the later nineteenth century, as Morris notes, it widened to include co-operative and political associations[48] and in the twentieth century liberal, conservative and labour clubs, all with associated leisure provisions, became common features of British urban life. Frank Prochaska has described this model as a buffer between the government and the citizenry, creating a moral environment in which civic virtues essential to social well-being may be expressed.[49]

The idea of civil society as a desirable social order is also relevant to this study. Ideas of the good society were contested and debated in social thinking, with capitalism, conservatism, liberalism, the new liberalism, Fabianism, idealism, feminism and socialism assigning different functions to both leisure and voluntary action. In this respect civil society was not a static formation but a dynamic pursuit of a good society, based upon a particular set of values and debated through a moral dialogue. Raymond Williams' observation of the necessity of cultural associations and socially democratic institutions to 'teach particular ways of feeling'[50] is highly relevant to leisure; cultural production was not historically limited to art and literature but included the wider leisure practices of what Hugh Cunningham termed as the secular leisure reformist culture found in Chartism, co-operative societies and the Left Book Club, which embraced rational change, political beliefs, mutuality and democracy.[51] Organized voluntary action was an important source of energy within civil society, not necessarily seeking change in capitalist economic production but aiming to improve social conditions and quality of life within its parameters. More radical change was advocated through socialist voluntary associations, not initially accepted into civil society, but that proposed alternative models of society through socialist clubs, worker sport organizations and associations celebrating alternative lifestyles through leisure.

Edwards' third version of civil society is that of an area for public debate on the common good and the promotion of active social citizenship. Drawing from the Greek *polis* and valuing associational life in terms of service to the community, this model gained ascendancy in the late Victorian and Edwardian period in which, as Jose Harris notes, social theory posited active citizenship and public spirit through voluntary association to be essential to a well-ordered society.[52] Young people's membership organizations such as Lads' and Girls' clubs and scout and guide associations typically had ulterior aims of creating good citizens through leisure clubs and activities. With the co-ordination of voluntary service in the early twentieth century through local Guilds of Help and Councils of Voluntary Aid the relationship between leisure and social citizenship became formalized. In the inter-war period the National Council of Social Service, Carnegie United Kingdom Trust, Pilgrim Trust and Church of England all adopted leisure as a field in which to produce the good citizen. Civil society was not, however, necessarily representative of society as a whole and in terms of leisure, socialist and radical voices were often marginalized on political or cultural grounds; furthermore certain sections of society, slum dwellers for example, had little collective representation.

The locating of leisure and voluntarism in civil society thus provides a framework of analysis in which to evaluate leisure and voluntary action in dialogues of social change and the imagination of the good society.[53] By the good society is meant the ethical and broadly socially democratic society imagined by progressive thinkers amongst whom William Morris, Thomas Hill Green, Robert Blatchford, John Hobson and Cecil Delisle Burns figured prominently. Their shared aim was to articulate modifications or alternatives to the society of industrial capitalism and although they did not necessarily agree on what this would be, it involved the potential contribution of leisure to a reformed social order. Some writers looked to Aristotle's philosophical works on social citizenship and leisure; others to a pre-industrial pastoralism or to Marx and a future socialist society. Ideas of the good society and the function of leisure within it were debated through scholarly reviews, monographs, newspapers, discussion groups, conferences and social service organizations. Importantly, the values of an imagined good society could be practised in leisure association; the Co-operative Holidays Association, Woodcraft Folk, worker sports clubs and co-operative society clubs, for example, operated according to the democratic and socialist values of a future society imagined by their founders. In modern sociological terms, leisure has similarly been argued by Karl Spracklen as a Habermesian space of communicative rationality, enabling experimentation in new modes of leisure to act out new ideas in response to social inequality and capitalist cultural production.[54] By no means all voluntary leisure intervention was grounded in terms of an idealized new society; much aimed to counter perceived, social, cultural and moral defects of popular and especially commercially provided leisure. The key shifts in the meanings of leisure and voluntarism, however, were produced in the moral dialogue of the good society.

1.4 Overview of content

Chapter 2 provides a pre-history to the main body of the book. It commences in 1830, a year described by F.M.L. Thompson as a turning point from an agrarian society of aristocratic rule and the cultural dominance of a leisure class to a new industrial and urban society in which political and economic power was passing to the middle classes and urban working-class leisure was becoming socially problematic in terms of morality, drunkenness and public safety.[55] Middle-class interventions in leisure were essentially concerned with morality and the maintenance of social order. However working-class leisure associations, notably friendly societies, teetotal temperance societies and working men's clubs, offered an alternative mode of reform through the creation of communities of interest with wider social objectives, thus establishing organic links between leisure, voluntarism and social change.

Chapter 3 reviews the influence of Evangelicalism, Christian socialism and the civic gospel in terms of the application of religious values to the creation of social communities through leisure. Through a study of John Brown Paton, a leading late-nineteenth-century Congregationalist, it demonstrates how models of German Christian social work were adopted in Britain and led into the formation of the British Institute of Social Service.

Chapter 4 argues that the importance of leisure to the settlement movement has been under-estimated. Leisure was a field in which the poorest sections of the working class could be brought within the ambit of the settlement's middle-class culture of clubs, concerts, socials, libraries and home-visits. Settlements foregrounded the idea of community, being based on the rationale that the city itself was a community fragmented spatially and socially by class divisions. Although the early settlements struggled to appeal to slum populations, they advanced the methods of social work and trained a cohort of predominantly young residential workers, many of whom later occupied influential positions in social service and government social policy circles. In the early twentieth century the Liverpool University Settlement helped bring both leisure and social work into the domain of the social sciences. Through Elizabeth Macadam, Fred D'Aeth and Fred Marquis it became a field laboratory for the University's School of Training for Social Work, articulating leisure as a field of social service.

Chapter 5 introduces the radical alternative to social work represented by socialist leisure associations committed to political change. Leisure was the core around which various organizations lived out socialist values in practice. These existed along a spectrum reaching from the mildly Fabian Co-operative Holidays Association to the politically active Clarion movement. Socialist leisure organizations were influenced by William Morris and John Ruskin. Morris in particular became an important figure in the theorization of the relationships between capitalist industrial production and leisure and in *News from Nowhere* portrayed a utopian commonwealth in which all men would live under equal conditions with a strong sense of a community. This chapter also includes a short case study of 'Red' Nelson, a Lancashire cotton town in which a strongly represented Independent Labour Party and a flourishing Clarion movement created a large and sustainable socialist leisure culture.

The narrative of this book hinges on the First World War. Chapter 6 presents a brief résumé of the changed nature and context of leisure in inter-war Britain, outlining the growth of the wireless and cinema and the increased sense of leisure as an element of modern life.

Chapter 7 is the most important of the book in terms of theoretical content. It presents an analytical account of the theorization of leisure and voluntary action in post-First World War social reconstruction, locating them in discourses of social policy. Reconstruction was not limited to industry and the economy; it also included a reappraisal of what civilization meant and a revival of moral energy to establish new socially constructive values and practices. It was an ethical project in which understandings of community and leisure were constructed around themes of social justice, well-being and social citizenship. The continuing influence of a leisure class was rejected as incompatible with a new democratic leisure culture and social constructs of leisure reflected contemporary interest in a more equitable community and a common culture.

A major influence on social reconstruction was the social idealism articulated in Thomas Hill Green's work on community and the obligation of the citizen. Bernard Bosanquet, a disciple of Green, re-visited Aristotle's distinction of leisure from recreation and entertainment to argue voluntary service to the community as a desirable use of leisure. Through social idealism, leisure and voluntary action were interpreted in terms of the ideal community and good society. John Hobson, a social economist and biographer of John Ruskin, defined leisure in terms of social as well as economic wealth, enabling it to be argued as a social asset to both communities and individuals. This chapter also reviews the contribution of Cecil Delisle Burns, writer and Stevenson Lecturer in Citizenship at the University of Glasgow, to the inter-war discourse of leisure. Unlike critics who looked backwards for the ideal society, Burns saw it in the process of being formed. Where writers such as Henry Durant and the Leavises saw leisure as a machinery of amusement, Burns welcomed the new leisure of inter-war Britain as a potential civilizing agent of modernity. Mass leisure forms, for example, were not alienating or conducive to passivity but created new shared interests by bringing the social classes into a closer relationship.

Chapter 8 provides an analytical comparison of the use of leisure in social reconstruction in urban and rural areas. The formation in 1919 of the National

Council of Social Service (NCSS) established a national forum for voluntary action and a co-ordination of voluntary effort in leisure, sometimes in partnership with the state. The NCSS placed a priority on community well-being and recognized leisure as an important element of community reconstruction. The new urban housing estates presented an opportunity for experimentation and under the direction of Ernest Barker a programme of community-centre building was implemented. Barker likened the estate to the Greek *polis*; the purpose of the community centre was that of a democratic meeting place for ordinary citizens to come together, without the intervention of a leisure class, to exercise the social duty of the management of the community. Leisure association was the intended catalyst for social citizenship. The extent to which this worked out in practice is discussed in case studies of the Watling and Becontree estates. In rural areas a radically different approach was adopted. As on the estates, village halls were built as focal meeting places but through the presence of a strong rural voice at senior levels of the NCSS, leisure was shaped by the revival of an imagined folk tradition, supported by funding from the Carnegie United Kingdom Trust.

Chapter 9 investigates the impacts of wartime measures to regulate young people's leisure and the extension of these measures into peacetime, notably through Juvenile Organizations Committees and the co-ordination of provision for youth at a local level. Although they provided leisure opportunities these committees also found leisure a useful field of surveillance and control. Outside social service radical youth movements, influenced by the German *wandervogel*, promoted pacifism and primitivism through woodcraft and an organic relationship with the land; the Kibbo Kift and the Woodcraft Folk are adopted as case study examples.

Chapter 10 discusses the impact of unemployment on leisure and the question of what leisure meant if there was no work. Through concerns that the unemployed might become a separated community the NCSS supported the government in occupying their time. Differences in the degree of resilience to unemployment were measured in terms of social capital and the extent to which leisure retained the active interest of the unemployed.

Chapter 11 reviews the growth of industrial welfare, a further retained wartime measure, and its expansive provision for leisure. In some areas the leisure amenities and programmes of large employers were significantly more extensive than those provided through voluntary and municipal effort. However, employer schemes were widely unpopular with trade unions and challenged by a worker sport movement that adopted sport as a socialist critique of capitalist society.

Associational Leisure and the Formation of Community in the Mid-Nineteenth Century

2.1 Introduction

The historical development of leisure and voluntary action corresponds with thematic approaches and periods in the historiography of social policy. Pat Thane adopted the sub-periods of 1870–1914, the First World War, and the inter-war decades;[1] Derek Fraser deployed a similar framework of an age of *laissez faire* from c.1780 to c.1885 and the emergence of a social service state c.1885 to1939.[2] Although no single model of voluntary action, or indeed leisure, was absolute at any given point, these temporal frameworks reflect broad phases of social, economic and cultural change and mark shifts of emphasis in voluntarism from paternalism and charitable philanthropy to social service and organized voluntary action. Modern meanings of leisure were similarly formed between the 1880s and the Second World War as rational recreation was superseded by scientific social understandings of leisure.

In the early nineteenth century responsibility for the regulation of popular leisure shifted from the landed gentry to the industrial middle class in what Roberts describes as a private moralizing effort in English culture.[3] However, in the 1840s aristocratic effort to regain control of leisure was contested by working-class agency in the formation of mutual and socially improving leisure associations. This chapter serves as a pre-history to the main body of this book, evaluating the growth of self-managed and largely working-class leisure associations and the formation of imagined communities of leisure at local, regional and national levels.

2.2 Industrialization, urbanization and community

The industrial revolution changed the dominant mode of work from hand to mechanized factory production. It involved a transition from an agrarian to an industrial and predominantly urban society with a new economic base and social order, described by Arnold Toynbee as a radical change from the simple social systems of the market town to those of a manufacturing town.[4] This distinction was, as Jose Harris notes, dichotomous; the organic rural community of *gemeinschaft* was bound together by ties of kinship, fellowship, custom, and the communal ownership of primary goods; in contrast, the *gesellschaft* society of the industrial city comprised free-standing individuals whose social interactions were formed through self-interest, commercial contract and rational calculation.[5] Urbanization created new social contexts for leisure and voluntarism. Patterns of leisure in pre-industrial Britain were shaped by custom and organically integrated in cycles of agricultural work, religious holidays and feasts;[6] in the new industrial town open space to enable continuity of traditional rural leisure practices was lacking as were public buildings and amenities for voluntary association and recreation. The requirements of a decent civic life, as John Hobson noted, were thus not replicated in the transformation of the medieval settlement into a modern manufacturing town.[7]

Surveys of the new industrial towns fuelled middle-class anxieties about popular leisure with graphic descriptions of a working-class culture lacking self-restraint and improving amenities.[8] Manchester – Asa Briggs' 'shock city' of Victorian Britain – was the epicentre of industrialization and a site of new values and a changing social order[9] which attracted interest across Europe. Peter Gaskell's account of the moral condition of its working-class population gave alarming insights to the grossness and vice associated with its one thousand beer houses and gin vaults.[10] The demoralizing effects of these were experienced by Engels in his encounter with drunken street crowds[11] and, as the French politician Leon Faucher reported, working-class leisure had made the city unsafe to the middle classes.[12] Pointing to the considerable geographical variations in popular leisure before 1830, Emma Griffin has warned against unsustainable generalizations.[13] However, parliamentary Select Committees and local reporting in the Lancashire textile towns were consistent in their portrayal of urban working-class leisure forms as incompatible with orderly social intercourse and civic improvement. In Bolton, for example, pedestrianism engendered large crowds and religious festivals were re-configured as wakes holidays and fairs. In

Figure 1 View of Bolton from Mere Hall. In the 1930s Mass Observation chose Bolton for its Worktown Study of an industrial town. Urbanization produced a space inimical to outdoor leisure activities but also created close-knit neighbourhood communities and a rich communal leisure culture.

Source: © Bolton Council. From the Collection of Bolton Library and Museum Services.

1841 the police were unable to maintain order at the Dean Wakes and bull-baiting was still practised in the 1840s, while in 1853 a midnight dogfight in nearby Horwich attracted hundreds of spectators.[14] Progressive thinkers advocated a persuasive rather than a coercive approach to leisure reform; William Cooke Taylor reflected a widely held view in proposing that moral education and improving leisure amenities would be the most effective resolution of what had become a problem of leisure.[15]

The industrial town of the early nineteenth century had numerous endemic problems of which leisure was only one amongst health, education, poverty and others. Voluntary efforts to resolve problems of leisure were, accordingly, not isolated from those that set out to address moral behaviour, education and the construction of civil society. Early nineteenth-century critiques of leisure, notably those by the evangelical educationalist Hannah More, were not directed towards the working classes but the failure of an aristocratic leisure class to set a moral example;[16] Alexis de Tocqueville too concluded that the traditional influence of the aristocracy on social life was in decline.[17] Young England, a Conservative group of the early 1840s comprising *inter alia* Benjamin Disraeli, Lord John Manners, George Smythe and Alexander Baillie Cochrane, sought to reverse this decline. A forerunner of later interest in the solution of the leisure problem through the re-creation of an imagined Arcadian past, Young England aspired to re-energize a national community of Christian responsibility and social harmony,[18] urging the aristocracy to demonstrate friendship to the industrial working class by building public libraries, opening parks and shared participation in 'traditional' sports and pastimes. Cricket was eminently suited to this; speaking at the opening of the Bingley Cricket Club in 1844 Manners described it as manly, bracing and capable of bringing the various social classes into harmonious contact. The Club would, he believed 'give place to cordial sympathy, to the performance of duties and responsibilities on the part of the rich, and to contentment and loyalty on the part of their less fortunate fellow-countrymen'.[19]

Young England was unsuccessful and the responsibility for setting standards in the leisure of the poor was transferred to an expanding urban middle class anxious to preserve social order and suspicious of democracy.[20] The shaping and regulation of leisure through philanthropic paternalism became a field of social intervention and moral regulation, seeking to integrate the middle and working classes through a set of leisure behaviours. Rational recreation was a classically utilitarian response to the problem of leisure, grounded in Jeremy Bentham's greatest happiness principle, which maintained that the merits of actions could be judged only by their propensity to increase or diminish happiness. It was, according to the Darwinian scientist George Romanes, 'not a pastime entered upon for the sake of the pleasure it gave but an act of duty undertaken for the subsequent profit it insured'.[21] Bentham also insisted that moral or religious opinion was not a basis for the determination of a right use of leisure. While this did not deter religious organizations from the moral reform of leisure, it invoked an alternative philosophical differentiation between uses of leisure. John Stuart Mill criticized Bentham's principle on the basis that it did not distinguish between preferable forms of pleasure and argued that as human conceptions of happiness transcended the 'lower' animal pleasures of sensual satisfaction, the 'higher' intellectual forms of pleasure were better. This distinction was not quantifiable in terms of Bentham's felicific calculus but was, Mill maintained, based on the fact that human beings had faculties more elevated than the animal appetites and once conscious of these, would only obtain happiness through them. Capacity to discern this distinction resided only with those who had experienced both lower and higher pleasures who would, according to Mill, always prefer the latter.[22] By implication, competence resided with middle- rather than working-class people whose lack of education and 'social arrangements' would, Mill believed, delimit their capacity for the higher pleasures.[23] Competence in leisure could accordingly be mapped in terms of Engels' two competing communities of a proletariat and a bourgeoisie,[24] with Mill implying the latter as the arbiter of cultural taste. Simon Gunn has more recently interpreted Victorian social distinctions of leisure in modern terms of Bourdieu's cultural capital, contrasting the 'higher' classical music concert with the 'lower' music hall.[25] It became axiomatic that the moral improvement and social reform of leisure could be achieved by middle-class voluntary charitable action to bring working-class cultural patterns in alignment with normative values. However this approach failed to acknowledge fully the fact that the better educated sections of the working class were able to create their own socially constructive and moral leisure associations.

Distinctions of competency in the use of leisure raised the question of what it meant to be 'cultured'. The impression gained from contemporary surveys and parliamentary reports is of a homogeneous working class leisure of dissipation, rough behaviour and immorality. This was not however the case; as Thomas Wright pointed out, although the working class was thought uncultured, it nevertheless included literate men who, through reading and intelligence, could correctly be described as cultured.[26] Furthermore, as Durkheim noted, community was not abolished by urbanism but assumed different forms and meanings; communal life and collective activity were found in both small and large social groupings.[27] As E.P. Thompson observed, by the early nineteenth century leisure and community were closely bound in a working-class culture of self-help and mutuality through associational formations, which nurtured self-respect and collectivist values.[28] As early as 1832 hobbies such as pigeon-fancying and tulip-growing flourished in Lancashire; evidence to Thompson of growth in self-respect and character.[29] Working-class leisure association, as a purposeful collective pursuit of sociability, conviviality and mutual interest, corresponded with what Kenneth Good has described as a pre-democratic culture of democracy,[30] not in a political sense but in terms of self-managed associations, communities of interest and collective identity. Examples include friendly societies, temperance associations and working men's clubs, all of which created an associational culture of mutual interest in which leisure was crucial.[31]

2.3 Leisure in mutual association

Described by Bernard Harris as the most important form of working-class voluntary association in the early nineteenth century,[32] friendly societies were organized around mutual interest and derived their social cohesion through conviviality; Good estimated approximately 25 per cent of all male workers to be a member of one.[33] An example of De Tocqueville's observation of an English propensity to create associations to pursue both political and recreative ends,[34] they became a common feature in the industrializing towns of Lancashire and Yorkshire.[35] Through club nights and dinners, better off working-class and middle-class people shared the same space, enjoying entertainment and conversation and fulfilling middle-class aspirations to a shared leisure culture with other classes.[36] As Gorsky notes, they also encouraged spatial identification with a local community, providing the good of social insurance while promoting civic engagement and a collective attitude to social welfare.[37] Most importantly, in terms of community formation, they nurtured the acts of listening, discussing and voting; skills that were viewed as essential to the foundations of any democratic community.[38]

Institutions combining leisure with instruction for working-class people were particularly valued by middle-class reformers. Appetite for education existed; Elizabeth Gaskell's novel *Mary Barton*, for example, described men in the Lancashire cotton industry who 'might have an open copy of Newton's *Principia* on the loom to be snatched at in work hours or revelled over at night'.[39] James Hole urged Mechanics' Institutes to do more to appeal to such men, arguing that a blend of education and leisure would meet a latent demand for instruction with conviviality.[40] The Miles Platting Mechanics' Institute was formed upon this principle, aiming to emulate the atmosphere of a club,[41] while the Accrington Mechanics' Institute, founded in 1845 by tradesmen together with professional men, combined a library with chess and billiards for 'social enjoyment as well as intellectual improvement'.[42] Lyceums similarly became popular for their newsrooms and libraries of light reading. By 1851 fewer than half of the lectures presented at the Manchester Athenaeum were on science and those on travel, history and the customs of foreign peoples attracted large and socially mixed audiences.[43]

2.4 Temperance, leisure and community

Drink was the most intractable aspect of the leisure problem in Victorian Britain. Although landed interests in parliament resisted political measures to reduce consumption, voluntary initiatives to address drunkenness exceeded those in any other field of leisure. Temperance created national leisure communities. By 1829 there were around 60 temperance societies in Ireland with approximately 3,500 members and 130 in Scotland with over 25,000.[44] The first temperance society in England was formed in Bradford, followed by others in Warrington, Manchester, Liverpool and Leeds;[45] nationally the Anglican-inspired British and Foreign Temperance Society was supported by both secular and religiously motivated philanthropists.

Initially temperance meant abstinence from spirits but the first teetotal temperance society, which excluded all alcohol, was founded in Dunfermline in 1830.[46] In England teetotalism resulted from tensions between the dominant Anglican control of the British and Foreign Temperance Society and its non-conformist members, particularly in northern industrial towns where dissent was strong.[47] The Preston Temperance Society, founded in January 1832, was initially committed only to moderation before becoming the first teetotal temperance society in England in March 1833.[48] This was not a middle-class intervention; Joseph Livesey, its originator, was a cheese factor; the occupations of the other founders included clog-making, carding, shoemaking and plastering. Through the Preston Society teetotalism spread on a regional and national basis,[49] aided by Livesey's temperance newspaper the *Moral Reformer* and the first teetotal periodical, the *Preston Temperance Advocate*. Members of the Preston society shared a similar social and cultural background to the northern working-class audiences they addressed; in 1840 Edward Grubb, for example, expounded the benefits of teetotalism to packed meetings on three consecutive evenings in Oldham.[50] Teetotalism challenged middle-class interpretations of temperance; in Bolton the Anglican-formed temperance society was forced to compete with a predominantly non-conformist teetotal society after a visit by the Preston Society in 1833.[51] Teetotalism's empathy with the intemperate was not paternalistic but mutual;[52] Livesey realized success depended upon the provision of alternative leisure amenities and through the *Star of Temperance* newspaper promoted a teetotal leisure culture of temperance hotels, coffee bars and reading rooms.[53]

The temperance movement blurred sectarian and class divisions in an associational leisure community of what Erika Rappaport describes as a sober consumer culture.[54] Temperance Halls were its focal social meeting place and from the late 1830s fulfilled many of the social functions of the pub in northern working-class towns – first in Burnley (1837) and Bradford (1838).[55] By 1853 there were approximately 350 beer houses and 174 public houses in Bolton but also over fifty dissenting chapels whose members rejected the leisure culture of the pub; the opening of its Temperance Hall in 1839 provided them with a cultural alternative for social gatherings, public meetings, concerts and juvenile gatherings.[56] Temperance societies invested considerable effort in the creation of a youth leisure culture, notably through the non-denominational Band of Hope. The first was formed in Leeds in 1847; by 1887 the United Kingdom Band of Hope Union had over one million members. Temperance values were inculcated through magazines, magic-lantern shows and images connecting drink to poverty and destitution.[57] The creation in 1855 of the Band of Hope Union brought local groups into a wider associational community of instruction and pleasure.[58] In 1861, for example, the Leicester Band of Hope, with the Sheffield and Nottingham Sunday School Bands of Hope, organized a grand Band of Hope Gala in Nottingham Arboretum attended by 5,000 young people.

Historians have observed that popular leisure was not necessarily a form of resistance or struggle but could equally be an expression of autonomy and self-reliance;[59] to socially progressive reformers this was an indication that self-managed working-class leisure associations might hold wider appeal than those controlled by the middle class. The temperance movement, especially in the form of working-class teetotalism, reflects this; its integration in a wider public culture was noted by Edward Baines in the House of Commons in 1861.[60] Teetotalism recruited from a respectable stratum of the working class to form and maintain a moral community through cultural practice. The idea of a self-managed temperance club as a non-alcoholic alternative to the public house was widely embraced; several were established in Oxfordshire villages and in 1860 the formation of the Westminster Working Men's club inspired Henry Solly's working man's club movement.[61]

2.5 Working men's clubs

Working men's clubs have sometimes been described as a form of rational recreation that failed when their teetotal principles were rejected by members who successfully challenged them and sold beer. More positively, however, they can be argued to have been important contributors to a moral dialogue of leisure. What the precursors of working men's clubs lacked, according to Henry Solly, was the opportunity for unrestrained social intercourse without an obligation to participate in cultural or educational improvement. Solly advocated self-managed clubs to reduce working-class dependency on middle-class philanthropy.[62] He was one of the earliest reformers to connect leisure to citizenship, imagining the club as an ideal community whose members, like citizens, were responsible for its continued existence and common good.[63] The idea of membership was central to this; as Raymond Williams noted, a member of any society was conscious of being a member, benefiting from membership and able to contribute to discussion on the operation and management of the institution.[64] Membership also implied co-operation and compromise.

Working men's clubs extended working-class agency in leisure, though not always without conflict and debate. Many of the early clubs were jointly managed by middle- and working-class men. The fact that a number of self-managed clubs were forced to close through incompetent management lent weight to a widely held assumption that the working classes were incapable of club management and by implication unfit to participate in a democratic society. The Preston Club, for example, founded in 1864, occupied a large building near the market-place with accommodation for over 600 local men, leading the Club secretary to doubt if working men had the experience or time to manage such an institution.[65] The Bolton club enjoyed a more harmonious relationship between working men and a 'few of the class above them'; the St. James and Soho club, on the other hand, floundered through the internal resentments of management by two committees, one comprising gentlemen, the other working-class men.[66] It was through self-management however that working men's clubs came to sell beer, an almost unimaginable step to contemporary middle-class reformers. When it became apparent that the movement could not survive under a teetotal regime, beer was gradually introduced and by 1883 was sold in 80 per cent of clubs.[67] This was not simply a response to a demand for beer *per se* but to significant middle-class resistance to its sale.[68] Some clubs however chose to remain teetotal; the Walthamstow Working Men's Club and Institute, for example, was founded in 1862 on this basis and remained teetotal until at least 1932.[69]

Working men's clubs appealed to respectable working- and lower middle-class men, offering a blend of leisure and education. The Borough of Hackney Working Men's Club, for example, had 1,600 members and provided social rooms, a large billiard-room, a library of 4,000 volumes, a reading-room, classrooms and a meeting hall.[70] They were also social centres of their community, especially from the 1890s when women were admitted on one evening a week or to attend lectures.[71] The balance between leisure and education was sensitive and, as Solly noted, clubs would have differing emphases according to location.[72] According to a survey in 1874, 21 per cent of clubs held classes in the arts and sciences; 33 per cent sponsored lectures; 64 per cent held educational and elocutionary entertainments and nearly all had lending libraries,[73] suggesting that even where recreation was dominant it was not to the exclusion of education. Although predominantly located in urban areas some rural working men's clubs were established, for example that in Hanley Castle in Worcestershire with reading room, library, classes and a band.[74] Working men's clubs fulfilled Solly's aim of becoming places that represented a 'fellowship formed for mutual benefit' with a mutual understanding of the need to promote the common good.[75] They were not, however, concerned with radical social change; although Conservatives and Liberals were permitted to form a club, socialists and trades unionists were denied this opportunity.[76]

2.6 Conclusion

The initial utilitarian response to the problem of leisure was the middle-class encouragement of rational recreation. However this approach assumed that working-class people did not possess the capacity to create and manage their own leisure associations. Although this was partly true, there is substantial evidence that the better educated and respectable working classes were able to organize their own associations of interest and leisure. Associational leisure practices nurtured a sense of community identity, conveying shared values and enabling a social life in which their members could participate. Although this occurred mainly at a local level, technological advances in communications created wider imagined leisure-based communities of interest. Where a crude utilitarianism attempted to impose cultural practices on working-class populations, enlightened reformers, notably Henry Solly, realized that agency and democratic self-management were necessary to the formation of working-class leisure association. Even when friendly societies and working men's clubs are argued to be essentially middle-class creations, it remains the case that their values of mutuality and collective ownership matched those of their working-class members who retained their independence[77] and more importantly developed the skills to assume control or establish new working-class associations. The temperance and teetotal movements and working men's clubs accordingly fit into Roberts' categorization of working-class people who were able to transform themselves from the objects of moral reform to its practitioners[78] and suggested that, given the right conditions, voluntary association and active social citizenship would be more productive towards the resolution of the leisure problem than middle-class intervention or state interference. As MacIver observed, free voluntary association was crucial to the development of community.[79] Community was, however, only possible because interests were realizable in common life and the expression of interests described above in terms of mutual societies, the temperance movement and working men's clubs show how in differing contexts leisure became a field in which working and lower middle-class groups contributed to an emerging civic culture.

Evangelicalism and the Inner Mission

Religion, Leisure and Social Service

Evangelicalism has been credited with the invention of the voluntary society;[1] by the end of the nineteenth century, as Pat Thane notes, it was the largest single inspiration of charitable effort.[2] Evangelicalism was a pervasive cross-denominational movement that proclaimed the responsibility of the church to apply the message of the gospel to social problems.[3] Its defining characteristic as a force for voluntary intervention was its emphasis on social ethics and welfare and from the 1830s it inspired a middle-class crusade to infuse social and cultural life with Christian principles,[4] prompting churches and socio-religious organizations to become providers and organizers of leisure. Puritan religion was suspicious of leisure as a source of sin and non-conformist denominations in particular imposed strict limits upon recreation. In the face of the new social problems of urbanization, religious attitudes to leisure changed. The extent to which they did so was varied; leisure remained a potential cause of sin and thus required moral regulation, but might also serve as the basis of a Christian social life. This chapter reviews the integration of leisure in a new framework of religious social service and evaluates the influence of evangelicalism on secular voluntary work in the early twentieth century.

3.1 Religion, the social mission and leisure

Religion has a strong historical relationship with sociability; from medieval times holidays, feast days and processions blended the religious and social life of the parish as a church community.[5] The post-Puritan revival of a social religion in the late nineteenth century owed much to the Christian socialist movement founded in 1850 by Frederic Denison Maurice, John Ludlow and Charles Kingsley. John Atherton helpfully describes this as a socialization of Christianity rather than a Christianization of socialism;[6] with few exceptions,[7] it offers deeper insight to evangelical effort to develop a Christian social community through leisure. As non-conformity gained urban prominence, religious missions adopted social objectives[8] and, like their temperance equivalent, mission halls became focal spaces around which a social community could coalesce.

Many non-conformist churches integrated leisure in their social works prior to Christian socialism; the Liverpool Domestic Mission, for example, founded in 1836 by the Unitarian William Rathbone, opened its first Mission house in 1838 with a mechanics' library, evening schools and a temperance coffee house.[9] Both Anglican and non-conformist Sunday Schools blended religious instruction with the nurturing of social life and a sense of community through leisure.[10] When John Wesley visited Bolton in 1786, 555 children were registered in Methodist Sunday Schools[11] and by 1834 most Bolton children belonged to a Sunday School in which recreation was a salient aspect.[12] Furthermore, as Doreen Rosman points out, Sunday Schools often included adults and became pillars of community social life;[13] their participation in ceremonial forms such as Whitsuntide processions blurred sectarian divisions and contributed to the civic life of northern industrial towns until the mid-twentieth century. Such parades were important; as Paul O' Leary notes, Irish processions in South Wales helped create public perceptions of Irish respectability, enabling civic integration through participation in the public life of the community.[14]

Religious influence on leisure was often mediated through municipal local government, which was itself shaped by religious values. In Blackburn, for example, a Conservative and Anglican dominated library committee purchased large proportions of popular fiction as a paternalist response to popular demand while in adjoining Darwen a Liberal and Congregationalist committee sought to raise cultural standards by promoting standard literary fiction.[15] Local government leaders often became leaders of voluntary organizations and brought with them a range of values; links with the temperance movement were, for example, particularly common in non-conformist dominated councils. Hardly anywhere was the influence of Christian socialism on leisure better illustrated than in Congregationalism, the denomination in which the civic gospel originated in Birmingham through George Dawson and the Congregationalist minister Robert Dale. Dale held active involvement in local civil society to be a Christian duty and the civic gospel became a powerful motivating force for socio-religious intervention and the construction of a provincial urban leisure culture.[16] The Congregationalist relaxation of strictures on leisure in 1879 retained an emphasis on its moral regulation[17] but Dale went further in seeing leisure as a positive component of human social life. Congregationalist, Unitarian and other non-conformist denominations became notable for their clubs, classes and tea parties, which nurtured social fellowship amongst congregations as well as providing a counterforce to the perceived moral dangers of commercial entertainment.[18] The latter was aided by the absorption of popular leisure forms; the growing popularity of spectator sport for example was countered with church football, cricket and other sports clubs for both men and women.[19]

Evangelicalism extended social projects in leisure beyond the church and congregation to society more generally. From the 1880s a distinctive Christian social mission formed, especially in non-conformist denominations, which possessed a stronger tradition of communal life and fellowship than Anglicanism,[20] and it was in the non-conformist denominations that leisure became particularly important to church social life.[21] Religious-based leisure association formed a good proportion of what F.M.L. Thompson described as a Victorian apparatus of social service.[22] Helen Meller's study of civic growth in Bristol demonstrated the prominence of Quakers, Congregationalists and Baptists in the development of a social community; the Anglican church was also active in this respect.[23] Church interventions were fundamentally local, creating opportunities for sociability and fellowship in urban populations in which dislocation and family dispersal were common features.[24] In London Booth noted how leisure helped religious organizations reach into neighbourhood communities, recording a Unitarian church on Highgate Hill with literary societies, sports clubs and a social institute. The Sunday Society, Sunday Lecture Society and the National Sunday League also provided a range of 'decent' occupations and pleasures whose appeal extended to 'non-church going respectable people'.[25] Beyond London, Victorian and Edwardian churches embraced sports and games, fairs, concerts and pantomimes and even the showing of films as part of their social provision of leisure.[26] This trend continued into the early twentieth century when nearly all denominations developed local social welfare schemes, which typically included youth clubs, men's societies, Boy Scouts and Girl Guides.[27]

National organizations blending social and religious objectives were also important providers of leisure. The YMCA (1844) and YWCA (1855) were prominent Christian young adult organizations with branches in nearly all major towns. Aiming to appeal to single young men and women in rapidly growing cities, leisure was crucial to their viability; in both Bristol[28] and Leicester[29] the introduction of recreational facilities was a factor of increased membership. This hard fact helped soften restrictive attitudes to leisure; the YMCA, founded by the Congregationalist George Williams, initially precluded leisure on moral grounds but by the 1870s found libraries, reading rooms and board games essential to recruitment.[30] The YWCA followed a similar pattern, initially focusing on girls' moral safety but eventually supporting girl guides and other girls' organizations. Some organizations were formed to retain Sunday School pupils; notable examples include the Church Lads' Brigade (1891), which by 1908 had a national membership of 70,000 in 1,300 companies, and the Church of England's Girls' Friendly Society (1875), a strictly denominational organization founded by Mary Elizabeth Townsend to prevent Anglican girls from mixing with those from dissenting denominations in the YWCA.[31] Achieving its peak membership in 1913 with 39,926 associates (leaders) and 197,493 members it was conservative in outlook and opposed women's suffrage. Its aristocratic leadership helped it spread in rural areas where it appealed to domestic servants and encouraged deference through recreation, but was less successful in the urban environment.[32] Many non-denominational young people's clubs were not overtly religious but nevertheless promoted spiritual development. The Salford Lads' Club, for example, aimed to advance 'Christ's Kingdom among working lads'; Brighton Boys' Club prepared 'God-fearing and intelligent citizens' and the St. George's Jewish Boys' Club at the Bernhard Baron Settlement developed 'labourers to establish God's kingdom on earth'.[33] Scouting similarly encouraged duty to God and attendance at church, chapel or church parade on Sundays.[34]

Interest in the organization of leisure within churches declined towards the end of the century. To some degree this reflected increased competition from an ever-expanding market of commercial leisure and a general decline in the status of religion. This was not, however, necessarily a process of secularization. The secularization thesis has been challenged in recent decades – Callum Brown for example has argued that it did not take a significant hold until the late twentieth century.[35] Secularization is problematic in other ways; as Jeremy Morris has noted, it has been differently interpreted in terms of church attendance and the associational culture of the church.[36] Taking the latter as a measure, although interest in leisure declined in theological terms, religion remained a major force in voluntary culture until at least the close of the inter-war period. In Congregationalism, for example, the social gospel of leisure became diluted as the previously highly valued Bands of Hope and cricket and football clubs were alleged to be detrimental to church attendance;[37] as a contemporary critic observed, despite numerous societies, guilds and crusades, the 'tone of religious life' was low.[38] Dominic Erdozain, however, has attributed the decreased religious interest in leisure provision to its success; instead of being ancillary to religion, leisure had come to dominate church life but without any apparent spiritual benefits. People enjoyed religious clubs and societies but leisure did not necessarily lead to conversion or even church attendance.[39] However, withdrawal from leisure was not absolute; Unitarians and Quakers founded the Leeds Association of Girls' Clubs in 1904.[40] On a wider scale, religious leisure-based societies not only survived but new ones emerged, concerned not with conversion but the maintenance of Christian values in leisure. The influence of Christian socialism did not diminish but became expressed in an articulation of a religious social service and a co-ordination of voluntary effort; as Graham Bowpitt has argued, Christian involvement in late nineteenth-century social work was not terminated by a secular take-over but survived in a different form in the voluntary sector.[41] The following section reviews the extent to which this argument was true of leisure and considers the contribution of socio-religious leisure organization to the formation of a twentieth-century model of social service.

3.2 Towards social service: John Brown Paton, leisure and the inner mission

By the end of the nineteenth century evangelicalism had built a complex framework of organized leisure for working people both in and outside of congregations.[42] Its enthusiasm for an associational culture was personified in the work of John Brown Paton, an ecumenical Congregationalist who infused secular social service with Christian values. A fellow student of Robert Dale at Birmingham's Springhill College, Paton was committed to the idea of the civic gospel and as the first Principal of the Congregational Institute at Nottingham encouraged ecumenical engagement with civil agencies to improve social conditions.[43] From Dale, Paton learned that although the municipal adoption of services previously provided through philanthropy might appear to be a process of secularization, the growing interest in social reform could be exploited to revive religious social intervention.[44] Paton applied this principle to leisure. An educationalist, he blended informal adult education with leisure to attract and retain working-class people, founding the Recreative Evening Schools Association (1885) and National Home Reading Union (1889) as national secular organizations. Both were aimed at young adults between school leaving age and twenty-five years old. Recreative Evening Schools interspersed instruction in subjects relevant to students' everyday lives with musical drill and magic lantern shows.[45] Supported by Robert Yerburgh, Conservative member for Chester, they were most successful in industrial urban areas and attracted a national weekly attendance of 81,068 by 1893.[46] The National Home Reading Union (NHRU) was conceived as a British replica of the North American Chautauqua Literary and Scientific Circle with secular and religious support from Arthur Acland, bursar of Balliol College, Charles Rowley, founder of the Ancoats Recreation Committee (later Ancoats Brotherhood),[47] Joshua Girling Fitch, lecturer at Toynbee Hall, and John Percival who as headmaster of Clifton College had led the civic renaissance of Bristol in the 1870s. The Union promoted the formation of local reading circles, which followed a prescribed list of books under the guidance of a voluntary leader. Circles were formed by churches, literary societies, co-operative societies, Sunday Schools, Adult Sunday Classes and Pleasant Sunday Afternoon Associations.[48] Initially some working-class circles were formed: one in a midlands factory studied in Carlyle; another in Aston read *Alton Locke*.[49] Several circles were formed in non-conformist churches.[50] By 1906 the Union's membership exceeded 13,000 but, like many initiatives intended to bring working-class people within the ambit of a middle-class culture, it became largely dominated by the middle classes themselves. After the First World War it declined under competition from BBC wireless talks and the expansion of the Workers' Educational Association.[51]

Paton's principal significance lies in his role in the creation of an ecumenical and co-operative Christian social service through which religion could influence leisure without the direct involvement of the church or a congregation. Paton was deeply influenced by the German social thinking on policy discussed by Hennock[52] and became a forceful advocate of the 'inner mission' of the German *Kirchentag*, or Church Assembly. Devised in 1848 as the basis of a German Evangelic Union, the inner mission emphasized provision for social needs through city missions and schemes of social welfare. Paton introduced the inner mission to Britain through a series of leaflets advocating the harmonization of social institutions and social life with the will of God.[53] The inner mission was, in Paton's term, to be a 'ministry of good' concerned with social as well as religious well-being and implemented through a secular Christianity.[54] Applying these principles to leisure, Paton established religiously inspired but outwardly secular Social Institutes to deliver educational classes and enable convivial social intercourse. These were non-sectarian, non-political and teetotal. The first was established at Dunscomb Road School in Islington in February 1894 under the supervision of Thomas A. Leonard,[55] followed by those at the Camden Street and Thomas Street Board Schools.[56] Several more were opened in London, including one exclusive to the employees of Welsbach Incandescent Gas Light Company, based in the schoolrooms of Westminster chapel, which recruited 230 members.[57] Social Institutes were also formed in Glasgow, with a combined membership of 1,500, and in Birmingham and Leicester.[58] Like the Recreative Evening Schools they blended education with leisure, organizing clubs for cycling, tennis, football, cricket and rambling while remaining teetotal. Affiliated to the Federation of Working Men's Social Clubs and open to both men and women, they hosted trade union and other mutual society meetings[59] and were widely reported in the public domain,[60] providing a prototype for inter-war community centres and continuing to flourish well into the twentieth century.[61]

Paton also adopted the German Elberfeld system of spatial division under which local inner missions would function as an organizing body comprising representatives of civic institutions and societies. Although secular, these would, according to Paton, retain a Christian spirit and an emphasis on ecumenical co-operative working.[62] In 1889 this became the informing principle of the Christian Social Union by the Anglican Christian Socialist James Granville Adderley and Henry Scott Holland, canon of St. Paul's and former student of T.H. Green. Through this prototypical council of voluntary aid, churches formulated and co-ordinated local social policies on a non-sectarian basis, which included the growth of an associational leisure culture.[63] With support from Charles Masterman, David Watson, founder of the Scottish Christian Social Union, and Sidney Ball, founder of the Social Science Club at the University of Oxford, the Union aided the Christianization of social reform as religion seeped into policy discourse through academic and social networks comprising both Christian socialists and socialist Christians. Important to this sharing of secular and religious ideas was the Rainbow Circle, formed in 1894 as a non-sectarian political and discussion group with a strong leaning towards the social philosophy of the new liberalism. Early members were drawn from leading social reform institutions and included: Percy Alden, Warden of the Mansfield settlement and co-founder of the Christian Socialist League; John Henry Belcher, its secretary; Percy Dearmer, Secretary of the Christian Social Union; the social economist John Hobson; Rev. Alfred Leslie Lilley, Canon of Hereford Cathedral; and William Pember Reeves, Director of the London School of Economics.[64]

Paton became an important influence on secular social work, promoting Civic Leagues, modelled on the Bradford Guild of Help,[65] as a 'municipal conscience' for civic authorities.[66] With his son John Lewis Paton he was instrumental in the establishment of the British Institute of Social Service in 1904.[67] By blending religion into the new world of social science, Paton helped ensure Christianity was represented in social policy debate on leisure. The Institute was not secular in the sense of being free of religious influence; it also included the Rev. Samuel Barnett, Percy Alden and Congregationalist Minister Benjamin Kirkman Gray of the Bell Street Mission in Marylebone. Other members included practising Christians with experience in leisure as a field of social improvement, notably George Cadbury, Joseph Rowntree and Mrs Humphry Ward. It also co-opted organizations including the Sociological Society, Working Men's Club and Institution and the Garden Cities Association, all of which brought leisure into social policy and debate.

3.3 Conclusion

Leisure was important to the implementation of the social gospel. Through the civic gospel, non-conformists in particular contributed to the growth of a dense network of church-based leisure associations and societies. Rather than ceding power to secular social science, religion retained a strong influence on secular social service. Providing the model upon which the National Council of Social Service was established after the First World War, the Christian Social Union and the British Institute of Social Service served as conduits of social thinking on leisure and voluntarism and extended the influence of Carlyle, Morris and Ruskin into the early decades of the twentieth century. They run counter to the idea that religion declined as a force of voluntarism in the face of secular competition and established a foundation upon which religion was to re-vitalize its social duty in the inter-war years, notably through William Temple's Christian Conference on Politics, Economics, and Citizenship in 1924. John Brown Paton made an important contribution to the development of voluntary leisure associations which incorporated informal education, and it was not coincidental that the first conference of the National Council of Social Service in 1919, organized by John Lewis Paton, adopted leisure as its theme.

Leisure, Community and the Settlement Movement

4.1 Introduction

Walter Besant's novel *All Sorts and Conditions of Men* and Andrew Mearns' *The Bitter Cry of Outcast London*,[1] published in 1882 and 1883 respectively, stimulated middle-class interest in the urban slum[2] as a separated community. Together with social surveys they contributed to a topographical imagination of the late-Victorian city, which, in Rosalind Williams' terms, posited the slum as a subterranean social underworld inhabited by a dispossessed class.[3] At a time when degenerationist theories were fashionable, the slum seemed to herald a collapse of civilization. Helen Dendy (later Bosanquet), a leading figure in the Charity Organisation Society, expressed a widely held view in describing its population as a 'residuum' characterized by lack of foresight and self-control.[4] To middle-class reformers the slum constituted a challenge to address the spatial and cultural distances between prosperous and poor communities.[5] Through Besant and Mearns, the leisure of the slum became a field of opportunity for intervention, the latter warning that despite the efforts of temperance societies and missions, the ubiquity of gin palaces, public houses and brothels had thus far rebuffed all reforming efforts.

The settlement movement aimed to establish a common ground on which working class populations could be brought under the cultural influence of the middle classes; to William Beveridge, a sub-warden of Toynbee Hall, it was an attempt by voluntary action to counteract the break-up of cities into preserves of the rich and leisured and the warrens of the poor and labouring.[6] Residential settlement workers, mainly young university-educated men and women,[7] lived alongside the poor, offering cultural guidance and developing their capacity to become active citizens. This chapter evaluates the settlements' adoption of leisure as a field of shared cultural experience and community building.

Late-Victorian understandings of charitable philanthropy and the city were shaped by the increasing complexity of society. There was, as Stephen Webb argues, a debate around modernist understandings of social work and a shared recognition within reformist discourse of the need for active citizenship to effect social change. Social work could not thus be constrained to the Charity Organisation Society's model of charitable philanthropy that focused on case work and the deserving individual.[8] The development of a community-focused model drew from Edward Denison who in 1867 had taken residence in the East end to live alongside the poor. Of equal importance was the social idealism emerging from Balliol College and the philosophy of Thomas Hill Green, which offered, as David Boucher and Andrew Vincent have argued, an optimistic, liberal and ethical theory of citizenship in which the state – in the wider sense – would enable a worthwhile life for all citizens.[9] Green was a major influence on social work throughout the period 1880 to 1930.[10] Appointed to the teaching staff of Balliol College in 1866 he was active in civic life as a Liberal town councillor, treasurer of the Oxford diocesan branch of the Church of England Temperance Society and from 1876 president of the Oxfordshire Band of Hope and Temperance Union.[11] Social idealism articulated the ethical community as an informative principle for moral dialogue on the good society. It extended the scope of social work beyond relief to the development of the community and posited active citizenship to be necessary, as Bernard Bosanquet argued, to enable a community to resolve its own problems through a democratic process.[12]

Although the high water mark of Green's influence came later, the Victorian settlement movement marked a stage in the transition to modern social work. Settlements were, in Sandra den Otter's terms, institutions to which the idea of community and a community life defined by a common good was a motivating force in a period of concern about the fragmentation of urban life.[13] Although religious principles underpinned the settlement movement they remained largely implicit, expressed through what Derek Fraser describes as a 'secular evangelicalism'[14] working through a widening of cultural horizons rather than preaching.[15] As a field of cultural practice leisure was ideally suited to this object. It is therefore of significant note that the use of leisure was incorporated in the first object of the Universities Settlements Association to provide 'education and the means of recreation and enjoyment for the people of the poorer districts of London'.[16] Although the moral improvement of leisure remained important, it acquired a social instrumentality in terms of education, class integration and citizenship. This was however a difficult task in a period of a rapidly expanding popular leisure. Described by Chris Waters as a 'unique moment in the history of popular culture' the late Victorian decades saw a continuing decline of 'traditional leisure' counter-balanced by an expansion of commercially provided leisure and the birth of a modern leisure industry.[17] Social reformers were consequently forced to compete with this. Being established by individuals and organizations with differing beliefs and values, settlements varied in their aims and methods. By the close of the nineteenth century they existed in major urban areas throughout Britain including in London Toynbee Hall (1884), Oxford House (1884), the Women's University Settlement, Southwark (1887), Mansfield House (1890), Bermondsey Settlement (1891), Browning Hall (1894) and Mary Ward's Passmore Edwards Settlement (1897). Those outside London included Chalmers (University) Settlement, Edinburgh (1887), University Students' Settlement, Glasgow (1889), Manchester University Settlement (1895), Victoria Women's Settlement, Liverpool (1897) and the Birmingham Women's Settlement (1899).[18] In Scotland the Glasgow University settlement was founded in 1886 through the idealist philosopher Edward Caird, later Master of Balliol College. In addition numerous small-scale settlements were established, for example that by Margaret Llewelyn Davies, general secretary of the Women's Co-operative Guild, in 1902 in a slum district of Sunderland above a co-operative society store. Here residential settlers lived on the first floor, organizing education and social work amongst its neighbourhood community.[19] However, the early London settlements merit more detailed discussion, being amongst the first to be established and setting the example followed by many others. The following sections compare the nature of social intervention in leisure at Toynbee Hall, Oxford House, the Mary Ward Settlement, Victoria Women's Settlement and the Liverpool University Settlement.

4.2 The Barnetts and Toynbee Hall

Toynbee Hall was established in Whitechapel in 1884 by Samuel Barnett and his wife Henrietta, named in recognition of Arnold Toynbee, a disciple of Green who had been foreman of Ruskin's road-repairing gang while at Oxford.[20] It adopted an open approach and relied on the aptitudes of residents;[21] by 1890 it housed fifteen residential workers, amongst them two curates, a school teacher and men who worked in the city and organized evening social activities. Its funding depended largely on charitable donors amongst whom Balliol College was the principal subscriber.[22] Like all settlements, Toynbee Hall was the expression of an ethical idea, an institution formed with a common purpose of bringing the poor and outcast into the social community. It differed from the Charity Organisation Society, according to Henrietta Barnett, in looking beyond material poverty to the poverty of a social life that lacked associational leisure forms.[23] Like the COS, it placed an emphasis on personal contact with the poor and upon the improvement of character because, as Samuel Barnett reasoned, reforms could only be effective if those towards whom they were aimed wished for them.[24]

In London, as in other cities, leisure was increasingly interpreted in spatial terms. Booth, for example, recorded betting to be more prevalent in poor areas with numerous gambling clubs and a high readership of sporting newspapers.[25] Social citizenship too was disproportionately low in slum areas and, as Percy Ashley noted, its development was an essential step towards communal self-help and management.[26] Leisure patterns and social citizenship thus became related in a sociological context. Samuel Barnett described leisure as a subject of greater importance than generally thought and a sign of whether the nation was socially regressive or progressive.[27] As the leisure of the poor was considered regressive, resident workers were to make personal contact with the people of the neighbourhood community and bring them into the settlement because, as Barnett believed, 'culture spreads by contact'.[28] The Toynbee Hall Entertainments Committee furthered this end with tea parties, recitals of classical music and art exhibitions[29] designed to create receptions of, in Barnett's adopted phrase, 'all sorts and conditions of men' in which students of its classes could exchange views and form friendships with residents.[30] Barnett had a realistic understanding of what could be achieved and encouraged residents to work with small groups and befriend only a few.[31] Visiting Toynbee Hall in 1890 the American social worker Robert Archey Woods found a vibrant hub of community life with educational classes and social clubs; it was a place where residents did not merely shake hands with the people they were trying to help but could invite to dinner anyone living in the East End at the expense of the Hall's entertainment fund.[32]

The Barnetts and leisure

The Barnetts showed little interest in developing a social theory of leisure and instead displayed a conventional middle-class tendency to approach it in terms of a deficit model. As Chairman of the Countryside Committee of the Children's Country Holiday Fund, which the Barnetts had founded, Henrietta Barnett personified late-Victorian charitable philanthropy rather than a new social work.[33] Much of the Barnetts' understanding of leisure can be gleaned from their joint manifesto, *Practicable Socialism*. This was anything but political in nature.[34] The slum, according to Samuel Barnett, had been created by the retreat of bourgeois society from working-class urban areas and with it that of friendship.[35] The effects of this absence were to the Barnetts readily evident in a degraded use of leisure. *Practicable Socialism* was replete with contemporary figurative descriptors of working-class leisure, for example, the 'swarming crowd', its 'love of excitement' and 'addiction' to passive amusement, the cheap music hall and spectator sport. However, the music hall and sport were, by the 1880s, not always undesirable forms of leisure and were arguably of greater symbolic than material concern. The Barnetts, however, had little understanding that popular leisure might enable convivial social intercourse and shared enjoyment; how, Samuel Barnett asked, could workmen participate in civic life if they had no other recreation than the spectacle of a football match?[36] Popular leisure was consequently perceived as an obstacle to social progress,[37] leading the Barnetts to focus on the encouragement of alternative forms.[38]

Like William Morris, Samuel Barnett harked to a 'Merrie England' and a recreation of fellowship and personal fulfilment[39] but unlike Morris believed this would come not through socialism but social intercourse.[40] Personal friendship and conviviality in shared leisure were at the core of settlement work. In theory this friendship was not paternalist but reciprocal; while the club boy might come under the 'sheltering cloud' of a 'ladye faire', a settlement worker could learn from the 'clear-visioned thoughts' of a lad.[41] Recent research has shown that it was indeed possible for durable affective relationships to form between residential settlement workers and working-class visitors.[42] However the nature of such friendship was inherently hierarchical; while the resident worker would gain insights to the lives of the poor, the greater benefit was to be change in the poor. As Samuel Barnett commented: 'Men who have knowledge may become friends of the poor and share that knowledge and its fruits as, day by day, they meet in their common rooms for talk or for instruction, for music or for play.'[43] A further expression of friendship was the invitation of the poor to the middle class home, idealized thus by Henrietta Barnett as a site of domestic leisure:

> In our English love of home is one of the hopes for the future; and not the least conspicuous as a moral training ground is the family dinner table. There the mother can teach the little lessons of good manners and neat ways, and the larger truths of unselfishness and thoughtfulness. There the whole family can meet, and from the talks over meals, during the time which, as things are now, is the only leisure of the busy mechanic, may grow that sympathy between the older and younger people which must refreshen and gladden both.[44]

In a discussion of place and space in late-Victorian social work Stephen Webb has differentiated the 'sacred' homefulness nurtured by middle-class life from the squalor of the single room home of the slums.[45] As a middle-class woman Henrietta Barnett understood the stark contrast between the leisure possible in prosperous homes and that in the small and overcrowded rooms of working-class houses where the cost of entertainment was a further barrier to domestic social intercourse.[46] Aiming to bring the 'townpeople' of Whitechapel into a domestic middle-class space she formed a network of families willing to entertain a party of Whitechapel residents in country houses. Visits were arranged through written invitations in accordance with middle-class protocol and conducted to replicate the social intercourse of a middle-class gathering. After a meal visitors could wander around the garden, hothouses, conservatories and ferneries, or play cricket, bowls or rounders.[47] Such offers of friendship were however transient. If the experience of the middle-class home was intended to encourage home-based leisure by working-class people, it was never likely to be successful; as the middle-class colonization of the National Home Reading Union demonstrated, domestic leisure practices could not be culturally disconnected from place.[48] 'At homes' similarly exposed the social gap between residents and the local community. Intended as a means of bringing local people into the middle-class space of the Hall or the homes of its supporters it was a gift that could be neither reciprocated nor replicated. Befriending might reduce temporarily the gap between the leisure of the rich and the poor and inspire aspirations of replication by the visitors. However as a longer term strategy it was reminiscent of Young England's aspiration to demonstrate cross-class friendship through a shared leisure and an assumption that this would be received.

The club

A contemporary survey of British settlements found the club to be the principal organizing unit for their work through leisure.[49] The idea of the club was integral to that of the settlement; both Samuel Barnett and Thomas Hancock Nunn saw the settlement itself as a club, being a 'community of men' prepared to work for a common cause.[50] The club, as Peter Clark shows, was a product of the early modern period that enabled a co-ordination of shared leisure interests; by the final decades of the nineteenth century it had become an instrument of personal improvement and social reform, facilitating social interaction, creating social bonds and engendering a sense of community.[51] School and college missions had organized communal activities around boys' and girls' clubs since the

1860s,[52] but the settlements rationalized club work in a more methodical fashion as a site of character building and training in social citizenship. The unifying principle of the settlement club was that it should have the maximum possible degree of autonomy. The club was simultaneously an inclusive and exclusive community; belonging was expressed through membership, which conferred benefits but invoked reciprocal duties and adherence to a set of rules and values. Membership implied active participation in a democratic process; self-managed clubs operated with elected officers and gave members opportunities for active voluntary support of the club. The settlement club was a specific form of voluntary leisure association, purposefully seeking to serve the interests of its members – albeit these were defined by others – through the organization of leisure activity. Activities were often determined by gender; boys' clubs typically emphasized sport while girls' clubs focused on games and domestic skills; adult clubs too formed around leisure interests and also blended these with sociability and informal education.

By 1888 fourteen societies had been formed at Toynbee Hall with clubs for chess, football, swimming, music and photography, plus an Elizabethan literary society, ethical society, Travellers' Club and Workmen's Travelling Club.[53] Barnett considered the self-governing Lolesworth club the most important to the aims of the settlement. Founded in 1887 it was teetotal and enabled social intercourse between resident workers and neighbours.[54] Through concerts, lectures, debates, excursions and Saturday 'Free and Easies' it was intended to nurture friendship between residents and local people and by 1890 had approximately 275 male and female members.[55] By encouraging members to participate in its management it aimed to develop the citizenship skills upon which Green and the social idealists placed such importance. However, the club's Athletic Association was obliged to rely on residents to act as officers as members' attendance at meetings was irregular.[56] By 1894 interest in lectures and debates had decreased markedly although entertainments and socials remained popular.[57] Neither were all clubs socially inclusive. The management of the Toynbee Travellers' Club, established to enable local people of limited means to undertake educational visits, was dominated by residents; one historian has noted how its trips were organized as an Oxford reading party rather than a holiday journey.[58] Although membership was theoretically open to all connected with the Hall, it was in practice regulated. Applicants were required to provide references personally known at the Hall and a probationary period facilitated the exclusion of anyone considered out of harmony with the spirit of the club. Honorary members, on the other hand, were nominated and elected in recognition of special service to the Hall and their near relatives and friends could join as associate members. Furthermore the club was effectively unaffordable to the average citizen of Whitechapel with visits to Switzerland and Florence costing over £12.[59] The excursions of the Toynbee Natural History Society were also beyond reach of most local people.[60] The establishment in 1902 of the Toynbee Workmen's Travelling Club for members of Trade Unions and Co-operative Societies resolved issues of cost but its socially segregated membership hardly provided a common ground for social intercourse between the middle and working classes.

4.3 Oxford House and the public school mission

The Oxford House settlement in Bethnal Green was established by the University of Oxford in 1884. Attached to St. Andrew's Parish Church, it was high Anglican and more outwardly religious than Toynbee Hall.[61] It organized a range of clubs and activities, which included a People's Entertainment Society, recreative evening classes and the Whitechapel Lads' Institute with classes in French, music and wood-carving. Late nineteenth-century men's clubs have been argued as sites of competing cultural policy agendas[62] and it was an objective of Oxford House clubs to offer a teetotal alternative to working men's clubs. The Oxford House club was designed for clerks and skilled artisans and aimed to replicate the ethos of a university with lectures, debates, branches of the National Home Reading Union and sporting activities.[63] University Club, on the other hand, was formed in 1887 for unskilled men with billiard tables, bagatelle boards, cricket and football clubs, and discussion and dramatic societies, and recruited over 1,000 members in its first year.[64] Oxford House clubs were intended to develop the skills of social citizenship and inculcate a 'higher ideal of club life' than politicized working men's clubs.[65] However, they were not fully democratic and even in 1895 officers of the settlement retained responsibility for their oversight, lacking trust in the capacity of their working-class members to manage them.[66] Antipathy to working men's clubs was further expressed through the establishment of a network of teetotal men's clubs. Adopting R.C. Buchanan's East End 'tee-to-tum' social clubs, Harold Boulton and James Granville Adderley, head of Oxford House, founded the Federation of Working Men's Social Clubs,[67] which by 1898 had around seventy affiliated institutions and included several of Paton's Social Institutes.[68] Overseen by the Oxford House Club[69] these clubs were regulated through the Federation and were, according to T.C. Collings, the only popular temperance public houses in London, with games of all descriptions, reading rooms and libraries.[70]

Boys, sport and the public school mission

Kate Bradley and Trevor Harris have identified an increase in juvenile delinquency as a significant influence on settlement work, foregrounding intervention in youth leisure to inculcate civilized values and social citizenship.[71] While the immediate concern was to modify delinquent behaviour, settlements were in the vanguard of what Roberts describes as a youth training movement in character-building and citizenship.[72] Late nineteenth-century literature on social work with young people reveals deep concerns about the physical and mental capacities of boys; a period, as Stephanie Olsen notes, in which concepts of manliness and character were formed in the contexts of social citizenship and imperial ambition.[73] Self-improvement through character, a forceful utilitarian idea of the mid-nineteenth century, was losing traction by the 1880s as social science suggested that character was also formed by social environment. However, as Stefan Collini has argued, idealist philosophy retained a focus on the individual as the primary object of voluntary intervention. Bernard Bosanquet, for example, insisted human action sprang from the individual mind and was to be explained rationally rather than causally.[74] Although this may appear to contradict idealism's concern for community, it is important to note that its realization of the good society was only possible as an expression of the general will; through the prism of liberalism, social change began with the individual. The typical aim of a boys' club was, as the Congregational Mansfield House expressed it, to develop character through dutiful citizenship, a recognition of collective responsibility and qualities of leadership.[75] Settlement workers quickly discovered that the young male East Londoner did not possess these attributes and was instead unruly, disdainful of authority and reluctant to join religious or middle-class organizations that imposed rules.[76] An illustrative example of this was Oxford House's Webbe Institute, a club of 400 boys of whom none came from the slums. Unlike Toynbee Hall there was an emphasis on football, cricket and boxing; sport was, as William Reynell Anson, chairman of the Council of Oxford House commented, the most effective means of changing the male youth's enjoyment of disorder by control and education.[77]

With increased juvenile delinquency, a facility to connect with working-class boys was an important quality in a resident worker. Those with previous experience of club work were better equipped to relate to slum boys to whom boxing held a special appeal. While barely within the parameters of middle-class culture, boxing was disciplined, orderly and popular in the East End[78] where its blend of masculinity, controlled violence and social respect appealed to rougher young males. Hugh Legge's Repton Club at Oxford House gained national recognition for its use of boxing to recruit the boy to whom club membership was abhorrent. Its sponsorship by Repton School was part of a public school mission to the urban poor. Georgina Brewis has shown how in the early twentieth century voluntary social work became an integral element of the education of middle-class girls as the British elites sought new outlets for service.[79] By the mid-1880s approximately twenty public schools had established a mission in London, most claiming religious objectives as their primary motivation. The provision and supervision of leisure-based activities became an important element of their work and for some schools attachment to an existing settlement was preferable to founding a separate mission.[80] Oxford House's St. Anthony's Club, for example – which recruited from the class of boys from which 'hooligans' came – was re-named as the Eastbourne Club when it was taken over as the School Mission of Eastbourne College.[81] Middle and higher class girls were similarly encouraged to embrace the service ideal through the United Girls School Mission, building character and developing skills useful to future employment.[82] Settlements might thus reach out to the poor and encourage self-reliance but the preparation of a younger and privileged generation for civic leadership ensured the continuity of a middle-class hegemony.

Not all settlements advanced the theory and practice of social work. University Hall, established in St. Pancras in 1890 by Mary Ward with support from the Unitarian James Martineau, James Drummond and Stopford Brooke, was modelled on Toynbee Hall. It was however more overtly religious[83] and its restricted emphasis on education and Biblical criticism[84] limited its appeal to working-class people.[85] Ward, daughter of Thomas Arnold, niece of Matthew Arnold and one of the most successful novelists of the late nineteenth century, shared few of the Liberal sympathies of the Barnetts, being politically conservative and staunchly opposed to the suffragette movement. She displayed little interest in personal contact with the local community, and resident workers, dissatisfied with the lack of opportunities for social work, founded Marchmont Hall in 1891 to develop community clubs and educational classes.[86] Ward was consequently obliged to adopt a more socially orientated approach and with funding from the library philanthropist John Passmore Edwards built a new settlement close to Tavistock Square in prosperous Bloomsbury.[87] Although this focused on the creation of an associational life by bringing people into building, there was little evidence that this was anything other than an end in itself; as its second annual report stated: 'The fortnightly socials in the Hall represent the most characteristic feature of this club life –the social is a party where people meet together and pleasant evening is passed in each other's company. The Hall is laid out with tables and the company sit in groups, or talks, or listen to music provided by the Associates.'[88] Mary Ward remained unenthusiastic about engagement with the poor and returned to the pursuit of philanthropically funded projects.[89]

The Victoria Women's Settlement was founded in 1898 in the Everton district of Liverpool. Like Toynbee Hall it adopted friendship as a conduit between the cultured English woman and the social outcast as a 'little oasis of education, refinement and sympathy' designed to make the poor feel that 'they belong to us'.[90] Supported by pupils from Liverpool's Belvedere School and Cheltenham Ladies College,[91] the Victoria settlement functioned as a club for working-class girls aged between ten and fifteen, opening each evening between 5.00 and 7.00 pm with tea, lessons in sewing, games and a National Home Reading Circle.[92] By 1904 a senior club provided instruction in the employment skills of cooking, fancy work and mending. Here, settlement workers visited the homes of club members, recording domestic conditions in the Victorian philanthropic custom through which middle-class women visited the homes of the poor.[93] Presented as an act of friendship, home visiting originated as an evangelical practice through the Stranger's Friend Association in the 1780s.[94] The offer of practical help was important but, as Frank Prochaska comments, evangelical religious motives remained dominant.[95] At the Victoria settlement visiting was also a means of surveillance of school attendance and the character of potential future domestic servants. Clubs and classes were graded according to social background; girls from the poorest homes were taught needlework and toy-making while a separate club existed for 'girls of a better class' and in all clubs the aim was to make girls more efficient in household management, which for many meant domestic service.[96] Although religion remained a potent force, modernizing concepts of social work also saw personal visitation necessary to forge links between individuals and institutional provision. Through the appointment of Elizabeth Macadam as Warden in 1903 and Eleanor Rathbone as Secretary in 1904 the settlement's objectives were re-defined in social terms. With Emily Oliver Jones, Macadam and Rathbone set out a new social approach, initiating a scientific study of the causes of poverty, a training scheme for settlement workers and a primary emphasis on social reform in place of charitable philanthropy.[97] When Macadam and Rathbone became associated with Liverpool University, these ideas were applied on a wider canvas.

4.4 The Liverpool University Settlement

The Liverpool University Settlement, established in 1906, pioneered the application of social science to the theory and practice of social work. Founded twenty-two years after Toynbee Hall its aims and practices were formulated in the light of advances in social science. Formed as a men's settlement connected to the David Lewis Club in the deprived south end of the city it integrated practical club work in the curriculum of the embryonic school of social work at the University of Liverpool. As with Toynbee Hall, leisure featured in its first objective of assisting in the means of provision for education and recreation; its second was to enquire into the social conditions of the poor and devise plans to address these.[98] Leisure was not thus simply a sphere in which the poor could be engaged on friendly terms but a field in which social objectives in education, employment and social citizenship could be scientifically pursued. The relationship between the university and the settlement was closer than that found at Oxford or Cambridge. Liverpool became a leading city in the development of voluntary social services and the integration of leisure in social work was aided by staff appointments to the University's School of Training for Social Work. Fred d'Aeth, lecturer in social work, was also warden of the David Lewis Club and had been instrumental in the establishment of the Liverpool Council of Voluntary Aid in 1909,[99] and the appointment of Elizabeth Macadam to a lectureship in 1910 further consolidated the bonds between academic research and the city's social services.[100] Fred Marquis, appointed in 1909, had been assistant general secretary of the Co-operative Holidays Association, an organization with strong connections to John Brown Paton's National Home Reading Union, and became Warden of the University's Settlement.[101] Leisure was thus connected to a department of social science and applied to social service in a community setting. Work with the children of the local Harrington School, for example, blended the formation and operation of clubs for both boys and girls with medical inspections, a dental clinic and an employment bureau for boys.[102]

Unlike Toynbee Hall, Liverpool actively sought out the 'residuum' of the poorest and worst-housed sections of the working classes rather than only those committed to self-improvement. Virtually all its work was conducted in external community institutions, principally the David Lewis Club. Inspired, according to Marquis, by Besant's *All Sorts and Conditions of Men*, the Club offered educational and recreational programmes.[103] When these failed to appeal to more than a minority of the desired population, Marquis undertook field research to explore to what extent contemporary attempts to replicate Besant's People's Palace had been successful. Lady Florence Bell's Winter Gardens in Middlesbrough provided games, a reading room and a café and attracted a daily attendance of 390, but the absence of alcohol limited its wider appeal. In Edinburgh, Thomas Nelson's People's Halls offered games rooms, gymnasiums and concerts while in Glasgow there was municipal provision of a Winter Garden and a Conservatory. In Birmingham some municipal buildings had been converted into Paton's Social Institutes, but again their teetotal regime limited growth.[104] Further obstacles to popularity included perceptions of a moralizing tone and over-ambitious expectations of the intellect of the population. Marquis concluded that a social centre could only succeed by eschewing improvement and enlightenment and simply allowing people to be made happy through social intercourse and leisure. The proposed Liverpool 'Palace of Delight' adopted Besant's claim that when people were happy it was easy to be good,[105] and would sell alcohol and reject a moralizing tone. Although the First World War prevented its construction, its rationale was innovatory, positing leisure as a source of happiness and pleasure rather than self-improvement and middle-class aspiration.

4.5 The settlement movement, social work and leisure

The settlement movement marked a transitional stage from charitable philanthropy to social work. Although Toynbee Hall was inspired by Green's ideals of social citizenship, these were not fully worked out in terms of the whole community and, as Ashley noted, although providing a higher tone of club, it failed to reach the poorest.[106] Recent criticism has argued that not always being located in slum districts, settlements catered for the respectable rather than the rough working class.[107] Nevertheless they were part of the moral dialogue of the philanthropic response to social injustice and innovative in developing a model of active social intervention within the community. However, settlements retained establishment connections that could not conceal the gap in social class between reformers and those to be reformed. Oxford House, for example, was led by influential social and political figures: William Reynell Anson, Chair of its Council, was a Fellow of Eton College, Chair of All Souls College and later the Vice-Chancellor of Oxford University; its head, Arthur Foley Winnington-Ingram, was educated at Marlborough College and Keble College, Oxford and later became the Bishop of London. Its residents – largely drawn from Oxford University – were also from this social stratum. For many of them, settlement work represented an opportunity for voluntary service to a lower social class rather than to effect meaningful social change. Furthermore, as Bernard Bosanquet observed, residents had few spontaneous connections with the poor as the formalities of the settlement precluded the citizen spirit of everyday life.[108] Residence was temporary and although hospitality was offered – at both Oxford House and Toynbee Hall working class people were taken on annual visits to Oxford each Whit-Monday to be met by members of the University and dine in a college – a shared leisure on common ground was a passing experience.

The practicable socialism of the Barnetts was a Liberal belief in strengthening the resilience of the individual rather than a social transformation of the collective.[109] Toynbee Hall and Oxford House were inherently paternalistic, and the naming of the Bermondsey settlement's club for disabled boys as the *Guild of the Brave Poor Things* surely harked to an earlier phase of philanthropic intervention. For the Barnetts, all music halls, seaside excursions and spectator sports of a 'pleasure-seeking generation' were empty of inner meaning and limiting to a progressive growth of English character.[110] Sport was an ambivalent form of leisure in this respect. Where settlement provision for sport and games was made, working class people appear to have found it appealing. Furthermore at the public schools and universities that provided the recruiting ground for settlement workers, muscular Christianity had invested sport with civilizing values of team spirit and leadership. Residential workers were thus able to establish common ground with their local communities in sport as a sphere in which working-class people could engage on relatively equal terms. Spectator sport may have displayed elements of unruly behaviour but the football crowd of the late nineteenth century was more respectable and socially mixed than its early Victorian counterpart. Barnett's suspicions of sport were, however, widely shared; speaking at the opening of the Passmore Edwards Settlement John Morley spoke approvingly of public lectures on Dante but hoped that sport and athletics would not become dominant.[111] The Barnetts' attitudes to urban working-class leisure betrayed a lack of understanding and an inchoate fear that its sheer popularity far out-stretched that offered by the settlement. Ernest Duckerschoff's report of working-class life in Newcastle, for example, presented a markedly alternative picture of a socially integrated urban community with friendly intercourse in numerous clubs and societies, harmless sport activity and mutual friendliness between the police, middle classes and workmen.[112] Although no direct comparison can be drawn from two contrasting communities, the account differs in tone and approach. It is perhaps of note that Duckerschoff was a miner with more acute social insight into working-class life. The construct of slum leisure found in some settlements corresponded not with the social sciences but with contemporary discursive constructs of the slum as the opposite of the ideal middle-class community. Yet, as Bill Luckin has pointed out, twentieth-century social scientific studies of the slums of Manchester and Salford discovered their inhabitants to be rational and socially aware of their situation;[113] nineteenth-century slum dwellers also resented middle-class representations of them.[114]

Thomas Hancock Nunn perceptively described the settlement movement as a leisured class for an industrial population.[115] A more recent critique has similarly likened settlements to a form of colonization[116] and as with political colonization, power resided with governing committees that, as described above, could be reluctant to relinquish control of their clubs. The work of the Victorian and Edwardian settlements exhibited a discernible sense of a ruling leisure class fulfilling a moral duty; contemporary observers saw Toynbee Hall to be filled with 'men of some culture and some leisure with public spirit and high aims',[117] and settlement work a worthy use of leisure by those who possessed it.[118] This was particularly so with the Mary Ward settlements, which were moulded to reflect her sense of charitable service. The sponsorship of leisure-based clubs by public schools and the training of a social elite in philanthropic duty further suggest a regime of charitable philanthropy by a leisure class rather than scientific social work. The former was discriminatory in approach, deploying a case-work model to help those who demonstrated the capacity to make the best use of whatever aid was provided. Samuel Barnett was a founding member of the Charity Organisation Society and approximately half of the Toynbee Hall resident workers served on its local committees, including Hancock Nunn who became honorary secretary of the Stepney Charity Organisation Society.[119] Furthermore, the practice of home visiting at both the Victoria Settlement in Liverpool and Toynbee Hall[120] was consistent with Victorian middle-class interest in the working-class home.[121] Settlement interventions in leisure were never completely free of the idea of rational recreation and, although encouraging working-class agency in the management of their clubs, they remained aloof from political clubs even though many supported trade union activity. The Liverpool University Settlement advanced the understanding of social work as a trained profession, grounded in the knowledge and techniques of the social sciences and the social meaning of leisure in the context of the community. Although retaining aspects of paternalism, it laid the foundation for the greater inclusion of leisure in social work and sociological theory in the inter-war decades.

Utopian and Radical Leisure Communities

5.1 Introduction

From the final decade of the nineteenth century evangelical religious interest in leisure was challenged by secular models of voluntary association, which defined leisure not primarily in moral terms but in those of an imagined ideal social community. Utopian thinking had historically associated leisure with ideals of community and the good society, notably through Plato and Aristotle and later Thomas More, whose Utopians devoted an hour to recreation each day and tended their gardens when not following Aristotle's guidance to pursue intellectual development.[1] In terms of the built environment, Patrick Geddes and Victor Branford, both connected to the Chelsea Utopians discussion circle on citizenship,[2] developed a sociological approach to urban living in which leisure and the cultural environment formed the seedbed of community in a new type of town. A different type of community was envisioned in socialism, which developed a leisure culture imbued with co-operative and collective values. Planners valued urban open space in terms of public parks, recreation grounds and the cultivation of a civic spirt; Fabian and radical socialists, on the other hand, influenced by a romantic imagination of the countryside as a pre-industrial organic society, saw the land as a contested leisure space and a common spiritual heritage.[3]

The garden city and leisure

Although the late nineteenth-century city raised concerns about over-crowding and social fragmentation it nevertheless retained its status of a centre of science, art and culture. Ebenezer Howard devised the garden city as a new type of town, harmonizing the civilized life of the city with the natural and healthy environment of the countryside.[4] Modelled in part on the industrial villages of Cadbury's Bournville and Lever's Port Sunlight, the garden city was simultaneously a planned space and a planned community.[5] By encouraging a new way of associational living it would be a social city, distinguished from the 'selfishness and rapacity' of the industrial city by its communal and fraternal spirit and voluntary effort.[6] A new leisure was central to this objective; communal amenities, social intercourse and restrictions on the commercial provision of licensed premises were all intended to nurture a new type of civilized life.[7] Letchworth, the first garden city, was built in 1903 with ample green space and civic buildings for community use. Designed by Barry Parker and Raymond Unwin, socialist and disciple of William Morris, its domestic and public buildings reflected Morris' belief in the moral purpose of art.[8] An infrastructure to facilitate communal activity and voluntary association was provided by public buildings and spaces for music, amateur theatricals and dances; there was however no planning permission for a public house in its working-class area.[9] Howard's belief that voluntary association in leisure would bring the social classes together was at least in part fulfilled at Letchworth. In other garden cities and garden suburbs too, for example Brentham in Ealing and Wavertree in Liverpool, the availability of gardens, parks and playing areas encouraged the formation of numerous sports clubs and horticultural societies.[10]

The garden city ideal informed urban planning for leisure more generally. The formation in 1903 of the Sociological Society, whose founder members included Branford, Geddes and John Hobson, provided a forum for the dissemination of theory and practice in planning and brought leisure further into public debate on urban social policy. Existing towns borrowed from the garden city ideal; the Moor Pool garden suburb in Birmingham, for example, provided sports and social clubs, a reading room and library, a central hall, a bowling green and tennis courts.[11] Immediately after the First World War the New Town Council, a planning group formed by the Society of Friends to build an experimental new town based on principles of co-operation and community service,[12] adopted leisure association as the principal means of creating civic life and community service.[13] The influence of William Morris was clearly evident in its proposals for a communal People's House for social intercourse and recreation and a Guest House to enable visitors to 'share for a time the life of association and comradeship' characteristic of the town.[14] Although few in number, garden cities consolidated the idea that a planned environment that supported voluntary association in leisure and civic engagement was an adjunct to a functional social and spatial community. This association of leisure and community later became central to post-war social reconstruction and the planning of new housing estates.

Socialist leisure associations

With the founding of the Independent Labour Party in 1893 socialism became a force in the creation of leisure association. More time for leisure was a political objective of trade unions but ethical rather than material issues were more significant to the formation of a socialist leisure culture.[15] The spread of socialism was driven not only by its economic arguments but also by its moral values and pursuit of a co-operative and democratic society. Leisure was a field in which collective and co-operative values could be expressed and disseminated through cultural practice. As Mark Bevir notes, this ethical brand of socialism flourished through local organizations, utopian communities and the Independent Labour Party, operating not through the centrist and scientific approach of George Bernard Shaw and the Webbs but through social fellowship and voluntary co-operative action.[16] The formation of a socialist leisure culture was in part formed by a belief that capitalist commercial leisure distracted workers from political activity,[17] but its primary objective was to develop the sense of belonging to a socialist community. By the early twentieth century it was possible to adopt the socialist leisure lifestyle personified in Alice Foley, a Bolton cotton operative, who was an active trade unionist and member of a Labour Church, a Socialist Sunday School, Bolton Socialist Club and the Clarion Cycling Club.[18] It is unlikely that Foley was unique in this respect. Socialists shared with idealists a belief in the well-being of the community and democratic participation in social citizenship. However they disagreed with idealists and liberals on how social improvement was to be effected, seeking structural change and a collective resolution of social problems by the state. In the mid-nineteenth century Chartism was socialized through instrumental and vocal concerts, amateur dramatics, bands and social evenings, which, as Malcolm Chase properly reminds us, leavened politics with fun.[19] The new socialist leisure continued to perform this function not through centralized imposition but, as Paul Salveson has shown, through numerous community-based Fabian, co-operative and later communist associations.[20]

A salient aspect of socialist leisure culture was its relationship to the land.[21] The countryside was the antithesis of the late Victorian city and had religious as well as romantic connotations; as Elizabeth Baigent has argued, evangelicalism had endowed nature with spirituality and a 'natural sanctity' by its association with religious experiences.[22] Many urban religious organizations adopted the countryside as a leisure space for Sunday School outings, children's holidays and temperance excursions. Its spiritual associations implied a leisure that was reverential to and consistent with the values it represented. As Henrietta Barnett asserted, a visit to the countryside was not an opportunity for exuberance by the crowd but a time for the quiet enjoyment of Nature.[23] The association of open space with spirituality was embedded in the Keswick Convention, an annual cross denominational gathering established in July 1875 through Anglican evangelicals, notably T.D. Harford-Battersby, Vicar of St. John's in Keswick and Hanmer William Webb-Peploe, a founder of the National Protestant Church Union and active member of the Anti-Socialist Union of Churches.[24] Drawing inspiration from the 'spiritual power' of the Lake District, it emphasized contemplation, moderate dress and a simple life. The countryside thus became associated with an enjoyment of nature and a non-ostentatious use of leisure. Radical socialism adopted these principles but also challenged the privatization of the countryside by a leisure class. Both strands were influenced by a cultural construction of the land in terms of what David Matless refers to as spaces of citizenship.[25]

The Co-operative Holidays Association (CHA) was established in 1893 by the Congregationalist minister Thomas Arthur Leonard, with help from John Brown Paton, to organize walking holidays in the countryside. It blended the Keswick Convention's concept of the countryside as a spiritual leisure space with an ethical Fabian socialism. The influence of Leonard's political socialism on its formation runs counter to the argument that socialism was a secular alternative to religion; to Leonard they were intertwined. In a sermon to his Dockray Street church congregation in the Lancashire cotton town of Colne, Leonard, a member of the Colne Valley branch of the Social Democratic Foundation, likened socialism to a new expression of Christianity, praising the work of trades unions and quoting from the Bible, Matthew Arnold and John Ruskin in a trenchant critique of capitalism.[26] Leonard contrasted the frivolity of the popular commercial seaside resort, typified by Blackpool, with a communal and non-commercialized walking holiday in the countryside in which class distinctions would be dissolved.[27] A CHA holiday party was assembled as a temporary community, embodying co-operative values and living collectively for a week. Centres were established throughout the British Isles, many located in the Lake District where the romanticism of Wordsworth and Coleridge resonated with critiques of urban industrial life. Strenuous rambles in the daytime were followed by sober entertainments and lectures in the evening. The CHA held a particular appeal to members of the Pleasant Sunday Afternoon associations, Bible classes and Sunday Schools of non-conformist congregations.[28] Innovatively it welcomed women, offering a safe cultural environment in which the financially independent new woman could travel unaccompanied as an equal member of the holiday party. Its clientele was socially mixed; as a journalist commented in 1897, each party was a small commune to itself with almost every class of society from the mechanic to the university professor;[29] like the majority of social interventions in leisure, however, it failed to attract the lower working-classes.

The CHA ideal of a communal leisure owed much to Ruskin and Morris, blending socialist values and spiritual beliefs. Drawing from Morris' vision of a commonwealth in which all men would live under equal conditions with a strong sense of community,[30] its approach to the countryside as a space to be enjoyed for its own sake reflected Ruskin's joy of nature and a spiritual sense of the land.[31] Although not religious holidays in any theological sense, religion interjected to ensure the CHA's holidays were never totally secular; daily morning prayers and Grace before meals were routinely conducted.[32] Furthermore, rambles led by professional and educated people were interspersed with hymn-singing and talks on natural history and the literary associations of the landscape. Hymn-singing on rambles, in Leonard's view, gave a mountainside an 'uplift' in terms of spiritual experience.[33] The CHA ideal of citizenship was one of communality and fellowship in leisure. Conspicuous display of class or wealth through dress or behaviour was forbidden and in its holiday centres, which it referred to as guest houses, residents undertook tasks that contributed to the collective good, for example the preparation of vegetables for dinner or boot-cleaning, adhering to Morris' insistence that in the ideal socialist community, all would do their share of 'rougher work'. Attempting to be a community of all classes, the CHA offered special rates through a Poor Folks Holidays scheme. This was however regulated in terms of respectability, its house magazine *Comradeship* noting that assisted holidays were designed for persons of 'taste and refinement' who would naturally visit a centre but were circumstantially unable to do so.[34] The Association never fulfilled Leonard's aim of replacing the working-class Blackpool holiday and as its membership became predominantly middle class, people with hobbies like photography, botany and geology would, as a popular magazine noted, find abundant opportunity to practise them.[35] Leonard resented the middle-class domination of the CHA, complaining of a 'smart set' influence with a tendency to unsuitable dress and a disparagement of robust and wholesome pursuits.[36] The simplicity and equality that had been the principal characteristics of the CHA became increasingly unacceptable to middle-class guests unwilling to tolerate cold baths and earth closets. In 1912 Leonard left the CHA to form the Holiday Fellowship, which retained the CHA's original standards of simplicity and strenuousness. Both organizations flourished in the inter-war period and remained active until the late twentieth century; the number of Holiday Fellowship centres in use during the inter-war period peaked at 34 in 1936, accommodating almost 40,000 guests.[37]

Through its federation of regional and local groups the CHA sustained communal activities throughout the year. By 1910 twenty-nine CHA rambling clubs had been formed, notably in northern towns including Blackburn, Bolton, Colne, Darwen, Manchester, Nelson, Oldham, Rochdale and Stockport.[38] Some, like the Bolton CHA rambling club, established a NHRU reading circle to pursue the Union's Open Air Course and nearly all held club days and New Year reunions.[39] The Huddersfield CHA Rambling and Reading Club for example, organized its own Reading Circle and Rambling Syllabus for its thirty members.[40] This pattern of organization continued through the inter-war period. The CHA was not a radical movement. Although Leonard shared the Wandervogel enthusiasm for experimentation in a non-bourgeois communal life, the CHA was constrained by considerations of religion and middle-class respectability to a more natural and simple life of rambles, singing and joy in nature.[41] It was however international in outlook and committed to peace-making, organizing holidays in Switzerland, Austria and Germany almost until 1914 to maintain social relations, particularly in Germany, where a CHA Association of Friends had been formed.[42]

Both the CHA and the Holiday Fellowship promoted the countryside as a democratically accessible leisure space though neither was actively involved in political campaigns for wider access. For almost a century they remained sustainable voluntary organizers of leisure in the countryside and influenced the establishment of the Youth Hostels Association, Workers' Travel Association, Ramblers' Association and the Pennine Way, all of which owed their existence to Leonard's social democratic beliefs and the aesthetic and co-operative leisure culture suggested by Ruskin and Morris.[43]

5.2 The Clarion movement

From the late nineteenth century socialist groups argued a radical alternative to liberal social reforming interventions, presenting, to borrow Maeve Cooke's phrase, the social arrangements of a differing social order that might be possible.[44] The historical tensions in the British Labour movement between accommodation within a capitalist system and the pursuit of an alternative model[45] were replicated in socialist leisure culture. Both strands reflected Ruskin's belief that co-operation and capitalism were not just differing economic models but different societies and that only the former would provide the worker with time for leisure for self-improvement.[46] Socialist leisure associations were thus significant to the process of moral dialogue, notably through the Clarion movement, which coalesced around the socialist weekly newspaper *The Clarion*, founded in December 1891 by the Manchester journalist Robert Blatchford.[47] Adopting a breezy and iconoclastic style this blended news and features with socialist propaganda, speaking to a collective readership and supporting the formation of a predominantly urban socialist leisure movement.[48] Blatchford's nationalism and class-consciousness resonated with working-class people[49] and, as Krishan Kumar observes, his stress on Englishness owed much to the English rural ideal.[50] His manifesto, *Merrie England*, was not however a re-invention of a pastoral idyll but a vision of how leisure would be re-distributed in a socialist society.[51] Addressing an imaginary John Smith, a working man in Oldham, Blatchford explained how capitalist production of luxuries for the rich denied him the leisure he deserved and presented an alternative socialist England of shorter working hours and increased leisure.[52]

The ideal citizen of the Clarion movement was not the peasant of an imagined bucolic England but an active contributor to the commonwealth from which he drew support.[53] Being a member of the Clarion movement gave identity as a 'Clarionet', or if female a 'Clarionette', a feminization disparaged by Henry Hyndman who nevertheless acknowledged the Clarion contribution to the spread of socialism.[54] Clarion membership was widely distributed across a range of leisure associations, which included Clarion Scouts, Clarion Vocal Unions, Clarion Glee Clubs, Clarion Handicraft Guilds and Clarion Field Clubs.[55] There were in addition Clarion sports clubs for swimming, football, cricket, hockey and rambling.[56] A salient feature of these clubs is that they represented popular contemporary leisure forms that the Clarion movement was able to claim and re-model in terms of socialism. On the one hand this was part of a wider labour movement to dissuade workers from engaging in capitalist leisure but more importantly it made it possible, through voluntary association, to build a socialist cultural community outside party political structures and thus relatively free from internecine disagreements. In Bolton, for example, the Clarion movement recruited from both the Social Democratic Foundation and the Independent Labour Party.[57] Nowhere was this undertaken more successfully than in the Clarion Cycling Club, which became the largest and the most important club to the spread of the movement.

In the final quarter of the nineteenth century cycling became an affordable means of escape from the industrial city to the countryside. Available to most working and lower middle-class people, cycling lent itself to the formation of clubs, notably, in 1878, the Cyclists Touring Club. By the 1890s over 300 cycling clubs operated in London alone.[58] The Clarion Cycling Club was initiated by Tom Groom in 1894 through the Bond Street Labour Church in Birmingham as a socialist alternative to the Cyclists' Touring Club and through the *Clarion*, 120 branches had been formed nationally by 1895 with a total membership of 7,000.[59] Annual meets, the first at Ashbourne in 1895, enabled Clarion members to socialize on a wide geographical basis; later meets were held primarily in the north and midlands from where the Club's national secretaries tended to be drawn.[60] The Clarion clubs developed a more explicitly socialist and secular leisure sub-culture than the CHA and it was a matter of pride to them that Christian socialism appeared hamstrung by its inability to declare affinity to political socialism.[61] The leisure culture of the Clarion clubs differed from that of the CHA and indeed that of other secular voluntary leisure associations with an interest in the countryside, for example the Cyclists' Touring Club (1878), the Polytechnic Rambling Club (1885) and the London Federation of Rambling Clubs (1901). Clarion cycling clubs were characterized by banter, high spirits and drink-enlivened runs from the town to the countryside and by summer camps with concerts, dances, recitations of comic songs, and boisterous socialist meetings. Nevertheless their proselytization of socialism embodied older Methodist practices; meets often included a socialist discussion[62] and Clarion Scouts and Vans travelled into the countryside for open-air meetings and the distribution of socialist literature.[63] Alice Foley, for example, recalled club rides in the wake of the Clarion van, helping form a nucleus for speeches and handing out socialist publications on village greens in an atmosphere of 'fun and comradeship'.[64] Clarion Rambling Clubs were also popular, foregrounding questions about land ownership and restrictions on access. The Sheffield club, founded in 1900, claimed to be the largest in Britain in 1920; its handbook inter-mixed details of walking routes with excerpts from socialist writers including John Ruskin, William Morris and Edward Carpenter.[65]

Although national organizations, the CHA and Blatchford's Clarion movement were strong in the north of England, both originating in Lancashire and contributing to what Paul Salveson identifies as a northern radical socialist tradition grounded in a co-operative and socialist leisure culture.[66] Writing in 1917, the social philosopher Cecil Delisle Burns observed the democratic ideal to be particularly evident in the north and midlands through a 'different feeling in social life'.[67] The strength of the CHA and the Clarion movement in north-east Lancashire supports this assertion. In the cotton town of Nelson, three miles from Leonard's Colne, a local socialist leisure culture became integrated with municipal political socialism. Nelson was not a large town; by 1900 its population was approximately 30,000 and non-conformity was dominant. These factors, as Jeffrey Hill notes, helped create a local identity and a community with a sense of itself.[68] Socialism gained a formidable presence in Nelson. The Nelson branch of the Independent Labour Party, founded in 1892, took control of the Town Council in 1905 and in the same period an active independent Clarion movement helped create a local leisure culture infused with socialist and democratic values. The integration of politics and leisure was eased by the ILP's ethical socialism, which committed it to cultural as well as economic change; in 1908, for example, Nelson council rejected the offer of a public library by Andrew Carnegie because of his anti-trade union working practices. Nelson had few large employers as its industry was based on the 'room and power system' through which small manufacturers rented space, obliging workers and employers to resolve disputes through personal dialogue. It was to this structural aspect of industry that Stan Iveson and Roger Brown attributed the growth of a radical and educated workforce, well versed in the techniques of self-advocacy.[69] Public life in late-Victorian and Edwardian Nelson was accordingly characterized by a co-operative and collective spirit; the local co-operative society, for example, had 7,000 members – approximately a quarter of its population – and provided cultural amenities that included a library and reading room, lectures, tea parties, billiards and accommodation for the societies and clubs of non-conformist churches that included a branch of Paton's National Home Reading Union.[70]

Like many northern industrial towns Nelson possessed a strong cycling culture. Despite heavy industrialization, Lancashire retained extensive open countryside and cycling from the town to villages and rural landmarks was a popular leisure pursuit. By 1882 the county had thirty cycling clubs, comprising mainly young middle-class men with the means to afford a bicycle. By the 1890s the availability of cheaper machines fuelled a growth of working-class cycling clubs: Burnley Wheelers, for example, recruited sixty-three male and eight female members within a year of opening in 1895.[71] Unlike the CHA, the Clarion movement was actively committed to the political labour struggle and in Nelson formed strong connections with the local branch of the ILP, which by 1912 had 1,000 members and a range of societies and clubs including a Socialist Sunday School and a Glee Club.[72] Many Lancashire cycling clubs established club-houses in the countryside;[73] the Clarion movement followed suit with club-houses at

Bucklow Hill, Knutsford in 1897 and Handforth in 1903.[74] In Nelson the Independent Labour Party established its first Clarion House in 1899 over a butcher's shop as a social meeting place for both men and women. In 1912 a new and larger Clarion House was built at Newchurch in Pendle with a loan of £350 from the Nelson Weavers' Association.[75] This became (and remains) a popular venue for both political and social purposes, providing a leisure amenity for walkers and cyclists from north-east Lancashire and beyond. In the inter-war years weekend attendances of 400–500 were normal and socialist organizations, including the Co-operative Women's Guild, held their meetings there.[76] In response to growing demand for socialist leisure provision, the Nelson ILP built the larger Ribble Valley Clarion Club House in Ribchester in 1913. This was a significant undertaking, enabled through the formation of an associated Land Society through which members of the ILP could buy one pound shares. With seating accommodation for 120 people and sleeping accommodation both indoors and in tents, the Club claimed to have 'all the necessary requirements of a Guest House' and became a regional centre for cycling, athletic and other sports and pastimes as well as providing access to eighteen acres of land and river-bank.[77]

Figure 2 Clarion House, Newchurch-in-Pendle. Situated only a few miles away from the north-east Lancashire cotton towns, Clarion House has been a popular venue for walkers and cyclists since its opening in 1912.

Nineteenth-century urban civil society was nearly everywhere constructed around middle-class interests, with the labour movement running in parallel rather than being integrated. However, in Nelson socialism effectively produced an alternative civic culture through the ILP, trade unions, co-operative society and the socio-political leisure associations of the Clarion and Co-operative movements. The cohesion of the labour movement in Nelson was made visible through the voluntary leisure activity it created; a socialist culture extended into everyday life through the trade-union movement, local politics and leisure.

5.3 The Co-operative movement

With three million members by 1914, the Co-operative movement was a significant institution in the promotion of collective and democratic values. Like the CHA and the Clarion movement, it originated in the north of England; the first society was formed by the Rochdale Pioneers Society in 1844 as a member-owned shop. By 1900, 1,439 local Co-operative Wholesale Societies had been established throughout England and Scotland. Following the decline of Christian Socialism the Co-operative Society became a mediator of socialist values and in many towns was the principal provider of social and cultural facilities. This provision was normally the responsibility of the local co-operative education committees. The Manchester committee, observing how leisure-based associations helped maintain church communities, advocated the formation of co-operative social clubs to create a co-operative social life and promote co-operative values.[78] The Huddersfield Industrial Society, for example, allocated 1 per cent of its profits to an Educational Fund for instruction, culture and recreation and opened the first free public reading room in the town in 1893. In the following year twenty concert meetings, a course of lectures, a rambling club and a choir had been organized.[79] As membership organizations, co-operative societies became integrated in local civil society and civic culture with the participation of co-operative choirs, orchestras and dramatic societies in the annual Co-operative Festival, which was held in London between 1888 and 1905, further enhancing civic identity.[80]

Beyond these national organizations a network of smaller local groups contributed to the growth of a socialist leisure culture. In Bolton, for example, the local branch of the Social Democratic Federation organized a mass land trespass in 1896 to reclaim right of way over the adjacent Winter Hill, privately enclosed for grouse-shooting. In many towns Socialist Clubs offered a political

Figures 3 and 4 Bolton Socialist Club exterior (left) and interior (right). Socialist clubs were important institutions in the late nineteenth and early twentieth centuries. Bolton Socialist Club still flourishes as a meeting place and hub of socialist political and leisure activity.

Source: © Adrian Greenhalgh.

Figures 3 and 4 Continued.

alternative to Liberal and Conservative clubs, nurturing a socialist leisure culture and providing a focal point for the local Clarion movement. The Bolton Socialist Club, for example, was founded in 1886 through Tom France and the local branch of the Social Democratic Foundation.[81] It blended leisure and politics with games, Saturday night socials, Clarion dances concerts and classes, lectures and discussions on socialism[82] and became a focal point for the socialist movement. Alice Foley recalled the Club as a home for a community imbued with visions of a new society.[83]

Through socialism working-class people produced their own leisure associations on collective and communal principles, rejecting the values of capitalism and the patronage of a leisure class. These associations reflected the broad spectrum of socialism with, at the Fabian end, organizations that, like the CHA, rejected capitalist competition and valued co-operation between social classes and, at the more politically active wing, those that, like the Clarion movement, used leisure as a campaign for political change and for which the socialist club was the epicentre of their activity. Socialism, which in part owed its existence to Christian socialism and the civic gospel, provided the foundations for an ethical and collective voluntary culture that was to flourish in the twentieth century and that stood in opposition to Liberal social philanthropy. The impact of socialism was, as Ernest Barker noted,[84] transformative rather than revolutionary; its reliance on what he termed as a 'slow growth of opinion' was consistent with the idea of a moral dialogue and gradual social change. Through the voluntary organizations discussed above, socialism gained a hold in popular cultural practice in which leisure was an expression of co-operative and collective values.

By 1914 MacIver's 'associations of social intercourse and camaraderie' represented an expansive range of leisure associations that served not only interests of sociability but of religious, political, economic and cultural values.[85] As such, leisure associations had become of central importance to the development of community and increasingly vocal in moral dialogue on the good society. Having for much of the nineteenth century been debated and shaped by religious and utilitarian principles, leisure was becoming theorized in terms of social science and policy. At the close of the First World War, emergent understandings of leisure, voluntary association and social change provided a basis for a re-energized social and political interest in voluntary action through leisure in both theoretical and practical contexts.

6

Leisure in Inter-War Britain

6.1 Introduction

Voluntary action in leisure in inter-war Britain was shaped by three principal forces. The most immediate and pressing was the need for social and cultural reconstruction after the First World War. The widespread demand for and expectation of a better post-war society stimulated interest in the potential contribution of leisure to this in terms of its more democratic distribution and of community-building. However the optimism of the early phase of social reconstruction was undermined by a series of economic crises that led to the mass unemployment of the 1930s and the 'enforced leisure' of the unemployed. The absence of work raised difficult questions about the meaning of leisure, fuelling fears of alienation and community breakdown. In areas of high unemployment voluntary action became not so much a question of deploying leisure to community reconstruction but of maintaining community cohesion to prevent the unemployed becoming a separated community. However, in the more prosperous regions of the midlands and the south, leisure opportunities expanded as living standards improved. The third force was the changing nature of leisure itself as new forms, notably the cinema, wireless and greyhound racing, gained widespread popularity. With the founding of the British Broadcasting Corporation (BBC) in 1927 drama and both light and classical music became increasingly available. The popularity of spectator sport also grew, providing an affordable leisure interest for everyone and especially working-class people. Welcomed by some critics as harbingers of an improved civilized life and a widening of cultural horizons of both children and adults,[1] these forms were reviled not only by culturally conservative critics but by some within the voluntary action movement.[2]

6.2 Social and cultural dimensions of inter-war leisure

By 1914 the more egregious aspects of the Victorian problem of leisure had been largely resolved. Education, more and better facilities, municipal provision, the civic gospel and the growth of commercial provision of socially harmless leisure opportunities had done much to produce a popular leisure culture that was not seriously problematic to society. The Education Act of 1870 had ensured virtual universal literacy, creating a mass market for light literature, while the expansion of a clerical and administrative workforce contributed to the growth of a lower middle class and a demand for respectable and affordable leisure. In inter-war Britain leisure became better integrated in social and civil life; with rising living standards and a shorter working week, it helped create a more homogeneous society and commonly shared culture.[3] There was by 1919 an increased sense of leisure as an entitlement of civilized society. By the 1930s the *New Survey of London Life and Labour* could confidently declare that since Charles Booth's survey, both time for leisure and the means of enjoying it had increased and observed that the worker's main centre of interest was increasingly shifting from his daily work to his daily leisure.[4] This pattern was not confined to London; even in Bolton, a town badly affected by poverty and unemployment in the 1930s, Mass Observation discovered that money was found to spend on 'cinemas, permanent waves, radio sets, drink, tobacco and similar "non-essentials" and on various forms of saving and gambling'.[5] A vast range of hobbies flourished, less historically visible but nevertheless important because of their proclivity to engender an associational culture. Gardening, photography, knitting, dog-breeding and other hobbies all had their clubs and societies. The men's club movement continued to expand; a survey conducted in 1925 recorded 10,712 clubs with a combined membership of 3,463,500. In terms of political affiliation Conservative clubs outstripped Liberal clubs by 1,321 to 526 although the largest single category comprised the 2,827 clubs run by Workmen's, Trade Union and Friendly Societies with 1,096,700 members.[6] In London, settlement clubs established by Toynbee Hall and Oxford House continued to operate but faced fierce competition from alternative attractions.[7]

The cinema, as Ross McKibbin has recorded, was the major medium of popular culture of the inter-war period and the single most important leisure activity of the English.[8] It was cheap and easily accessible; in Liverpool in the early 1930s, sixty-nine cinemas had an aggregate 73,000 attendances per week.[9] In 1937 Bolton had forty-seven cinemas, none further than five miles from the town hall; musical romances, drama and tragedy were the most popular type of film.[10] By the end of the period approximately 20 million tickets were sold nationally each week and it is important to note that these were not just for films shown in the new large-capacity town-centre cinemas but also those in the small cinemas in neighbourhood communities and suburban villages, which had consolidated the cinema as a cornerstone of everyday popular culture by the late 1920s.[11]

Sport too expanded after the War both in terms of participation and spectatorship. The demand for outdoor sports and physical exercise, in view of the New London Survey, was one of the outstanding features of the period with calls for more cricket and football pitches and tennis courts, the latter sport being the fastest growing with four times as many games played in 1926, when London had 781 tennis courts, as in 1905 when it had 450.[12] Interest in sport extended beyond those who played it; both national and local newspapers devoted several pages to it and in 1927 the BBC began to broadcast sport, making it not just a leisure interest but part of civil culture for all classes.

New forms of sport such as greyhound racing, speedway and All-in wrestling emerged and quickly became popular. Greyhound racing – seen within social service as a new cause for heart-searching in a country that claimed to be civilized[13] – gained a cross-class appeal but was particularly popular with working-class people because it built upon an existing culture of whippet breeding and dog racing and also because gambling was legally permissible at the greyhound track. In 1927 eighteen tracks drew five and a half million attendances; by 1938 there were thirteen and a half million.[14] Speedway – dirt track motor cycle racing – was introduced in1927, again appealing to working-class people for whom a motor-bike was both a form of transport to work and of leisure interest and was widely presented in greyhound stadiums; the five London tracks attracted over one million spectators annually in the early 1930s.[15] All-in wrestling was established in 1930 and like greyhound racing was imported from America. It quickly gained notoriety for excessive violence and its transgression of sporting norms and values. It was highly popular with working-class audiences; in Bolton Mass Observation found its followers to hold manual and mainly unskilled jobs such as storekeeper, labourer and foundry worker and several were unemployed. Virtually ignored by the national press and attracting the disdain once accorded to the cheaper type of music hall it nevertheless provided a popular and relatively harmless entertainment.[16] Although many of these new forms of leisure may not have met with middle-class approval, their acceptance as part of the fabric of popular culture reflected a far greater degree of tolerance than existed in the late nineteenth century. Drinking and gambling – major *bete noires* of nineteenth-century reformers – similarly received less criticism. Drinking was better regulated through licensing laws and new legal forms of gambling enabled working-class participation. In Bolton, for example, Mass Observation reported that in the late 1930s people drank less but, more importantly, showed the pub to be an epicentre for much community-based leisure with sports and games teams, clubs for pigeon-flying, fishing and saving and excursions and parties enjoyed by women and children as well as men.[17] Gambling remained contentious and subject to criticism, mainly from religious sources, but was increasingly more legally available, notably through the introduction of the football pools in 1923.[18] Churches continued to be major organizers of leisure; the Bolton Sunday School Cricket League, for example, resumed post-war competition in 1922 and remained an important sporting organization throughout the inter-war period.[19] Large employers also became significant providers of leisure with sports grounds and social amenities accessible to employees and sometimes their wider social community.

In 1919 popular leisure no longer raised the deep moral concerns of the Victorian age; neither was it credible to argue that it was a potentially destabilizing social force and for most people the inter-war years saw rising living standards and increased consumption in leisure.[20] The Holidays with Pay Act of 1938 affirmed government approval of leisure – even when commercially provided – as a social good and something to be enjoyed.[21] Inter-war leisure thus offers a good prism through which to explore the formation of a distinctive twentieth-century modernity. It was a period in which mechanization and mass culture changed the nature of both work and leisure and in which the demands of post-war social reconstruction engendered a social policy discourse that argued for a new society radically different from that of the Victorian–Edwardian social order. In 1919 social inequalities remained evident in the distribution of leisure and social reconstruction looked to leisure in terms of social policy and community building. Despite the expansion of leisure opportunity in the inter-war years, social concerns about the perceived effects of passive participation associated with the cinema and an 'Americanization' of culture became of concern to educators and social critics. From the late 1920s social service organizations supported the government in addressing the use of spare time by the unemployed but radical leisure associations, for example the British Workers' Sports Federation, Woodcraft Folk and the Kibbo Kift Kindred, created leisure practices with specific and alternative social and political values.[22] The use of leisure and the role of voluntary action in shaping both social and spatial communities were thus widely contested in both theory and practice.

Theorizations of Leisure and Voluntarism in Post-First World War Social Reconstruction

7.1 Introduction

During the First World War the social and cultural orthodoxies of the late-Victorian and Edwardian era came under severe critical attack and by 1919 there was widespread demand for fundamental social change through post-war social reconstruction.[1] When the government established a Ministry for Reconstruction in 1917, it was emphasized that this was not a rebuilding of society as it had existed, but of moulding a better world from the social and economic conditions that had come into being during the War.[2] The demands of reconstruction embraced several long-standing concerns of social policy, notably housing and health, and it is instructive to recall George Orwell's description of the War as a heightened moment in an almost continuous crisis.[3] This was particularly true in terms of leisure and voluntary action, in which its effect was to re-energize interest and debate in the meanings of leisure and social work initiated by social philosophers before the War. That there was a need for social renewal was not contested; the question was what type of society should be aimed for. Many critics believed more than an adjustment of the social and cultural values of pre-war society was necessary; as 'Demos' expressed it, reconstruction presented an unparalleled opportunity to overhaul national life in accordance with the ideals of a new age.[4] There was a consensual view that the new society should be more democratic and less unequal than pre-war society and many reformers broadly shared the Labour Party's vision of a new social order of fraternity, co-operation, equality and democratic participation in political power.[5] The discourse of reconstruction, which remained active until the mid-1930s, is important to an understanding of how and why leisure acquired changed social meanings after the First World War and of how these were interpreted in terms of voluntary action.

Reconstruction was concerned not only with industrial and economic recovery but also with enhancing the quality of life.[6] Leisure was integral to this. The

King's speech to parliament in February 1919, for example, called for a more equal distribution of leisure,[7] as did the Labour Party,[8] and time for leisure became part of wage bargaining.[9] Trade Union campaigns for an eight-hour working day in the 1880s[10] had met resistance from employers concerned by the economic cost of lost production. At the close of the War, Lord Leverhulme proposed a utilitarian six-hour day under which industrial machinery would operate for twenty-four hours and be supervised by workers on a six-hour shift basis, claiming this would, at no economic cost, increase both production and happiness.[11] Social idealist, new liberal and Fabian rationales for leisure, however, did not recognize the economic quantification of leisure in terms of industry's profit but valued it for its own sake. Leonard Hobhouse, a leading Liberal theorist, maintained the true value of the shorter day was to enable the working man to enjoy an active leisure outside work,[12] and through Seebohm Rowntree this was adopted in 1918 as Liberal Party policy.[13] Paid leisure time, as Sandra Dawson notes, became symbolic of a new political democracy and social citizenship.[14] However, the question of whether working-class people would make a constructive use of additional leisure time became part of public debate. In the late nineteenth century Sidney Webb[15] argued that more leisure would allow workers to join evening classes, debating societies and gymnasiums. The economist John Hobson further argued more leisure time to be a condition of effective social reconstruction; when used for voluntary service to the community it could be construed as industry's contribution to the common good.[16] In 1918 a government committee on adult education recommended a reduced working week[17] and in early 1919, following trade union and Labour Party campaigning, several major industries adopted an eight-hour day.[18] To social reformers this 'new' leisure was a sphere in which social reconstruction and community building could be nurtured.

In the discourse of post-war social reconstruction leisure and voluntary action were re-interpreted in terms of the good society and democratic community. The relationships between work and leisure developed by Ruskin, Morris and their disciples acquired a fresh relevance as the Victorian primacy of work and economic growth was challenged by a moral case for more leisure and the recalibration of work to allow for personal development and cultural enjoyment.[19] The increasing social status of leisure was reflected in the *New Survey of London Life and Labour*'s allocation of a full volume to it.[20] The nature and function of leisure in the new post-war society were debated across several policy fields and became integrated in progressive thinking on social service and community well-being. Unlike some European countries, Britain did not have a state ministry with an overall responsibility for leisure.[21] Consequently, the contribution of leisure to the making of a new post-war society was debated not primarily through parliamentary channels but the institutions of civil society, notably academic and policy circles, religious and secular voluntary bodies and civic organizations. Discussion was shaped by cultural criticism and Fabian and Christian socialism but most importantly by social idealism and T.H. Green's interpretation of the common good and social citizenship. Social idealism was the dominant philosophical school of social thought in British universities between 1880 and 1914 and was particularly associated with Balliol College. It was, as Jose Harris has argued, well-suited to a period in which classical Liberalism and utilitarianism were losing force and social theorists were searching for new theoretical approaches to society and social reform.[22] Its impact on inter-war welfare policy in Scotland has recently been demonstrated[23] and was further reflected in the establishment of the Stevenson Lectures in Citizenship at Glasgow University in 1921. Elements of social idealism were absorbed into ethical socialism, new Liberalism and Christian Socialism;[24] all placed a priority on a common good although with varying nuances in terms of what this meant and how it might best be realized. A salient feature of social idealism was that it was never intended to be a purely academic exercise; its proponents expected it to be applied to practice and Green encouraged his students to engage in social work. Although of diminished philosophical appeal in the inter-war period, social idealism remained a potent force in social policy on reconstruction and community well-being.[25] It is within this context that new social meanings of leisure and voluntary social service were formed.

Green outlined the application of idealist philosophy to social practice in *The Principles of Political Obligation*, published in 1882.[26] The good of the individual was, he argued, identical with that of the community. Civic action was accordingly to be directed towards moral ends; any activity that benefited the individual at the expense of the common good was unethical.[27] Social idealism challenged classic Liberal notions of rights and the understanding of leisure as untrammelled individual freedom to pursue hedonistic pleasure and offered instead one of leisure as virtuous activity towards the common good. Similarly, voluntary action in the service of the community was redefined as not simply an act of kindness but a moral responsibility; in Green's expression, 'my duty is to be interested positively in my neighbour's well-being'.[28] In short, the good citizen was obligated to contribute to the good of the community. In idealist terms a virtuous use of leisure would be some form of engagement in voluntary action in the service of the community. Social institutions, notably industry and education, also had social obligations in which the good of the community was their primary object.

Idealism owed much to the social philosophy of ancient Greece, which, as Henry Stead and Edith Hall have shown, became an important motivating force of reformist discourse in early twentieth-century Britain.[29] It promoted an active citizenship derived from Greek and Roman republicanism, which, in Eugenia Low's terms, assumed a communal consensus of values and a positive conceptualization of a common good.[30] Borrowing from the social philosophy of Plato and Aristotle, social idealism developed theories of civic and social reform, connecting social philosophy to voluntary social service and leisure. Idealists believed the state had a moral duty to promote the conditions under which the common good could be realized by encouraging the civic spirit.[31] This was important in terms of rationales for voluntary action because, as Melvin Richter has argued, Green presupposed the existence of voluntary associations, for example, friendly and co-operative societies formed by working-class people, to undertake collective action that was beyond the resources of the individual.[32] Jose Harris similarly comments that to social idealists a progressive community depended not so much on the state as on voluntary co-operation by individuals with a common moral purpose and expressing a conscious will,[33] although it is important to note that Green did recognize the need for direct state intervention where voluntary effort could not be effective. However voluntary effort was preferable because it pre-supposed a moral action by the individual. In sum, idealists believed the good community could be realized through the co-operative voluntary association of individual people, social citizenship and democratic principles of equal rights. Its emphasis on ethics invested the state with a moral responsibility to nurture community well-being by ensuring the conditions in which active citizenship and voluntary associations such as friendly and co-operative societies and similar reforming movements and interventions could flourish.[34] Its principal tenets, as Michael Freeden notes, were the notion of the common good and the enabling of individuals to contribute to it.[35] Unlike Morris, who contextualized his discussions of the good society, work and leisure in politicized and collective terms, idealism couched its interpretations in philosophical and ethical terms.

Green's model of the good community was hugely influential on social thinking on voluntarism in the Edwardian and early inter-war years. To Edward Caird, who like Green was associated with Balliol College, the idea of organized voluntary action as social service to the whole society distinguished it from the personal charitable philanthropy of Victorian case-work.[36] This marked a radical point of difference: whereas social work had, under the influence of the Charity Organisation Society, focused on helping the deserving individual, social idealism posited a model of social work in which individual action focused on the good of the community as a whole. The key importance of this to leisure was that it too became valued less as a field for the moral improvement of the individual and more a sphere for the pursuit of the good of the whole community. Idealism was diffused and adapted across several theoretical domains of social policy; as Jose Harris pointed out, it 'united people who differed widely on political tactics [and] generated a vocabulary of social reform that transcended political parties'.[37] Through Green's influence, voluntary association and co-operative intervention in pursuit of the good society gained currency in progressive social thinking. Although his social philosophy was intellectually complex, Green's ideas were diffused through social philosophers, notably Bernard and Helen Bosanquet, and were influential in the early twentieth century in the formation of new voluntary service organizations such as Guilds of Help, Councils of Voluntary Aid and the National Council of Social Service, all of which adopted leisure as a field of instrumental action in community building. Many of idealism's leading proponents were speakers at the South Place Ethical Society where its social applications could be debated.[38] Together with the visionary socialism of Morris and Ruskin and the more grounded socialism of the labour movement, idealism competed to shape theoretical approaches to social reform. Social service thus acquired, as Clement Attlee commented, both scientific and aesthetic appeals with utopianism and rationality each having their place in the construction of a new post-war society.[39]

With idealism came optimism that change was possible, altering the tenor of public debate on leisure from one that focused on its problematic aspects to one that positioned leisure as a social good and an agent of social reconstruction. The influence of classicism on the reform of the industrial city and indeed on Edwardian culture more widely has been recently noted;[40] its importance to thinking on leisure has been less remarked upon. However, Peter Womack has identified a mid-nineteenth-century intellectual idealization of leisure, motivated by Newman's anti-utilitarian insistence that knowledge was valuable in itself and not only for what it did. This contributed to an idea of leisure as dialogue and the basis of a scholarly life at Oxford University where, under Benjamin Jowett, Master of Balliol College, Plato's *Republic* and Aristotle's *Ethics* became set texts.[41] In the *International Journal of Ethics* in 1911, Bernard Bosanquet, a student of Green at Balliol from 1866 to 1870, drew on this classical tradition to argue a social idealist case for leisure which became a central tenet of post-war debate on its social meaning.[42] Referring to Aristotle's *Ethics*, Bosanquet distinguished leisure from recreation, noting that while recreation and amusement enabled men to work and were therefore necessary and instrumental to an end, leisure was an end in itself. Leisure thus acquired a theoretical meaning beyond that of recreation as something valuable for its own sake. Leisure could also be directed towards the good of the community. Idealism assimilated Aristotelian ideas of duty and service to the community, drawing on the concept of practical wisdom, described in the *Ethics* as a 'reasoned state of capacity to act with regard to the things that are good or bad for man'[43] and positing the use of leisure in voluntary social work as a virtuous act. As Bernard Bosanquet argued, the man of practical wisdom was one able to guide the organization and education of the community to sustain the 'highest' and most virtuous activities in leisure.[44] The idea of leisure as something to be enjoyed for its own sake corresponded with what George Sabine referred to as idealism's 'self-realization ethics'[45] and implied intellectual activity and creativity. The realization of a 'true' leisure consequently implied its more democratic distribution and the education of people, as citizens, in its use. The basic tenets of social idealism influenced debate on the post-First World War social reconstruction of society and were particularly important to leisure and voluntary action. Idealism was, as Sandra Den Otter comments, pre-occupied with the idea of community.[46] In this respect it was eminently fitted to a basic object of social reconstruction and offered a theoretical rationale for post-war social service and the role of leisure in community development. The following sections review the theorization of leisure in inter-war Britain to give context to the discussion of voluntary action in community-building through leisure which forms the subject matter of Chapter 8.

7.2 Leisure in the new society

The discourse of social reconstruction was imbued with idealist values of spirituality and the belief that social reform required a moral basis.[47] Civilization itself was seen as a spiritual entity;[48] in MacIver's terms it was a manifestation of the conscious co-operation of its citizens in a 'great common life'.[49] H.A.L. Fisher, Liberal MP for Sheffield Hallam, architect of the 1918 Education Act and Stevenson Lecturer on Citizenship, summarized the application of Green's moral community to post-war reconstruction thus:

I shall ask you to assume there is such a thing as morality and that morality consists in the disinterested performance of self-imposed duties. And I shall ask you further to assume [with Green] that the real function of government is to maintain conditions of life in which morality should be possible.... Let us assume for the present that man is a social animal, that it is his duty to perfect his being, that this he can only do as a member of a commonwealth so instituted and organized as to maintain conditions under which it is possible to lead a moral life.[50]

Reconstruction was in this sense an ethical undertaking and consequently discussions of community and leisure were constructed around themes of social justice, community well-being and social citizenship. Inequalities in time for leisure and the perceived limitations placed by routine automated work upon workers' engagement in active leisure were consequently constructed as social injustices. Like Bosanquet, Bertrand Russell believed that, while amusement and diversion were functionally important, they did not have the capacity to create a good life; leisure, on the other hand, was central to it.[51] The revival of Aristotle's philosophical distinction between leisure, recreation and amusement was a pivotal step towards its formulation as a social abstraction that could be applied to inter-war modernity. Amusement was instrumentally valuable in terms of relaxation and entertainment, but leisure was a more elusive conceptual abstract, amenable to philosophical discussion in the social sciences. Following Bosanquet's example, the application of social idealist ideas to leisure drew heavily from Athenian philosophy and in particular from Aristotle and Plato who both saw leisure as a sphere for virtuous individual activity and human flourishing.[52]

Social idealism posited leisure as eudemonic and not hedonic. *Eudaimonia* is a contested word but is generally associated with happiness, personal development and human flourishing. For Aristotle leisure was essential to *eudaimonia*; happiness was achieved not through amusement but through virtuous activities desirable for their own sake.[53] More specifically, happiness depended upon activity of the mind; it was not a state of mental euphoria but the flourishing found in excellent intellectual activity.[54] Aristotle in particular associated the use of leisure with social citizenship, connecting the active leisure of the individual to the social good; the *polis* was not just a social formation but the 'perfect and final association',[55] a community defined by citizens sharing common activities. If happiness meant flourishing then the active life would be best both for the whole community and for the individual.[56] Therefore, education in the use of leisure in civilized pursuits and a socially constructive enjoyment of leisure were necessary to the well-being of the community.[57] Plato too distinguished leisure from idleness and argued that the best forms of leisure were those enjoyed for their own sake, such as music; he also believed service to the state a virtuous use of leisure.[58] These ideas were appealing to social philosophers and policy theorists attempting to navigate a pathway to a new society and a reformed social order through an enhanced sense of civic duty. The distinction between eudemonic leisure and hedonic pleasure provided a philosophical basis for the articulation of a right use of leisure that would, in theoretical terms, lead to both individual and community well-being while avoiding the pitfalls of Bentham's greatest happiness principle. It was encapsulated in the *New Survey of London*'s differentiation of cultural and non-cultural pursuits as those aiming at self-improvement and those ministering to evanescent enjoyment.[59] Ernest Barker, an authority on the political thought of Plato and Aristotle applied this distinction to post-war planning by defining leisure as employment in some activity desirable for its own sake such as listening to good music or poetry, intercourse with friends or the exercise of the speculative faculty.[60] In contrast, hedonic pleasure, easily found in the passive consumption of entertainment and amusement, had an important instrumental value in terms of relaxation but lacked a capacity for self-development and did not imply social duties of citizenship. Veronica Huta has suggested a modern interpretation of this distinction in terms of hedonic happiness as the pleasant life of as many pleasures as possible and eudemonic life as meaningful and fulfilling.[61] In terms of leisure, the role of voluntary action began to focus on the latter while remaining suspicious of the former.

Social theorists and policy makers of the inter-war decades were able to draw from a substantial body of theoretical debate and practical effort in social intervention reaching back to the final third of the nineteenth century. Many were familiar with the social critiques of Karl Marx, John Ruskin, William Morris and T.H. Green and were well informed in terms of Aristotelian philosophy and social idealism; several had also practical experience of residential settlement work. Through a blend of various schools of thought leisure became connected to ideas of community, the common good and social well-being. The concept of community was a central theme of social reconstruction. The communities of the Greek city-states were bound together not only by economic forces but by a psychological sense of being a community, or possessing a community consciousness. Aristotle, as we have seen, held that leisure was essential to the citizenship necessary to the maintenance of such a community.[62] In terms of the twentieth-century community, this citizenship was not restricted to active participation in the political process but included any action that in some way contributed to the community as a holistic organic system. Bernard Bosanquet, for example, imagined a community in which everyone could fulfil the obligations of citizenship and cited as an example a tradesman of his acquaintance who devoted his leisure time to the management of local working-class clubs and societies.[63] The active involvement of working-class people in community-orientated social citizenship was a primary aim of idealists and after the War idealist understandings of community found a resonance amongst many inter-war social theorists. However, as Harold Laski, a theorist of the pluralist society pointed out, this ambition could only be realized under certain conditions which the state would need to ensure, particularly a greater amount of leisure for and education in the fulfilment of the duties of citizenship to enable people to form voluntary associations directed towards the good of the community.[64]

Greek understandings of leisure and community influenced thinking on the building of a democratic society and the ways in which a right use of leisure could contribute to communities with high levels of social citizenship and a civic consciousness. Ernest Barker, for example, argued for a more democratic distribution of leisure as the 'noblest thing in life';[65] Fisher called for a revival of Aristotelean thinking on citizenship and a greater sense of social citizenship and service to the community, asking his reader to assume with Aristotle that it was only through a life 'passed in the Commonwealth and for the common weal' that he could use his talent to the best advantage and realize perfection.[66] The social philosophy of the Edwardian and early inter-war period thus presented a cogent case for a social community in which a democratically shared associational leisure would be an important means of enabling and encouraging social citizenship. However the application of these ideas to the shaping of a new community faced notable challenges. Leisure was not democratically shared, a leisure class remained culturally influential, popular new forms of hedonic mass cultural production were thought to increase passivity and advanced industrial automation was believed to incapacitate the worker from a true enjoyment of leisure.[67]

7.3 'New leisure makes new men'[68]

In 1919 the social structure of Britain retained the hierarchical model of Edwardian society and Thorstein Veblen's analysis of consumption as a gauge of wealth and class remained an accurate measure of social differentiation in leisure.[69] Before the War Masterman had condemned the 'leisured life' of the new wealthy, or 'Conquerors', whose position had remained unchallenged by the 'futility' of philanthropic efforts to improve the lives of the lower classes with chess, coffee and bagatelle.[70] It has more recently been argued that the British establishment remained almost unchanged by the War with power and influence remaining with a social and economic elite.[71] After the War the leisure class remained in evidence in the small coterie of wealthy 'Bright Young Things' who sought notoriety through outrageous breaches of standards of leisure behaviour. Orwell's assessment of England as the most class-ridden country of the world[72] was validated by the continuing patronization of leisure by the Crown, with horse racing at Royal Ascot, royal boxes at Wimbledon, the theatre and the opera, and Cowes Yacht race all under-pinning the social position of their participants and reinforcing pre-war patterns of leisure.[73] The leisure class was numerically small: working-class people formed 78.29 per cent of the population of England in 1921[74] with the main proportion of males employed in the heavy industries, as they were in Scotland and Wales. Leisure remained undemocratically distributed and Labour's campaign for better social conditions achieved only moderate gains in time for leisure; neither was there any significant expansion of public facilities. It was the task of reformers to explain why these inequalities in something as seemingly mundane as leisure represented a social injustice.

John Atkinson Hobson, an important and overlooked figure in the historiography of leisure, argued the effects of industrial capitalism to be social as well as economic in nature. A left-leaning liberal, Hobson maintained economic policy should be concerned with the social impacts of industry, particularly those affecting the quality of life. As a biographer of Ruskin[75] he was familiar with Ruskin's belief that political economy should study not only the material necessities of life but also factors of human health and happiness. Wealth was to be valued not only in financial terms but in those of a full human life;[76] in Ruskin's famous dictum, there was 'no wealth but life'.[77] Hobson, who quoted Veblen extensively, believed the true economy of leisure was only beginning to be recognized in theories of consumption.[78] In *Work and Wealth*, published in 1914, Hobson developed Ruskin's ideas in near-idealist terms, arguing that although leisure had a social as well as an economic value, time saved by mechanical production in modern industry had not been re-distributed to the working classes as leisure but diverted, through increased profits, to employers, thereby increasing the leisure class.[79] R.H. Tawney too, following the ethical anti-capitalist tradition of Ruskin, Carlyle and Morris,[80] argued that the organization of the economic system had created the social injustice of a hierarchy of leisure[81] which denied labour a just share of wealth by constraining time for leisure.[82] Following Veblen, Hobson argued that social and economic inequalities between the rich and the working classes were diffused through leisure, citing the former's parasitic life of idle travel, racing, hunting, motoring, golfing, yachting and gambling.[83] The social injustice of this lay in the fact that leisure, the 'opportunity of opportunities' for personal development and human enjoyment and a form of communal wealth, was not equally distributed.[84] At the root of this inequality was the capitalist economic system under which the shorter working hours necessary to energy and time for leisure could be gained only through reduced demand in the wasteful consumption of the leisure class. Equality in leisure was, in this light, socially and ethically desirable to enable the worker to engage actively with voluntary organizations and the life of churches, friendly societies, trade unions, co-operative societies, clubs, musical and educational associations, which made up the social life of Britain. Leisure would then, Hobson believed, 'yield rich nutrient to the organic life of society, because the individual will find himself drawn by the social needs and desires embedded in his personality to devote portions of his leisure to social activities which contribute to the commonwealth as surely as do the economic tasks imposed upon him in his daily industry'.[85] Hobson, an economist who referred to his own discipline as 'mechanical',[86] articulated a social economics and alternative measure of value that depended on qualitative rather than quantitative data and remains a seminal figure in the formation of a modern social concept of leisure as a field of individual and community well-being.

The enduring influence of a leisure class became a totemic obstacle to a democratic re-distribution of leisure; in theoretical terms it was incompatible with a democratic society and, as Hobson had noted, social equality could be achieved only if culture, or leisure, were more equally spread.[87] To progressive thinkers, a democratic distribution of leisure was impossible without the abolition of a leisure class.[88] The substitution of the leisure class by a democratically formed culture held wide appeal in the inter-war period; it was for example a policy adopted by the Conference on Christian Politics, Economics and Citizenship in 1924 at which the leisure class was described as ignorant, extravagant, a menace to social stability and in need of replacement by the church and voluntary social service organizations as community leaders in the field of leisure.[89] In socialist terms the novelist Storm Jameson, a member of PEN, an organization formed in 1921 for the advocacy of human rights, also argued for a classless leisure state and education to restore the creative uses of leisure in the time saved by machine production.[90]

The inter-war period produced a rich seam of writing on the democratization of leisure that has remained largely unnoticed. Henry Durant, whose doctoral thesis was one of the first in Britain in the sociology of leisure, exaggerated in claiming Lads' and Girls' clubs and the Settlements to be dominated by aristocratic patronage but the accusation nevertheless contained a degree of truth.[91] There remained a question, however, of how moral and cultural standards in leisure could be exemplified if the leisure class were to be abolished. The danger existed of a return to Benthamite utilitarianism through which leisure forms seeming to contribute to the greatest happiness would be encouraged, invoking the question of whether a eudemonic leisure was possible in an age of the cinema and mass spectator sport. Cecil Delisle Burns, a progressive liberal thinker also largely absent from the historiography of leisure, argued that it was. Drawing from Hobson, Tawney and Veblen, Burns blended socialism, Athenian philosophy and social idealism in a broadly progressive liberal and left-wing critique of leisure in inter-war Britain. With Hobson, he was a member of the Rainbow Circle and also of the Romney Street Group, founded in 1917 to discuss post-war social reconstruction, whose members included R.H. Tawney, J.J. Mallon, Warden of Toynbee Hall, Arthur Greenwood and Alfred Zimmern. His obituary[92] recorded his interests to be speculative rather than practical, and this was reflected in his visionary imagination of a society changed through leisure but that left its realization to others.[93] He was educated at Christ's College, Cambridge and worked in the Ministry of Reconstruction from 1917–1920, later becoming assistant secretary to the Joint Research Department of the Trades Union Congress and Labour Party. Following a period as lecturer in social philosophy at the London School of Economics he was appointed to the Stevenson Lectureship in Citizenship at Glasgow University where his public lectures on democracy, citizenship and industrial questions were influential and attracted large audiences. Before and during the War he was a contributor, as were many social idealists, to the *International Journal of Ethics*;[94] after the War he served on that journal's management committee and published several analyses of leisure in the context of an inter-war modernity of changing social attitudes, women's emancipation, mass culture and youth movements. Although only one of these was devoted exclusively to leisure,[95] it was a prominent theme in his other works on civilization,[96] democracy[97] and industry.[98] He cited amongst his friends John Hobson and A.J. Toynbee and was a lecturer at the South Place Ethical Society, founded in 1787 as a radical Congregationalist body but that by the twentieth century had become a forum for humanist discussion and debate on social matters. His work on leisure was consequently informed by his position within the intellectual vanguard of early twentieth-century Britain and derives importance and relevance from this.

Burns argued leisure to be a prime agent of social change. With other progressive critics he believed that the removal of a leisure class influence would create a cultural environment in which ordinary people would collectively demonstrate leadership in leisure.[99] Like Tawney,[100] Burns argued not for an equal culture but for an equal opportunity to cultivate creative and intellectual faculties through a new leisure:

> Our use of leisure should not involve attempting to turn everybody into a lady or gentleman on the old model – that is to say we should be concerned not with living up to the old ideal but with establishing in practice a new ideal. That is what is meant by the phrase 'new leisure makes new men': the new kind of leisure can make men and women just as good as the ladies and gentlemen of an earlier age, if we know want we want and have skill enough to get it. The use of leisure being the architecture of our character, our new architecture ought not to be based upon the old 'orders' – classical or gothic, Greek or mediaeval.[101]

Drawing directly from Morris he advocated wider participation in active leisure through creative production, arguing in the *Social Service Review*, for example, that as capacity for the enjoyment of art was not determined by social class and therefore not confined to a leisure class, a more democratically distributed involvement in art through the efforts of voluntary action could aid social change.[102]

7.4 Leisure, modernity and social change

In *Leisure in the Modern World* Burns expounded a democratic and socially constructive leisure for a modernizing society. In contrast to contemporary leanings towards a romantic pastoral revival,[103] Burns saw the post-war world as new, modern and full of possibilities, characterized by a new kind of community life, democratic institutions and ideals.[104] In this sense the modern world was not simply the end of an old civilization but the beginning of a new one.[105] Sensing cultural changes in post-war forms of leisure, Burns discerned signs of a new leisure in women's institutes, the increased numbers of women playing sport, the new working and lower-middle class influence on the outdoor movement in rambling, cycling and camping and, perhaps most controversially, the shared enjoyment of the cinema and wireless. These forms were not revolutionary but gradual changes, representing a moral dialogue of leisure in which new cultural forms and standards were being negotiated in the context of the evolutionary process of social change outlined by Todd.[106] To many critics, however, modernity constituted the antithesis of an idealist-informed leisure with mechanized production and standardization of taste seen as harbingers of a collapse of civilization.

The machine became central to inter-war debate on leisure and work in both Great Britain and America,[107] producing dystopian visions of a civilization determined by technology. In E.M. Forster's story *The Machine Stops*,[108] for example, a subterranean population is dominated by a machine above it. Fritz Lang's urban dystopia *Metropolis* similarly depicts a privileged leisure class supported by a de-humanized working class employed in subterranean mechanized factories, while in Charlie Chaplin's *Modern Times*, assembly-line workers are constrained to the repetitive performance of a task. Concern about the machine was not limited to fiction but debated in cultural criticism and social philosophy. In a paper 'The Fear of Machines' published in the *International Journal of Ethics* in 1917 Hartley Burr Alexander echoed Carlyle in arguing that the mechanization of industry had led to an erosion of humane values by 'social machines' of politics and industrial economics.[109] The anti-machine discourse was however counter-balanced by the fact that mechanization could increase time for leisure and enable a greater shared enjoyment of cultural production. The debate on leisure consequently ran across a spectrum of optimism and pessimism. Pessimists tended to associate modernity with collapse and crisis; optimists equated it with positive social change.

Resistance to modernity: leisure

As the *New Survey of London* noted, the machine represented a revolution in popular entertainment, posing the question of whether the cinema and the wireless were positive or negative forces in working-class life.[110] To Henry Durant the new mass leisure constituted a 'machinery of amusement' of vicarious thrills and displays of wealth and power,[111] which, as Storm Jameson suggested, encouraged the passive consumption of capitalist forms of entertainment.[112] Empirical surveys lent weight to these claims; the *New Survey of London* found that although the cinema and wireless provided a more varied and less coarse amusement than was common in Booth's time, they nevertheless fostered passive receptivity at the expense of an active use of leisure.[113] Passivity was the antithesis of idealist eudemonic leisure and active social citizenship; Durant, for example, believed the cinema distracted audiences from the problems of everyday life[114] and as Fisher remarked, passivity was inconsistent with citizenship.[115] The cinema and wireless were consequently seen by many social reformers as opposing forces to the education of future citizens;[116] to Edith Neville, Warden of the Mary Ward Settlement, they represented an aimless leisure, lacking spiritual and mental stimulus.[117] The effects of the cinema on juvenile behaviour were of particular concern, even though the Home Office believed the cinema was more conducive to the prevention of crime than its commission and teachers found it to increase children's knowledge.[118] The cinema also presented unwelcome competition to voluntary social service clubs; in London, where 41 per cent of children aged between eight and fourteen years went to the cinema at least once a week, societies formed around popular film stars such as Greta Garbo and Ramon Novarro.[119]

To conservative cultural critics the modernity of the new popular and mass leisure undermined the values and standards of civilization. For F.R. and Q.D. Leavis, custodians of a humane literary tradition, civilization and mass culture were antithetical terms. The Leavises resisted modernity and saw in American mass culture a force for cultural disintegration;[120] Queenie Leavis, somewhat anachronistically, imagined the destruction of a traditional working-class leisure of country arts, games and singing by the 'kill-time' interests of the radio, gramophone, cinema and spectator football.[121] Unable to understand the appeal of popular culture, conservative critics retained the belief that a leisure class was necessary to the preservation of civilization. For Clive Bell this was not necessarily a ruling class but, similar to Matthew Arnold's aliens, a civilized and civilizing elite, distinct from the materialistic middle classes.[122] Bell and the Leavises personified the resistance of the intelligentsia and 'Bloomsbury highbrow', which persuaded Orwell that there could be no holistic common culture.[123] Mechanized leisure was also perceived to lack a social function; as Mass Observation remarked in its study of inter-war Bolton, older leisure institutions always included co-operation. The pub, for example, was not simply a place for drinking but for convivial conversation and a home for mutual aid societies, sports clubs, collective outings and celebrations. In the pub a man was a participant rather than a spectator, whereas the newer institutions of the motor car, cinema and dance hall did not create a social group of people consciously sharing the same experience and lacked common feeling and conversation.[124]

Work

The debate on work and leisure built upon the nineteenth-century discourse of the mechanical society. John Ruskin and William Morris had argued mechanized production to be a regressive and de-humanizing process that incapacitated the industrial worker to enjoy leisure.[125] After the War both Henry Durant and Arthur Clutton Brock, a biographer of Morris, identified the division between work and leisure as the 'outstanding aspect' of the problem of leisure.[126] For Morris, mechanized industrial work was the chief obstacle to the enjoyment of an active leisure of artistic or intellectual engagement;[127] *News from Nowhere* portrayed a utopia in which machine production had been abolished and leisure was understood not in terms of recuperation for work but of self-development and fulfilment.[128] Morris did not, however, embrace modernity; as a medievalist he desired a restoration of the communal culture of the pre-industrial craft guild and its harmonized blend of skilled work and conviviality. More realistically, he advocated a co-operative mode of work that would maximize opportunities for creative and constructive uses of leisure rather than profit.[129] Like Ruskin, Morris understood leisure as a form of wealth that was social as well as personal and advocated a collective leisure within a collective life, supported by a communal hall that would enable a common social life.[130] Both work and leisure would be undertaken for the benefit of the community:

> And I may say that as to that leisure, as I should in no case do any harm to any one with it, so I should often do some direct good to the community with it, by practising arts or occupations for my hands or brain which would give pleasure to many of the citizens; in other words, a great deal of the best work done would be done in the leisure time of men relieved from any anxiety as to their livelihood, and eager to exercise their special talent, as all men, nay, all animals are … it is clear that if I am a member of a Socialist Community I must do … that share of work necessary to the existence of the simplest social life.[131]

Following Morris, Hobson associated the work–leisure antithesis with the problematic cultural dichotomies of art and mechanism, spontaneity and routine, and qualitative and quantitative production.[132] Monotonous work left the worker too tired for active forms of leisure and the active citizenship necessary to a democratic community.[133] Documentary social evidence supported this belief; in Bethnal Green passivity and apathy in leisure were attributed to monotonous machine-minding and its inability to provide satisfaction to the worker.[134] A scientific investigation by the National Institute of Industrial Psychology also found the physical and nervous fatigue resulting from work to affect the enjoyment of leisure.[135] The concerns enumerated above were not confined to Britain; in the United States of America Lewis Mumford connected the absence of humane values in the mechanization of industry to an increased demand for compensatory functions[136] and Paul Frankl noted how those who worked with machines tended to passivity and the consumption of the 'machine-made toys' of the radio, cinema and spectator sports.[137]

Modernity and opportunity: leisure

Many critics, however, believed modernity need not come at the expense of democratic and collective values. Burns saw modern civilization as a transformative process rather than a product; the machine, mass culture and leisure were not absolute but elements of modernity that had not yet realized their full social effects. Although not uncritical of its potential abuse, Burns argued that technology had created a more democratic leisure, equalizing without degrading the taste of all members of a community. The so-called standardization of taste was, he maintained, an accidental outcome of the improved standard of life for the majority.[138] In other words, the leisure of mass culture was not a diminishment of a 'higher' culture but an enhancement and democratization of popular culture; the radio and cinema, by bringing all classes together, could stimulate conversation between people who otherwise had no common interest.

Modernity, he argued, was dynamic and brought vitality,[139] encouraging experimentation in leisure, particularly by the younger generation, that could inform and change the dominant attitudes of a community. Notable examples of such experimentation in inter-war Britain included the Kibbo Kift and Woodcraft Folk (see Chapter 9) and working-class leisure associations devoted to artistic creativity, for example the Ashington pit painters and more avowedly left-wing cultural organizations such as the Unity Theatre and the Workers' Musical Association.[140] By the early 1930s, the Worker's Theatre Movement was established in London and Dundee, using drama as a critique of the capitalist system and preparing the ground for the co-operative Unity Theatre, formed in 1936 in Kings Cross.[141] This performed to local working-class organizations on the principle that drama should speak to the everyday lives of ordinary people.[142] In Manchester the workers' theatre movement was an off-shoot of the Young Communist League led by the Red Megaphones under Jimmy Miller (later known as the folk singer Ewan McColl).[143] As later did Raymond Williams, Burns believed in the primacy of the individual in the mass, not the mass as a whole. Experimentation in leisure was therefore to be encouraged to reveal new standards of art and culture that would also be those of men and women in a 'new kind of community'.[144]

To modernizers, the mass consumption of mechanized leisure was not without merit. In America the Lynds noted how the cinema, automobile and radio were not exclusively passive enjoyments but expanded the horizons of Middletown, bringing classical music and sermons into the home.[145] Sir John Russell, in an Essex Hall lecture in 1931, similarly acknowledged that the gramophone and wireless had made classical music and topical discourse more accessible than ever before.[146] Whereas many social reformers remained unable to understand the appeal of mass culture in working-class life,[147] Burns perceived that the tendency of modernity was to bring people into closer relationships. Through a shared mass culture the mental world of both adults and children was widened, providing an active leisure of intellectual engagement for workers undertaking repetitive jobs.[148] A further sign of modernity was the increased use of leisure for enjoyment, not only by the leisure class but by ordinary people finding in ephemeral singing, dancing or holiday-making an experience that had no reason for existence except itself – according to Burns the 'the sort of life which alone can be called civilized'.[149] In some instances Burns appears to be

Figure 5 Hemming towels. The workforce of the Lancashire cotton industry was dominated by women. Although the boredom of repetitive work was believed to encourage passivity, Mass Observation found the factory a site of informal leisure with workers' conversations expressing critical judgement on films and wireless programmes.

Source: © Bolton Council. From the Collection of Bolton Library and Museum Services.

close to Walter Benjamin's idea of leisure as what Chris Rojek[150] terms a place of hidden wonders, enlivening mundane experience, such as boring work, and reading mass culture in imaginative ways. To Burns even mechanized industrial production could be interpreted as a positive development of leisure; where the physical actions of the machine operative became unconscious, day-dreaming could fulfil the psychological need to alleviate boredom and jobs with a fixed habitual pattern could allow informal conversation with fellow workers.[151] This was not purely speculative; as Mass Observation discovered in its study of life in Bolton's cotton mills, popular leisure provided a common interest for conversation in the work place on, for example, films, wireless programmes, clothing and other leisure activities.[152] A wider survey by the Industrial Health Research Board found similar evidence.[153]

Although mass culture was not a democratic culture, it nevertheless had democratizing tendencies; as Le Mahieu argued, the BBC heralded a more egalitarian culture and mass leisure potentially embraced all social classes even though they remained deeply divided in other ways.[154] These were not, as we shall see, beliefs widely found in voluntary social service.

7.5 Conclusion

By 1919 the Victorian debate on recreation had been superseded by one on leisure. Inter-war theorists built upon this and were accompanied by American social philosophers and sociologists with an interest in leisure. In Britain the influence of social idealism on policy on community building and an associational culture helped create new social thinking on leisure. The influence of Balliol College, Green's academic home, was significant; leading theorists and practitioners who had imbued Balliol's emphasis on public service included Percy Alden, Bernard Bosanquet, R.H. Tawney, Ernest Barker, William Beveridge and William Temple. Beyond idealism, socialism had by the inter-war period become established as a major voice in social policy. While both domains shared a similar broad goal of a democratic society, they disagreed fundamentally on the way in which this might be realized. Furthermore an innate conservatism was presenting a durable barrier to democratic social change. These similarities and differences were played out in voluntary action through leisure.

Reconstruction, Social Service and Leisure

8.1 Introduction

The First World War re-energized the Edwardian voluntary spirit and placed new demands on post-war voluntary action.[1] The discourse of post-war social reconstruction was not a sterile intellectual debate but an analysis of need and a call to action.[2] In keeping with the new interest in social reconstruction, the focus of voluntary service, according to James Heighton, President of the National Association of Guilds of Help, had to change from personal case-work to civic engagement, community well-being and greater co-ordination.[3] In some fields of social policy, notably housing and health, state intervention was forthcoming. This was not the case with leisure, in which the principal agent of intervention was the voluntary social service of A.J.P. Taylor's 'great army' of volunteers'[4] who administered the societies and clubs of Orwell's stamp-collectors, pigeon-fanciers, amateur carpenters and other manifestations of an English addiction to hobbies.[5]

Voluntary action was important to social reconstruction. With growing state interest in national and regional planning, social reformers anticipated a greater role for voluntary organizations. Plans to train a new cohort of social workers prepared by the Collegium, a social reform group emanating from the Student Christian Movement, helped shape the religious and secular strands of inter-war social service. Chaired by William Temple this group included E.J. Urwick, founder member of the Sociological Society and Head of the Department of Social Science and Administration at the London School of Economics, J. St. G Heath, Warden of Toynbee Hall and Lucy Gardner, later secretary of Temple's inter-war Christian Conference on Politics, Economics and Citizenship.[6] The social profile of inter-war volunteers has been debated and earlier accounts of a middle-class withdrawal have been contested.[7] In terms of leisure, voluntary social workers – an umbrella term that ranged from casual help in a girls' club to the leadership of large organizations – were largely drawn from the middle classes; Madeline Rooff's survey of girls' organizations revealed a heavy reliance on church and settlement workers, married women, teachers and leisured women.[8] In the 1930s, as social work became more bureaucratic and professionalized, senior positions in social service often required a qualification in social work or a degree in sociology.[9] However, at the executive levels of national organizations it was not uncommon to find representatives of the landed gentry and higher middle classes in positions of power and patronage. Consequently, although both idealism and socialism theorized leisure as an agent of social change, reformist objectives had in practice to be worked through structures and networks of competing interests and power.

Civic societies, service clubs and Women's Institutes

Post-war social reconstruction re-invigorated interest in the application of sociology to the creation of civic life.[10] In 1920 Arthur Greenwood, then a civil servant in the Ministry of Reconstruction, re-iterated the importance of voluntary action to the development of social citizenship.[11] It became a task of civic societies to construct an infrastructure within which leisure could perform this function. The idea of civic associations had been mooted through John Brown Paton's proposed Civic Leagues.[12] The first civic societies of the late nineteenth century were concerned to engage citizens in activating the public life of a local community in terms of the aesthetics of the urban environment and town planning.[13] Post-war civic associations fulfilled similar functions, encouraging the provision of parks, open spaces and cultural venues and extending the meaning of voluntary action to include the enhancement of quality of life.[14] Addressing the Civic Association in 1921 Sybella Branford, a housing reformer and organizer of community revival schemes, called for a regeneration of the idea of citizenship to energize the civic and cultural life of the community.[15] A renewed spirit of voluntarism was much in evidence in the years immediately following the War. The Birmingham Civic Society, for example, incorporated the city's Civic Recreation League and provided open spaces, parks and theatres; that in Richmond created opportunities for recreation, music, open spaces and gardening.[16] In Bradford civic voluntarism established a Civic Theatre with amateur actors and professional producers, one of several across the country and described by Priestley as a genuine popular and spontaneous movement.[17] Complementing the work of civic societies, relatively newly formed secular organizations including the Women's Institutes and British Legion offered new opportunities for leisure association,[18] the former encouraging women to take a more active part in the democratic process.[19] Service organizations, for example the Rotary Club, Round Table and the Soroptomists, a women's organization formed in America in 1921 to address social problems faced by women, similarly combined middle-class conviviality and social citizenship in their contribution to the urban public sphere.[20]

Religion

In 1917 the Interdenominational Conference of Social Service Unions produced a prospectus for Christian Social reconstruction to ensure religion would remain a motivating force in inter-war voluntary social service. Richard Tawney promoted the application of Christian values to reconstruction[21] and William Temple organized the cross-denominational Conference on Christian Politics, Economics and Citizenship (COPEC) in Birmingham in 1924 to re-articulate Christian social ethics as a basis for social regeneration and a new ideal of corporate life.[22] Motivated by a re-invigorated Christian socialism, COPEC, as we have seen, explicitly rejected the idea of a leisure class. Its report on leisure,[23] compiled by a committee substantially drawn from the settlement movement, blended pragmatism, social science and spirituality and urged churches to become social as well as religious centres, organizing leisure to provide a common meeting ground for social gatherings.[24] Many churches had already moved in this direction; the Farnworth Parish Church of St. John Mutual Improvement Society in Bolton typified COPEC's blend of the spiritual with the social. A female cotton worker recalled how:

> It had a big influence over me and it brought all kinds of things to us. Travel and music had opened the world to us. Lantern slides and many famous men came to speak to us, it certainly enriched our minds. A big day was the New Year's Tea Party, there was a scramble for tickets and there used to be two sittings, it was hard work but everybody enjoyed it. We worked for a lot of bazaars, we used to have potato pie socials and dances and whist drives almost every Saturday evening. New Year's Eve dance was a big success. We would dance until 11.30 p.m. and then go into Church for the midnight service and resume dancing until 2.00 a.m. The school used to be used to the full in those days, always something going on, dances, whist drives, concerts and tea parties.[25]

Reciprocity was important and COPEC emphasized the Christian duty to engage in social service to the wider community, suggesting the devotion of Sunday to the supervision of youth leisure as a desirable Christian act.[26] Many

Figure 6 Bolton St. Thomas' Church Garden Party, 1914. Churches were important providers of leisure. The pictured event clearly involved a cricket match but for many it was simply an opportunity for social intercourse, enjoyment and a sharing of identity as a member of a congregation.

Source: © Bolton Council. From the Collection of Bolton Library and Museum Services.

churches consequently made extensive provision for young people, their clubs and societies contributing to the civic identity of the community in the Whit processions that survived in Lancashire until the 1960s.[27]

8.2 The National Council of Social Service – leisure and community well-being

The co-ordination of social service, as noted above, became a goal of reformers in the late nineteenth century. Spurred by Stanton Coit's *Neighbourhood Guilds*, published in 1892,[28] Guilds of Help and Local Councils of Voluntary Aid had established some local co-ordination before the War; the Halifax Council of Social Welfare, for example, had a Playing Fields and Open Spaces Committee and incorporated the Halifax and District Amusement Association. These guilds and councils, together with the British Institute of Social Service, formed the template for the establishment in 1919 of the National Council of Social Service

(NCSS) to co-ordinate voluntary action on a national scale and provide a forum through which its theory and practice could be debated. The NCSS aimed to promote civic, social and industrial betterment through the formation of local councils of social service in urban areas and rural community councils in rural districts.[29] Although with only spasmodic acknowledgement of Green and social idealism, the NCSS was from the outset, as its historian noted, concerned with all aspects of the life of the community.[30]

The NCSS was the principal representative body of voluntary social service in inter-war Britain. Its conference on Reconstruction and Social Service, held in Oxford in April 1920, was a rallying call for the voluntary spirit, social citizenship and the social service movement.[31] As an embryonic field of social service, leisure was not the province of the state but of local and national voluntary organizations. The organization of clubs and community centres, the development of social citizenship and youth work consequently became fields of opportunity for voluntary intervention through leisure.[32] Leisure itself became a field of social policy and practice; in a seminal statement W.G.S. Adams, the Chairman of the NCSS, declared leisure to be as much a social service as housing, health and education.[33] Leisure thus acquired recognition as an agent of community well-being, equal, in theory, to other services.[34] Its centrality to social service was further reflected in the corporate membership of the NCSS, which included the Boy Scouts, Girl Guides, Church Lads' Brigade, YMCA, YWCA, and numerous secular and socio-religious organizations with an interest in leisure.[35]

An immediate manifestation of the new sociological status of leisure was the National Conference on the Leisure of the People, held in Manchester in November 1919. This was the first conference of the NCSS. Organized through the local Temperance Council by John Lewis Paton,[36] it mapped the scope of intervention in the new leisure of an eight-hour day for voluntary and municipal organizations.[37] Attended by 400 delegates, suggesting an extensive interest in leisure, it encapsulated the nature of social service concern in leisure at the beginning of the inter-war period. This included the changing social meanings of leisure and voluntary action, leisure as a field of citizenship, community centres and village halls, the role of the state in leisure and the effects on leisure of work. It did not however embrace Burns' idealist vision of leisure in a new world, with its discussions exposing underlying tensions between the idea of leisure as a social good and as a sphere of regulation and control. In terms of the former leisure was articulated as an agent of community well-being, working through social citizenship in social centres, churches and social welfare organizations to create and sustain community identity and spirit. In contrast, juvenile delinquency and the new mass leisure of the cinema and dance hall were interpreted in terms of regulation and discipline through Juvenile Organizations Committees and critiques of commercial leisure.

As G.D.H. Cole observed, the NCSS had to foster a spirit of community among a generation that had lost much of its social cohesion.[38] Community building thus became a core task of the NCSS through its stated commitment, reminiscent of Green's idealism, to create an 'association of citizens united for the common purpose of securing the fullest and freest life for all' with the 'old fashioned' view of social work as an effort to help other people being superseded by a new conception of social service as a common effort to achieve social well-being.[39] As we shall see, these aims were only partly fulfilled. Nevertheless, as a field of social association, leisure became linked to community building through discussion in the NCSS *Monthly Bulletin*, which dedicated a special issue to the questions of what use people would make of the 'new' leisure and how leisure might confer both individual and communal benefits.[40] From the outset tensions existed between a prioritization of the active use of leisure as a building block of the new democratic community theorized in liberal and social idealist thinking and the prevention of its use in the consumption of the mass popular culture of commercial enterprise.[41]

Although the NCSS introduced a national framework for its co-ordination, voluntary action worked principally at a neighbourhood level and planning for social service required detailed knowledge of local communities and their needs. To this end the social survey was, as Victor Branford and Patrick Geddes, noted a prerequisite of progress.[42] Surveys of leisure were commissioned by the NCSS, some being undertaken by local councils of social service, and the sociological status of leisure was further enhanced by its inclusion in regional surveys. Their reports give insight to social scientific understandings of leisure in the context of the urban community and the nature of voluntary interventions in leisure. The Liverpool Council of Voluntary Aid survey in 1923, for example, recorded that social service had recognized leisure as a newly discovered need of ordinary citizens and that through the Liverpool Citizens' Institute Association, clubs, holiday camps and other forms of active leisure had been organized.[43] The Bethnal Green report was less positive, finding apathy, gambling, excessive drinking and little desire for 'real' culture.[44] However, although recording a growth of mechanical organizations that fostered passive receptivity, the *New Survey of London Life and Labour* found an increase in active leisure in walking, dramatic societies, gardening, dancing, adult education and especially a rise in demand for outdoor sports and physical exercise.[45]

In Liverpool, the city in which social work in leisure had been supported by the university settlement, social service had positioned leisure as an integral element of a new civic modernity and an aspect of everyday life. As the Social Survey of Merseyside discovered, work was increasingly seen a means of providing resources to spend in leisure time.[46] Although commercial provision was substantial, nearly every church in Liverpool organized social clubs and cultural activities of some kind. This may have owed in part to Church of England policy on social service, which committed it to establish a Director of Social Studies in each Diocese and the use of the vicarage as a home for leisure organizations and sports clubs.[47] Social centres also provided a wide range of informal leisure opportunities; the Kirkdale Citizens' Institute, for example, had a mixed membership of 600 and opened each evening between 6.30 p.m. and 10.00 p.m. with concerts and facilities for billiards and football. Through the university settlement, the David Lewis Club organized sports and educational classes and both the Victoria Settlement and the Liverpool Domestic Mission continued to provide social amenities.[48] Need was measured by differences in wealth and capacity for civic action, with poorer inner districts, being more dependent on social service support, given priority in the provision of a club as a social centre. Leisure was also integrated in campaigns for civic action; the St. Anne's Citizen's Institute, for example, combined agitation and propaganda to address local deprivation with club rooms, playgrounds, singing and dramatic groups and classes in nursing and woodwork. In outer districts, for example Aintree and Aigburth, where capacity for self-organization was greater, social institutes were formed by Tenants' Associations; the North East Liverpool Association, for example, co-ordinated dances, concerts, a debating society and numerous sports clubs.[49]

Notwithstanding the growth of a progressive social scientific approach to leisure,[50] regressive narratives of degeneration and a civilization in crisis remained influential. Although declinist narratives are more generally associated with the later inter-war years, concerns about capacity for social citizenship were widespread and often associated with leisure. The adequacy of the adult manual worker as a responsible citizen was the theme of a survey conducted by the St. Philip's Settlement, based in the Sheffield YMCA.[51] Almost one quarter of respondents were categorized as well-equipped, being socially active, coping with life and possessing intellectual, moral and aesthetic capacities, three quarters were inadequately equipped, muddling through life and seeking immediate gratification while one tenth were mal-equipped, incapable of active social citizenship and, in the language of the report, a 'positive evil for the community'.

The use of leisure was a determining criterion of this categorization. As a 'well-equipped' male, 'Hoppitt' was self-taught, read public library books, visited the Mappin Art Gallery and Ruskin Museum and spent his leisure time painting, drawing and making model aeroplanes. The 'inadequately equipped' Miss Yen, a twenty-four-year-old shop assistant, liked the cinema, dancing, meeting men and stayed in bed until noon on Sundays. The 'mal-equipped' Ollis, a thirty-year-old furnace-man with a wife and children, was rarely at home and frequented the music hall or the public house on a daily basis. The report concluded that the well-equipped – those with active leisure lives – were more likely to pursue self-culture and personal development and to contribute to society through active social citizenship while the mal-equipped, whose passive leisure was dominated by drinking, gambling, sport, the 'pictures' and music halls, took no interest in trade unions, politics or their community. The cumulative evidence of social surveys revealed spatial patterns of practice and an uneven distribution of the social capital that enabled some neighbourhoods to develop and maintain their own leisure association and institutions. The challenge to social service was to establish how, in other neighbourhoods, voluntary action in leisure could create a sense of community and a duty of reciprocity and active social citizenship.[52]

8.3 Re-constructing the rural community: leisure, village halls and folk dance

The historiography of social service and leisure has tended to focus on their urban context. However, their role in rural social reconstruction has recently been explored by a number of historians.[53] Interventions in rural leisure by the NCSS and Carnegie United Kingdom Trust (CUKT) were shaped by the differing social and cultural contexts of the countryside and the town. In rural areas the term 'reconstruction' was appropriate to the regeneration of a community in decline; on urban estates, however, it was not a question of restoring something that had previously existed, but creating a new community amongst spatially displaced people who barely knew each other. The differing approaches to leisure and community well-being in rural and urban areas reveal historically contrasting concepts of community and leisure within social service. Concern for the countryside was not limited to those connected to it; instead, as John Stevenson notes, its preservation became part of a wider cultural re-imagination of the rural in terms of national identity and the safe-guarding of supposedly unchanging values in a new age of American mass cultural production.[54] Distinction of the rural was simultaneously one of the urban, creating what David Matless terms as geographies of reconstruction.[55] Reflecting what Matless describes as cultures of landscape, contrasting constructs of leisure were created on rural and urban lines in terms of modernity, democracy and citizenship.

Re-construction in rural areas was concerned with the re-vitalization of a sense of community in villages where the agricultural depression and rural depopulation of the late nineteenth century had fragmented social communities.[56] In *The Rural Problem*, published in 1917,[57] the agricultural economist Arthur Ashby argued that the economic reconstruction of agriculture was dependent on a revival of rural social life. Although the sense of the village as a social community was aided by its small size, the War, as Henry Rew observed, had created new fractures in class relationships and petty snobbery. With its diminishing leisure class, the corporate life of the village seemed to be fading and, as the *Times* commented, young people were increasingly allured to the town by the football match, cinema and trade union meeting.[58] The threat of further depopulation and diminution of village social life signalled to the NCSS a need to develop a more active participatory leisure culture in rural areas.[59] Its focus on leisure found wide support; Henry Wolff, a founder of the International Co-operative Alliance and the Agricultural Organization Society, agreed that the regeneration of social life in villages required a co-ordinated approach to the development of leisure.[60] This would, as Rew commented, require village halls and clubs as catalysts of a rural revival through an associational culture.[61]

Although progressive social thinking provided the theoretical base for community building, the CUKT was crucial to the funding, planning and building of village halls and urban community centres. Adhering to Andrew Carnegie's personal interest in public libraries and church organs, the Trust supported campaigns for a rural public library service and the music competition festivals organized by the Village and Country Towns Concert Fund.[62] The revival of a shared associational rural culture through leisure was led within the NCSS by W.G.S. Adams and Grace Hadow, a Somerville educated social worker who had been influential in the formation of the Women's Institutes and became Secretary of Barnett House, an institution founded in Oxford in 1914 to study social and economic questions. Hadow's pioneering scheme of rural social work in adult education and cultural activity, notably music and drama,[63] was adopted by Rural Community Councils, the first of which was established in 1920 in Oxfordshire with financial support from the CUKT.[64] In 1923 the CUKT, working through the NCSS, agreed to finance the formation of others and by 1934 they were established in twenty counties.[65] Through Rural Community Councils the NCSS and CUKT became a dominant influence on community building and the development of an associational leisure culture in rural Britain to the extent that they earned arguably justified criticism of being more interested in rural than urban social service.[66] A contributory factor to this was a prominent and inter-connected network of influential figures at senior levels of both organizations. Adams had produced the CUKT report, which led to rate-supported rural public libraries under the Public Libraries Act of 1919.[67] The Trust subsequently funded rural library buildings and supported the extension of the National Home Reading Union into rural areas.[68] Horace Plunkett, a member of the CUKT Executive Committee, had been a former colleague of Adams at the Irish Department of Agriculture and Technical Instruction, while Adams was a founder of the National Federation of Young Farmers' Clubs. Grace Hadow, who had been asked by Adams in 1920 to work at Barnett House, also served on the National Council of Social Service; her brother Henry was commissioned by the CUKT to prepare the report on British music that secured grant funding for rural community development through music. Oxford itself was a further unifying theme; Adams had been a student of Balliol College and was later Gladstone professor at Oxford and active in the Oxford Preservation Trust; Henry Hadow was classics tutor and Dean of Worcester College, Oxford, while the Somerville-educated Grace Hadow was a lecturer at Lady Margaret Hall, member of Somerville College Council and served on both the university's extra-mural delegacy in Oxfordshire and Oxfordshire's county education committee. Also important was the cultural milieu in which rural regeneration operated. Bill Luckin, for example, has written of a powerful anti-urban discourse and a loss of belief in the city as a sustaining force of an urban civilization,[69] which generated resistance to urban cultural influence within the Council for the Preservation of Rural England and the CUKT.

Policy on social reconstruction in both urban and rural communities focused on the encouragement of an associational leisure culture, but this required a communal space for social activities and meetings. Many villages lacked such premises, and even where they existed, for example village reading rooms, had in nearly all cases been provided through philanthropy. After the War, as Carole King notes, there was a demand for independence and self-governance.[70] Lawrence Weaver, an organizer for the village hall movement, insisted the benevolence of the local squire was not wanted; rather the new village community should be self-governing in all aspects.[71] It was therefore considered crucial to the development of a democratic and sustainable rural community that there should be an alternative non-paternalistic source of funding.[72] In 1923 the NCSS formed an Advisory Committee on Rural Affairs and in 1924, with the CUKT, established a fund to support village communities to build a hall.[73] Henry Mess estimated approximately 1,800 village halls to have been constructed between 1918 and 1939.[74] Funding was conditional on community involvement and democratic management.[75] As Ashby commented, the revival of village life should not to be a return to the maypole but a progression to the modern co-operatively run village club and recreation ground.[76] However, the idea of the maypole retained a strong appeal to an influential artistic and cultural coterie who saw in the village a traditional rural community threatened by a modernity of industrialization and urbanism. F.R. Leavis regretted the loss of a living communal culture in which folk songs and dances had represented a way of social life,[77] while artists such as Stanley Spencer and John Piper focused on the English landscape and village. The travel guides that proliferated with the spread of the motor car encouraged such imagination, eulogizing natural features and historical market towns while virtually ignoring the modernity represented by industrial regions. The tensions between an imagined rural England and a modern democratically organized village were reflected in rural reconstruction and leisure.

Effort to establish a re-vitalized and sustainable rural community owed much to women who, through the Women's Village Council Movement,[78] Women's Institutes, and the Village Clubs Association were instrumental in the construction of a community-based rural leisure.[79] Village halls provided a social space for activities organized through the Women's Institutes. The first was established in Anglesey in 1915; by 1917 199 had been formed[80] and in 1928 the Women's Institute had 240,000 members across 4,000 branches.[81] By the mid-1930s Madeline Rooff found Women's Institutes to be centres of village life,[82] widening country women's horizons, emphasizing an understanding of what community meant[83] and, importantly to social reconstruction, encouraging women to take an active role on local councils.[84] The NCSS established a Joint Committee with the National Federation of Women's Institutes to develop village music and drama through Rural Community Councils.[85] With financial support from the CUKT, producers and conductors were trained as teachers and organizers by the British Drama League and Village Drama Societies.[86] As it was the policy of the NCSS Rural Advisory Committee that Rural Community Councils should foster festivals in arts that were traditional in the countryside, representatives of the English Folk Dance Society and the Federation of Musical

Festivals were co-opted to them.[87] Furthermore, exemption from Entertainments Duty was granted for events that had the objective of reviving a national pastime.[88] Policy thus leant towards a conservative rather than a modern leisure culture and an emphasis on folk and tradition, which encouraged the re-creation of an imagined pre-industrial agrarian community.

Pursuing a revival of indigenous music, the CUKT[89] commissioned an investigation of musical activity by Henry Hadow[90] who recommended a revival of English folk culture to recreate a village communal life through folk song and rustic dances. English cultural identity and community were to be further promoted through performances in Competition Festivals and village halls of music by Elgar, Walford Davies and Vaughan Williams,[91] – composers associated, as Luckin comments, with soundscapes with an anti-urban sentiment.[92] From 1923 the CUKT funded the English Folk Dance Society to deliver classes in rural areas. Women's Institutes helped organize these in seventy-six villages for over 2,000 pupils and single middle-class women formed a large proportion of the teachers of folk dance.[93] The ground for a folk revival had been prepared before the War by Lord Lytton's Association for the Revival and Practice of Folk Music[94] but more influential was Cecil Sharp's field research in rural southern England where remnants of a folk tradition were thought to have survived. The rural essence of folk dance was emphasized in Sharp's publications, which referred to it as country dance.[95] Insisting upon the preservation of continuity, Sharp demanded technical accuracy and an undeviating adherence to a prescribed style of performance. However this rigidity was challenged by Mary Neal, a folk dance collector and social worker at the Mary Ward Settlement, who, with Emmeline Pethick, formed the Esperance Guild of Morris Dancers from the Esperance Girls' Club.[96] Neal believed enjoyment of the dance more important than technical accuracy and toured England with the Esperance dancers, often at the invitation of rural clergymen anxious to relieve the 'apathy and dullness' of village life.[97] However, it was Sharp's approach that became dominant through the formation in 1911 of the English Folk Dance Society, which promoted folk dance as an authentic form of English culture.[98]

The English Folk Dance Society thrived in rural areas, attributing its popularity to the sense of communal life embodied in the country dance. It was strongly represented in the south of England: Dorsetshire, for example had fifty branches and Kent forty, whereas Lancashire North had four and Sheffield two.[99] To Sharp, folk dance was an inherently English cultural form, closely linked to identity. Krishan Kumar has suggested that in the inter-war period ideas of Englishness became less nationalist and more retrospective in character. The positioning of English folk dance at the centre of a revived village culture corresponds with this interpretation, representing both a retreat from pre-war jingoism and a re-imagined cultural Englishness as a response to a popular culture increasingly influenced by American forms.[100] To Sharp, jazz, with it its 'merciless tom-tom rhythm' and 'negro influence' emanated from an urban black culture of America whereas the roots of folk dance were fixed in the real England of the countryside.[101] Its rural associations separated it from the urban dance hall and as Douglas Kennedy, Director of the Society, argued because folk dance had emerged from English yeoman stock it was 'peculiarly suited to the conditions of village life'.[102] The advocacy of folk dance as a leisure form specifically appropriate to a village endowed the village hall with a cultural significance that did not reflect contemporary cultural patterns; instead it was a reconstruction of an imagined past as, since the arrival of the railway in the countryside, urban musical culture in the form of music-hall songs and commercial popular music was displacing a pre-existing oral tradition.[103] Perhaps the harshest criticism of the imposition of a folk culture came from Sir A.D. Hall, Technical Adviser of the Ministry of Agriculture in reminiscing that the greatest contribution to village life had been the spread not of the morris but of 'ordinary' dancing with the waltz, one-step and tango.[104]

Hopes for a democratization of rural community life through a shared leisure remained largely unfulfilled. Not least important, as Emma Griffin observes, was the fact that leisure had never been perceived to be as destructive of the social order as in urban areas and a culture of paternalism consequently enjoyed greater continuity.[105] The dominant agricultural leanings of the National Council of Social Service have been mentioned, but this pattern was replicated in Rural Community Councils that, as Burchardt notes, were effectively the social wing of the agricultural interest;[106] a rural leisure class was also predominantly represented on the NCCS by landed brigadiers, rear-admirals and deputy lieutenants. Even the nominally classless Women's Institutes were governed by the gentry at county and national levels; in 1925 their national Executive Committee, led by Lady Denman from 1917 to 1946, included three Ladies, an Honourable Mrs and a former Member of Parliament.[107] Women such as these, as Beveridge noted, could only be drawn from a social stratum whose economic and domestic circumstances allowed the necessary leisure.[108] The working-class agency that might have been expressed through trade unions and working men's clubs was absent, partly by self-volition as in Oxfordshire, for example, the former would not work with the Oxford Council of Social Service.[109] Instead, the leisure-class functions of the Victorian and Edwardian middle classes were subsumed within the rural work of the NCSS and CUKT. In small and tightly knit village communities class distinctions remained important and as Councillor Peel from Wells in Norfolk expressed it, Mrs Shilling would not associate with Mrs Sixpence.[110] Moreover, the supposed retreat of the squire and parson has arguably been overstated; as both Martin Pugh and Nick Mansfield have argued, paternalism declined rather than disappeared from rural England.[111] Mowat too noted that while village halls held dances and whist drives, older traditions survived in the form of flower shows and fetes on the rectory lawn and at the manor house.[112]

In practice village halls were about much more than folk dance; like their urban counterparts they housed sports and social clubs, gardening societies, WEA classes and general leisure activities. Nevertheless the co-ordinated adoption of folk dance as a symbolic rural leisure practice was driven by a small network of individuals and institutions who sought to impose a particular form of associational leisure on rural communities. It placed the custodianship of folk song and dance with middle-class voluntary associations that, following Sharp, offered it to the agricultural labouring class as a traditional rural leisure form. As a middle-class re-invention of 'folk' this corresponds with Robert Colls' interpretation of the revival of folk culture as one with the people put in but their agency left out.[113] In a period when the commercial dance hall industry was booming in popularity[114] the valorization of an alternative and minority interest form of dance as a socializing force represented a prioritization of the perceived cultural values of an ideal imagined community through voluntary leisure association. The function of leisure as an agent of social change in inter-war rural England was articulated not in terms of a democratic community, nor, except for a small number of women organizers, the development of skills in social citizenship,[115] but of a conservative desire to retain stability in social relations and cultural values. Folk culture in Scotland and Wales, on the other hand, expressed a more widely shared cultural nationalism and was valued as a means of retaining identity within the political construct of the United Kingdom.

8.4 The new estates and community centres

In urban areas voluntary action in leisure progressed from a different starting-point to that in rural areas, being grounded in a more developed infrastructure of voluntary social service and building upon the pre-war practices of model factory villages and the garden city movement. Urban housing policy prioritized the replacement of slum housing and over one million council houses were built between the Wars.[116] Inter-war planning inherited from the garden city movement an awareness of the importance of the formation of a social community. The government's Tudor Walters committee, commissioned in 1917, recommended that new housing estates should aspire to a mix of social classes and the provision of private gardens.[117] The new post-war urban estate was thus a theoretical construct as well as a material reality and its planning involved not just the construction of housing but the creation of a self-managed and sustainable community.[118] However, few estates were built with the necessary facilities for social intercourse. Unlike rural reconstruction, which aimed to re-energize a moribund but existing spatial community, the challenge on the new estates was to create a new community from a population of strangers. The physical conditions of estate life were generally superior to those of the slum housing they replaced and conducive to private domestic leisure activity. However, social networks were weak as previously existing community and family structures were fragmented and estate residents, especially women who did not leave them to work, were often lonely and prey to mental illness.[119] Brad Beaven has noted how to conservative critics estate communities raised fears of alienation and social and political unrest.[120] In 1929, for example, the *Liverpool Daily Post* reported a mood of anger, depression and resignation amongst residents of the city's council housing schemes.[121] Although estates were intended to become stable social communities, few provided leisure amenities or had a community centre. As Richard Alston has observed, in architectural terms they were built not for a new society but for no society, offering no institutional support to the formation of a community.[122] Rooff reported how on Birmingham's Acocks Green and Perry Common estates the lack of a central focal building frustrated attempts at leisure association with the only meeting place being the school, which was often unavailable or unaffordable.[123] This pattern was widely replicated. In Liverpool, the Norris Green estate housed 30,000 people but, as the *Survey of Merseyside* discovered, the historical associations and institutions that gave cohesion were almost entirely absent; the formation of a social unit from a heterogeneous collection of people had, as its report noted, failed to take place.[124] As Liverpool Corporation refused to allow the erection of licensed premises on its estates, residents were deprived of a public house, the typical locus of informal associational leisure. Mass Observation described how on a Bolton estate this practice removed a customary social institution and left much social life to be conducted on public transport; the last bus home from town on Saturday night was effectively the estate's only meeting place.[125] The historiographical narrative of alienation and community breakdown on estates has been relatively unchallenged until recently[126] and many were successful in developing communal leisure forms that at least in part supported a sense of community and civic engagement.[127] However not all estates were the same in terms of social composition and facilities and some required more external social service support than others.

The idea of leisure as an agent of community well-being was well-suited to the planning of estates. To the NCSS their tenuous social life and lack of serious commercial competition opened a field for experimentation in the constructive use of leisure in community building. In 1928 the NCSS, with the Educational Settlements Association and the British Association of Residential Settlements, formed a New Estates Community Committee, chaired by Ernest Barker and including Cecil Delisle Burns.[128] Whereas voluntary associations normally formed naturally through common interests, the community centre movement adopted residence as the unifying force of an estate, aiming to develop the social interaction and social citizenship necessary to a functional community through the creation of an associational leisure culture.[129] The idea of a community centre drew from a number of sources: one was Morris' communal hall as a space for a common social life and a collective leisure.[130] Barker, however, adopted a different approach. A classicist, historian, ex-chairman of the National Home Reading Union and, like Adams, a product of Balliol College, he articulated the social function of leisure on the new estates in Hellenistic terms of community and citizenship. A disciple of T.H. Green and an authority on the philosophy of Plato and Aristotle, Barker conceptualized the estate as a community modelled on the *polis*.[131] Through Barker, Athenian social philosophy became the dominant theoretical paradigm for the organization of leisure on the estates. The estate was to be imagined in conceptual terms as 'some form of grouping, of which the object is a higher life, a great spiritual growth, on the lines of voluntary association.'[132] Barker's understanding of leisure was that of a sphere in which voluntary association could be encouraged[133] and democratically re-distributed,[134] a view in harmony with Burns' confidence in the capacity of ordinary people to create their own leisure associations and community consciousness if given the conditions to do so. The NCSS defined a community centre as a building that served a community, organized in an association responsible for it, which provided facilities for the development of the recreational, cultural and personal welfare of the members of that community.[135] To Barker, however, it was not only a building but an institution as a 'true power-house of new social life . . . controlled by those who use it through a Community

Association, that is to say, an association both of individual residents and of the organized clubs and groups established in the neighbourhood which it serves'.[136]

Voluntary association and leisure were to be the catalyst of a civic life; to one critic the new estate could become the modern counterpart of the ancient Greek city-state with a corporate life of its own.[137] In *Greek Political Theory* Barker likened the city to a club as a public space where people met to discuss common public interests.[138] By providing a space in which estate residents could associate, a community centre would function as a 'House of Leisure' – like the *agora* it would be a public space for social intercourse and activity, making leisure a common possession and enabling shared enjoyment.[139] The popularity of amateur dramatics on the estates even encouraged Barker to anticipate plays produced and acted in public, as in fifth-century Athens.[140]

The building of community centres for leisure association was a widespread practice of inter-war urban development.[141] Community Associations were needed to manage these; at Liverpool's Norris Green estate, for example, around thirty local societies together with a brass band and orchestra were federated in a Community Council.[142] Social capacity to develop communal associations was influenced by the demographic composition of the estate; on socially mixed estates residents were more likely to do so, while external help was needed on single class estates. The Watling estate belonged to the former category. Opened in 1927, it was not a slum clearance estate but housed relatively prosperous working-class families of semi-skilled workers and members of the police and armed forces.[143] In 1928 a Watling Residents' Association was formed by people with previous experience of active involvement in public life to co-ordinate community-based activities, a first step in making the estate the unit of association.[144] Through the NCSS, the Pilgrim Trust funded the building of a community centre and a full time organizing secretary.[145] Opened by the Prince of Wales in January 1933 this combined various social services with leisure, housing a Poor Man's Lawyer, Distress Fund and Personal Service Committee and providing a catalyst for the formation of voluntary associations as a meeting place for clubs and societies.[146] Ruth Durant found women to be leaders in the organization of voluntary life, particularly in churches, co-operative societies and the social and educational activities of the Women's Neighbourhood Guild, Adult School and Guild of Players.[147] Religion was a potent force of community formation; all Watling churches organized a social programme either to increase their congregation or to fulfil the social responsibilities stated by COPEC.[148] Church-based clubs, with 2,500 members, were the main providers of children's leisure.[149] A similar pattern prevailed on Manchester's Wythenshawe estate where the development of spiritual life was integrated through social associations such as the Mothers' Union, Church Lads' Brigade, Girls' Friendly Society and Salvation Army.[150]

By 1938 the programme of the Watling Community Centre involved numerous leisure associations, which included the Watling Guild of Players, Watling and District Rose Society, Weight Lifters' Society, Veterans' Club, Youth Club, Scouts, Cubs and Brownies. In addition, informal cultural and social events were held on a regular basis and included Sunday evening 'Free and Easies', lectures, public concerts and a range of educational and vocational classes.[151] Folk dancing, however, was not commonly found on the estates, partly as the English Folk Dance and Song Society organized classes only if requested.[152] To this extent Watling seemed to correspond with Barker's ideal of a Centre through which social association in leisure enabled an estate population to form a sense of itself as a community.[153] Ruth Durant found the Centre to be an 'exceptional institution', free from patronage, which had revived common enjoyment not by external persuasion but by internal effort and a culture of friendliness and ease.[154] It reflected Burns' belief in the capacity of people to create their own shared leisure without a leisure class and in terms of adult education, as E.W. Woodhead noted, it realized a spiritual rather than a political democracy, promoting a constructive use of leisure by meeting new social needs.[155] However, Durant concluded that as Watling grew it had become less a traditional community of people; with a constant turnover of residents its societies did not reduce but reflected social atomization. It remained, she noted, inconclusive whether leisure could supplant work as the source of community.[156] Elizabeth Roberts' oral history of working-class women later supported this assessment in noting that although 'urban villages' provided a sense of place and unity they often lacked the necessary capacity to develop into a fully functioning community.[157]

The Becontree estate, built by the London County Council close to Dagenham, required greater social service intervention than Watling. Its population increased from 11,837 in 1923 to 103,328 by 1933 and it was, as Terence Young noted, a small town rather than an estate.[158] It was predominantly working class with 95.34 per cent of male and 96.47 per cent of female residents employed in manufacturing, building and transport. Most households comprised married couples aged 30–45 with children under school leaving age and social work was consequently constrained by a shortage of volunteer helpers.[159] Although a number of voluntary leisure and educational organizations were established, there was no community centre.[160] In a paper to the International Conference of

Settlements in 1922 Walter Mabane, Warden of the Liverpool University Settlement, had argued a settlement's most effective contribution to neighbourhood communities – which he saw as the foundations of a new state – was to enable them to become self-organized. Neighbourhoods, he claimed, were anxious to develop a community life but needed initial training in the organization of leisure and education as a basis for political and industrial organization.[161] Victor Branford and Patrick Geddes observed towards the close of the War that the settlement movement was progressing from the acceptance to the transformation of social conditions.[162] This was particularly so with educational settlements, many of which had started to shift their focus from education to community development, becoming, as Mark Freeman notes, more akin to social settlements by providing training for citizenship and social leadership.[163] In 1929 the CUKT funded the Educational Settlements Association's Pettit Farm at Becontree. Although a settlement rather than a community centre, Pettit Farm performed several of the functions associated with the latter and changed its emphasis from bringing people into the settlement to extra-mural work. Supported by the East End Kingsley Hall settlement, it helped residents form voluntary organizations.[164] However, as Andrzej Olechnowicz's study of Becontree discovered, although Pettit Farm became the headquarters for the Becontree Residents' Association and approximately a further thirty organizations, further growth was hindered through political and religious antagonisms between community groups.[165]

The growing popularity of sport was reflected in numerous sports associations, which included at least forty football clubs, many with associated cricket clubs. Several were connected with churches and factories and competed in local competitions and leagues. With assistance from Pettit Farm the Dagenham Boys' and Girls' Club opened in 1933[166] as the only institution to provide facilities solely for young people, with a gymnasium, clubs and a membership of c. 80–100 boys and 80–200 girls. Its Trustee Committee included representatives of the NCSS, but all clubs were administered by committees of local people. Mutual associations also flourished; the Dagenham Socialist Sunday School organized an alternative range of clubs for rambling, swimming, cricket and football and there were four licensed working men's clubs with rooms for games, meetings and socials.

At Becontree too churches were significant contributors to the creation of social life with over half of the estate's 590 societies and organizations attached to a religious body or a church.[167] Although Young considered Anglican churches to make a significant contribution towards the social life of the estate with men's organizations, women's fellowships, scout troops, Brownie and Guide companies and Church Lad's Brigades, some restricted their membership to congregations and Sunday Schools. The involvement of the Anglican Mother's Union in the formation of societies corresponded with its endorsement of COPEC's emphasis on active citizenship and supports Caitriona Beaumont's assessment of its wider encouragement of recreational activities as a form of Christian citizenship.[168] The London City Mission also operated branches of the Girls' Guildry and Girls' Life Brigade.[169] As at Watling, women were active in the development of community life, organizing women's clubs and societies, meeting in the afternoon and sometimes establishing links with political parties.[170] Many women participating in church-based social activities claimed to have avoided contact with churches since childhood. This contrasted sharply with male membership of societies; while approximately 15 per cent of women on the estate were a member of an organization, the corresponding figure for men was 3 per cent, most of which was based on membership of social clubs.[171] The cinema, greyhound track and public houses on the estate were the primary leisure attraction for adults aged over twenty-five and appeared to Young to erode older ties to community clubs and societies.[172] Although alternative forms of commercial leisure distracted from volunteering, as critics had anticipated, a further obstacle to community was transience; by 1929 over 10,000 people had left the estate.[173] The most salient aspect of associational leisure formation and community development at Becontree was that almost all societies concerned with helping people in distress originated externally, supported by churches and the settlements, whereas co-operative and political societies, tenants' associations and sports organizations were initiated by local enthusiasts.[174] Although leisure interests could be served through self-initiated association, this did not necessarily create the social leadership necessary to the well-being of the whole community. Reviewing progress on the new estates towards the end of the 1930s, Ernest Barker regretted the general lack of capacity for social leadership and the insufficiency of men and women with the technical or professional skills to organize community life.[175] Effective voluntary social service on a housing estate, he concluded, required the external intervention that could be provided by local authorities under the 1936 Housing Act and 1937 Physical Training and Education Act 1937, which permitted them not only to build a community centre but to employ a full-time organizing secretary.[176]

To what extent did practice in rural and urban reconstruction correspond with theoretical policy discourse? The conceptualization of the community of the new housing estates in terms of classical Greek philosophy, and especially Aristotle, drew in part from social idealism and was expressed through the intended function of the community centre as a democratic and public forum for leisure association and social citizenship. However, as the development of Watling and Becontree demonstrated, without the necessary levels of social capacity, leisure association did not necessarily mature into a wider community-wide social citizenship without external assistance. Rural reconstruction on the other hand displayed no overt connection to idealism and neither was there a serious effort to democratize the village leisure culture. The village hall was not articulated as a democratic forum in the same way as the estate community centre, and the word 'community' here seems an important indicator in the distinction between urban and rural reconstruction.

Young People, Youth Organizations and Leisure

9.1 Introduction

Much voluntary work with young people in the inter-war years focused on those aged between fourteen and twenty years old who had left school but were not yet fully equipped to enter the world of adult leisure. Its overall aim was to intervene in the transition to adulthood to encourage a preference for active leisure and to develop the skills of social citizenship. In this context character became important in sociological rather than moral terms; its improvement, as the National Conference on the Leisure of the People noted, was the foundation of intelligent employment and citizenship.[1] Central to social service with young people was the self-managed club; as B.A. Campbell, the leader of a London boys' club remarked, in a time of democracy and democratic government, the boys had to be allowed to govern themselves.[2] The juvenile, or adolescent, was, as Mike Brake has argued, a cultural construct, variously identified as respectable, delinquent or culturally rebellious.[3] Much intervention in the leisure of young people reflected not idealism but a perceived need for control and regulation; Pearl Jephcott, a senior organizer in the National Association of Girls' Clubs, conceded that inter-war voluntary social service for youth never transcended the idea of a social ambulance.[4] Nevertheless, through experimentation, social research and state-voluntary partnership, a modern twentieth-century approach to provision for young people emerged that led to the publication in 1942 of *The Service of Youth* and its recommendation of the establishment of youth committees by local authorities.[5] However new experimental youth movements emerged after the War that operated outside the framework of social service to focus on personal development through nature, romanticism and an idealistic socialism.

9.2 Leisure, young people and industrial welfare in the First World War

The recruitment of young adults to munitions factories in the First World War placed new demands on voluntary youth organizations. In May 1915 the government established a Ministry of Munitions to control factories engaged in war production.[6] Its responsibilities included the well-being of the workforce through the governance of the Health of Munition Workers Committee formed in September 1915 under George Newman, Chief Medical Inspector for the Board of Education. Based on empirical research of factory conditions it recommended the appointment of factory welfare supervisors to co-ordinate workers' use of leisure time.[7] As Dorothea Proud's seminal text on factory welfare demonstrated, leisure was an increasingly prominent element of welfare schemes on an international basis.[8] Persuaded by Proud that welfare provision would create factory troops of Boy Scouts and Girl Guides with strength of character and less need of supervision at work, Lloyd George instituted welfare work in the munitions industries[9] through a Department of Welfare in the Ministry of Munitions with Seebohm Rowntree as Director.[10] The munitions factory welfare supervisor was responsible for the oversight of behaviour both inside and outside the workplace and for the co-ordination of recreation for boy, girl and women employees. In some cases the munitions factory itself became a provider of leisure; the Woolwich Arsenal, for example, organized classes in gymnastics, physical exercise and country dancing as well as numerous hockey and football clubs.[11] This required co-operation with local voluntary organizations, typically lads' and girls' clubs, and municipal authorities.

Boys' leisure was seen to be particularly problematic. Responding to a sharp rise in juvenile delinquency, Charles Russell, a pioneer of the lads' club movement, advised the Home Secretary that voluntary social work would reduce delinquency.[12] The government consequently created a central Juvenile Organizations Committee in the Home Office in 1916, under Russell's chairmanship, to promote the co-ordination of leisure provision through local Juvenile Organizations Committees comprising representatives of voluntary and municipal organizations.[13] Although a wartime measure, this was a significant development as the first government intervention in the leisure welfare of adolescents. A local Juvenile Organizations Committee (JOC) typically included delegates from boys' and girls' clubs, the local education authority, churches, local councils of voluntary aid and the probation service. JOCs co-ordinated young people's sport on a community basis and were encouraged by the Home Office to extend their scope to the adult working population. Through a donation of £6,000 from the Maharajah Scindia of Gwalior, *aide de camp* to King Edward the Seventh, some towns formed Central Schemes of Recreation for all workers; that in Birmingham operated as a Civic Recreation League, financing and co-ordinating the use of recreation halls, playing fields and open air concerts. JOCs were retained with a wider remit in 1918, when responsibility for their co-ordination was transferred from the Home Office to the Board of Education, symbolizing a policy shift of focus from the containment of delinquency to education in the use of leisure and the encouragement of socially constructive activities.

By 1920 JOCs existed in several towns and under the 1921 Education Act, which empowered local education authorities to promote social and physical training for young people, became a hub around which voluntary and municipal provision for juvenile leisure could be jointly organized and grant-funded.[14] Some JOCs operated under a different name; the Bradford Federation of Young People's Societies, for example, was chaired by the municipal Education Officer and opened the authority's playing grounds and camp to play centres, clubs and brigades.[15] Reports from local JOCs reveal a huge demand for leisure and especially sport among young people; the Wigan JOC for example, had twenty-one football and four girls' hockey pitches, while at West Ham a football league of twenty clubs with a membership of over 1,000 men was formed along with a range of other sports, including netball, for girls.[16] JOCs worked most effectively where there was an active local council of social service. The Bristol JOC, for example, formed in a city with a strong tradition of active social service and civic consciousness, amalgamated with the Bristol Social Centres Association and operated as the Bristol Recreation Council,[17] incorporating youth organizations, the Civic League, Rotary Club, Co-operative Society, major employers, the Juvenile Court and Probation Office.[18] Its 'Scheme of Recreation' embraced all industrial workers, dividing the city into five areas and undertaking a survey of local needs in each. Though seemingly mundane, this was crucial to the enabling of much everyday leisure and indicative of the paucity of resources available; it enabled, for example, the purchase of a billiard table for the Brooklands Institute of Boys' and Girls' Clubs and the rent of a playing field for the Horfield Baptist Institute Clubs. JOCs made a largely unrecognized contribution to the provision of leisure, especially sport, in urban communities and as Kathleen Dewar, Secretary of the Glasgow Council of Juvenile Organisations noted, they gave a collective voice to leisure that would always receive more attention that the individual club.[19] In so doing they contributed to policy objects of limiting delinquency and acquired a regulating oversight of young people, being represented on Juvenile Employment Committees, which maintained records of character and employability.

9.3 Educating the young citizen

The NCSS annual report for 1930, published as *Constructive Citizenship*, signalled a renewed emphasis on social citizenship in both secular and church-based social service. Religion remained a potent influence on voluntary provision for young people, working through girls' and boys' clubs, Junior Temperance Societies and other interdenominational groups with a Christian ethos.[20] The Girls' Life Brigade was nominally inter-denominational but particularly strong in non-conformist churches where it maintained a tradition of training girls as Sunday School teachers and promoting an internationalist spirit.[21] National socio-religious bodies such as the YMCA and YWCA, and nominally secular

Figure 7 Scout Parade in Bolton, 1938. This photograph, taken by Humphrey Spender as part of Mass Observation's Worktown study, shows the appeal of uniformed boys' organizations and also provides a reminder that without the active social citizenship of leaders, such organizations would not have existed.

Source: © Bolton Council. From the Collection of Bolton Library and Museum Services.

Figure 8 Guides and Brownies in Procession in Bolton, 1938. Another Spender Worktown photograph, this shows how youth leisure organizations contributed to a civic identity while also enabling older girls to develop citizenship skills by assisting in the leadership of clubs and projects.

Source: © Bolton Council. From the Collection of Bolton Library and Museum Services.

groups such as the Boy Scouts and Girl Guides, also promoted Christian values and were often connected to church communities. As Rooff discovered, mixed gender clubs were uncommon and the single sex principle hampered the recruitment of older girls.[22] Platonic friendship remained an ideal; the Church of England sponsored Girls' Friendly Society, for example, which had 2,256 branches by the mid-1930s, retained a focus on purity and, although rarely allowing the admission of boyfriends, recruited upper- and middle-class girls as 'associates' to form friendships with working girls.[23]

Democratic club management through committee membership and elections provided training in social responsibility and, as Rooff suggested, encouraged members to feel that the well-being of the club depended in part on each individual. Despite contemporary middle-class enthusiasm for civic participation, club leaders were in short supply on a national scale with many clubs relying on women already involved in church-based social organizations.[24] In the depressed Lancashire cotton town of Burnley, however, political antipathy to interference by 'leisured people' undermined the credibility of social service clubs and was blamed for low levels of recruitment[25] and it seems improbable that Burnley was unique in this respect. Nevertheless, clubs struggling to find leaders were obliged to depend upon leisured people for support.

Inter-war voluntary youth work did not divest itself of Malthusian fears of over-population; Bill Luckin, for example, has noted how reformist discourse in Manchester and Salford continued to display Edwardian imaginations of the urban slum in terms of immorality, fecklessness and sexual profligacy.[26] All cities, Robert Gunn Davis had declared before the War, housed a vast population, devoid of character and afflicted by hereditary moral and physical imperfections, whose spread was exacerbated by early marriage and that remained stubbornly resistant to reforming effort.[27] Early marriage, according to Helen Dendy, was a sign of recklessness and weakness of character which led to poverty.[28] A reduction of the birth rate in slum areas was widely advocated as a means of addressing a perceived problem of over-population and was adopted as an object of the clubs established by Maude Stanley, a leading figure in the late nineteenth-century girls' club movement in London and founder of the first Club for Working Girls in 1880. Stanley's clubs were socially graded and differentiated in the type of leisure they provided; those for the poorer girls believed most susceptible to early marriage placed a special emphasis on member retention to limit population growth.[29]

Although in the twentieth century the slum became a sociological construct,[30] the Victorian discourse of degeneracy remained active. The urban adolescent, according to Stanley Hall, inherited a 'genetic psychology' of urban life that produced tendencies to moral insanity, delinquency and lack of respect for others.[31] Deviance was associated with lack of character that, as Stefan Collini notes, implied the qualities necessary to deal with life, typically team-work, self-reliance, concentration, obedience and initiative.[32] Rationales for the development of character were consequently expressed in terms of the cultural deficit of the crowded industrial city.[33] Collini demonstrates how the Victorian idea of character fed into a belief that working-class populations lacked the virtuous middle-class characteristics of self-restraint and maturity and were consequently unable to resist the temptation of excitement.[34] After the War, Lawrence Pearsall Jacks, Unitarian minister and Stevenson Lecturer in Citizenship, attributed social degradation to uneducated leisure and the skills and attributes to use it wisely.[35] This could be a dangerous weakness; in Bethnal Green young males were notoriously difficult to attract to lads' clubs but expanded significantly the membership of the Young Fascists, described by a resident as the real youth movement of the district.[36] If the ideal boy could not be found in the urban slum, the public schoolboy could be called upon as an embodiment of the character and public spirit lacking in rougher working-class boys. Public schools had long emphasized character formation through sport with boys destined to become leading future citizens.[37] In 1929 the Prince of Wales, patron of the NCSS and the Duke of Gloucester, President of the National Association of Boys' Clubs[38] urged clubs to emulate the public school spirit of comradeship, good fellowship and loyalty.[39] By the late 1930s Henry Durant found almost every large public school had formed a service club.[40]

The public school adoption of boys' clubs did not correspond with either the anti-leisure class discourse of reconstruction or new sociological understandings of leisure. Even the Liverpool University Settlement interpreted delinquency and intolerance of authority not in sociological terms but as pathological 'diseases' to which unemployed boys were prone;[41] its booklet *Character* likened the mind of the average working man to a national menace and his attitude towards the home and family relations as dangerously near to being animal.[42] The settlement's York House Boys' Club, opened by the Duke of York in 1926, was adopted by Liverpool College, whose pupils and old boys took control of its management. Following the principles established in Toynbee Hall there was an emphasis on friendship between public school boys and club members; the slum boy would be trained in character by exposure to the public school spirit of service.[43] In an institution committed to social science, the deployment of public school intervention in a slum district club reflected a regressive adherence to a leisure class. Although public schools valued their adoption of boys' clubs as a manifestation of paternalist social duty, the mission organically connected a future ruling class with a slum population in a period of political instability and social unease. Through service, public schoolboys were introduced to the social and economic conditions of urban youth; in 1928, for example, boys from Sherborne School, Dover College, Eastbourne College and St. Edmund's School Canterbury were taken to the East End to visit a Juvenile Employment Exchange and the Oxford and Bermondsey settlements' boys' clubs.[44] Although desire to improve social conditions may have been genuine, social change was not in the interests of public schools and service was rather a display of friendship to the poor and an impression of solidarity with those served.[45]

Voluntary social service organizations for youth struggled to come to terms with the new modernity of inter-war youth. Much recent historiography has documented the extent to which young people's leisure consumption reflected new modern tastes and attitudes.[46] Although mass popular culture may not have corresponded with Arnoldian standards, much of it was socially harmless and preferable to street loitering. By the 1930s the cinema was a potent counter-attraction to the lads' club, although surveys of juvenile cinema-going in Edinburgh, Liverpool, Sheffield and Newcastle found it had no significant negative aspects. However, rather than embracing the new leisure, many club leaders perceived it as an obstacle. At the NCSS conference on reconstruction in 1920, for example, C.E. Clift, Secretary of the Board of Education Juvenile Organizations Committee, likened cheap cinemas, music halls and herbalist shops to a form of delinquency,[47] while in *The Girl* Katharine Dewar advised club leaders to respond to requests for rag-time music with trips to concerts of classical music.[48] In her survey of Bethnal Green, Constance Harris found school leavers wanted no mental effort in leisure and preferred the most lurid cinema films and dance-halls.[49] Class distinction underpinned much of this bias; to Edith Neville, warden of the Mary Ward settlement, commercial leisure was inseparable from the incivility of the popular crowd with its lack of restraint and self-assertion.[50]

9.4 Cultural rebels and radical leisure association

Between the 1880s and 1914 uniformed conformity was widely adopted by youth organizations through codes of dress, ritual and discipline to create a shared identity and regulate behaviour. Examples include the Boys' Brigade (1883), the Church Lads' Brigade (1891), Catholic Boys' Brigade (1896), Baden Powell's Boy Scouts (1908) and the Girl Guides (1910).[51] The militaristic nature of some uniformed organizations, particularly the Boy Scouts, was criticized for its imperialist and jingoistic tone. In a period of popular nationalism and imperial pride the young Edwardian male was subject to a pervasive model of masculinity, mediated through popular magazines and stories of selfless patriotism, imperialism and duty.[52] Scouting, with its uniform, discipline, games and outdoor pursuits, encouraged these values, motivating socialists and pacifists to create counter-associations. One of the first examples was the British Boy Scouts, founded as a reconstitution of the Battersea Boy Scouts in 1909 to promote pacifism. Adopted by churches, especially the Quakers,[53] its growth was accelerated when Francis Vane left Baden Powell's scouts to become president, supported by a committee that included the prominent liberals Charles Masterman, W.T. Stead and Barrow Cadbury.[54] In 1910 the British Boy Scouts, with John Brown Paton's pacifist Boys' Life Brigade, federated as the National Peace Scouts and increased its membership to 50,000.[55]

Other breakaway voluntary youth organizations formed through a growing cultural rejection of Edwardian social values and an emerging moral dialogue around militarism and imperialism. In the early post-war years the Kibbo Kift Kindred, Woodcraft Folk and Urdd Gobaith Cymru contested the conventional idea of British citizenship. The latter, formed in 1922 by Ifan Owen Edwards, promoted a specifically Welsh citizenship through summer camps of trekking, boating and cultural evenings.[56] All three embodied a sense of social dislocation and operated in the outdoors, assigning to the land values different from those of the CHA and Holiday Fellowship and reflecting what Sarah Mills has referred to as a geography of voluntarism.[57] The Kibbo Kift and Woodcraft Folk emphasized the purity of the primitive life and a mystical view of nature. Founded by young people disillusioned with the conservatism of social service, both were influenced by Ernest Thompson Seton, the English-born Chief Scout of America. Seton had assisted in the formation of Baden Powell's scouts, having established the Woodcraft Indians for boys in North America in 1902 in response to the suppression of the indigenous American Indians.[58] His cultural re-imagination of the outdoors also influenced Ernest Westlake's middle-class and anti-urban Order of Woodcraft Chivalry, founded in 1915.[59] The Kibbo Kift and Woodcraft Folk were part of an early twentieth-century English radicalism described by Jon Savage as a reaction to a perceived spiritual decay. At the forefront of this movement were the Neo-Pagans, a Fabian-orientated circle formed around Rupert Brooke, which challenged conventions of gender, deference and adulthood.[60]

Drawing inspiration from the pre-war German *Wandervogel*, the Kibbo Kift and Woodcraft Folk adopted the outdoors as a site for a leisure culture grounded in a spiritual reconnection with the land. The Kindred of the Kibbo Kift was founded in 1920 by John Hargrave, formerly the Boy Scout's Commissioner for Woodcraft and Camping.[61] Disappointed with the militarism of the Scouts and sceptical of the capacity of organized voluntary action to effect social change,[62] Hargrave rejected establishment patronage and created the Kibbo Kift to promote pacifism and alternative cultural norms through both its adult and junior sections.[63] Whereas social service emphasized citizenship and conformity, the Kibbo Kift (meaning 'proof of strength') prized a radically alternative model of citizenship for a similarly alternative commonwealth through experimentation in communitarianism with camping, 'naturecraft' and handicraft as expressions of personality and self-reliance. To anyone disenchanted with conventional uniformed organizations it presented an almost intoxicating alternative; one of its members, Leslie Paul, likened it to a new wind blowing through a young country and recalled being 'carried away' with its vision of a new movement to cure the diseases of civilization through co-operative woodland communities, the revival of native arts and the promise of a new pagan religion.[64] Although not fully in accord with Morris' view of leisure and work, the Kibbo Kift recognized its debt to him, comparing its camps to Kensington Wood in *News from Nowhere* where children came to play in the summertime, living in tents and learning to do things for themselves.[65] Its dress code of hooded jerkin, cloak and shorts was copied, through Ruth Hargrave, from the American Camp Fire Girls whose native ceremonial costume and emphasis on woodcraft and service informed Kibbo Kift's ideals. The Kibbo Kift was not democratically organized, something widely considered essential to sustainable voluntary association, but worked through a complex structure of ritual and ceremony, which John Hargrave argued to be more appropriate to the creation of group harmony than bureaucracy and military discipline.[66] This proved its downfall as Hargrave's autocracy was unacceptable to members with connections to labour and co-operative movements and thus prevented the Kibbo Kift's expansion as a mass left-wing scouting movement.

Kibbo Kift claimed to be the guardian of a Britain that had lost spiritual direction under the competitive ethos of industrial capitalism.[67] Spirituality in this context was not religious but like Rolf Gardiner's arose from the 'cultural soil' of an ancient England of old straight tracks, Neolithic barrows and older civilizations. Gardiner, described by David Fowler as one of the prime inter-war developers of youth culture in Britain, associated himself with the Kibbo Kift in 1923 hoping to connect it to German youth movements but was prevented from doing so by Hargrave's suspicions of nationalism. Gardiner later organized his own folk dance tours to Germany and the north of England with his 'Travelling Morrice', describing them as communion with places and people.[68] Although remaining small – its membership rarely exceeded 1,000 – the Kibbo Kift attracted support from prominent socialists and liberals.[69] Its Advisory Council (Annebella Pollen notes there is no record that this ever met[70]) included Mary Neal, Emmeline Pethick Lawrence, who had been associated with Percy Alden's Mansfield House settlement in Canning Town, and Henry Nevinson, founder member of the Men's League for Women's Suffrage.[71] Neal, at least, would have found Gardiner a welcome contrast with the English Folk Dance Society as like the Kibbo Kift she believed folk dance to be a primary form of expression rather than a regulated technical replication of an imagined tradition.[72]

The Kibbo Kift was the template for the Woodcraft Folk, formed in South London in 1925 by the nineteen-year-old Leslie Paul and Sidney Shaw. Paul left the Kibbo Kift to form the Woodcraft Folk as the Labour scout movement he had hoped the Kibbo Kift would become. In this context, as Paul explained, folk meant not the English 'art and crafty sense' but the German sense of *volk*, co-operation and the welfare of the community.[73] As David Prynn notes, its self-identity as a folk movement owed much to the *Wandervogel* interpretation of the land as a life-giving force.[74] Drawing from the Kibbo Kift's alternative Englishness of anti-urbanism, pacifism and mysticism, Woodcraft socialism was, according to Paul, a blend of Edward Carpenter's Millthorpe with pantheism, paganism and the mystical vision of England found in Richard Jeffries' green roads.[75] The new civilization of the Woodcraft Folk was not the modern progressive society imagined by the National Council of Social Service but one that, like the Kibbo Kift, drew from the ideal society of *News from Nowhere*.[76]

Aided by a donation from the Royal Arsenal Co-operative Society[77] it was not party-political but imbued with Morris' socialism, seeking the welfare of the community through communal ownership of the means of production, communal responsibility and the prioritisation of service over private greed. Reliable quantitative data on the Woodcraft Folk are scarce; although Paul acknowledged that it failed to develop into a mass movement it nevertheless offered an alternative approach to the countryside as a leisure space and branches were formed throughout the country. The reluctance of social service youth organizations to relinquish a policy of single-sex membership has been noted above; the Woodcraft Folk was one of the first youth associations to pioneer a mixed-gender membership. It was more successful than the Kibbo Kift in establishing a broad social appeal; as Madeline Rooff reported, it had a natural affinity to co-operative societies, many of which adopted Fellowships and Lodges of both the Woodcraft Folk and the Order of Woodcraft Chivalry.[78] The Bristol Co-operative Wholesale Society, for example, operated three groups of Woodcraft Folk with a total membership of eighty, approximately a half of whom were under twenty-five years of age.[79] The Independent Labour Party too organized Woodcraft groups; in Nelson these were organized through local Clarion groups.[80] In Leicester a Woodcraft Folk group for girls offered 'undenominational and socialistic' though not party political activities, which included woodcraft, camping, hiking, sun-bathing, swimming, craft work, folk-dancing and singing.[81] For adults it was a space in which Paul's emphasis on the unit of the family could be developed, an innovative development in voluntary youth work.[82]

The Kibbo Kift and Woodcraft Folk symbolized a desire for radical cultural and social change that was not possible through more conventional outdoor organizations, particularly the Co-operative Holidays Association and the

Holiday Fellowship, and brought a radical voice to the moral dialogue of leisure. Both embodied the spirit of Burn's revolt of youth, seeking not a nostalgic pastoral recreation but a radical leisure through which to teach and act out a new type of society. Common to both and in keeping with contemporary thinking was the perception of a sickness of civilization in need of radical reform; in the case of the Woodcraft Folk this necessitated training men and women in physical fitness and mental independence and the survival of the race.[83] Although corresponding with other interventions in young people's leisure that saw the countryside as a temporary restorative place from which a return to the city was inevitable,[84] the leisure practices of the Kibbo Kift and Woodcraft Folk represented a radical imagination of the countryside as a primeval space and a rejection of the values of industrial capitalism.

Leisure, Unemployment and Social Service

10.1 Introduction

Long-term unemployment was a persistent feature of inter-war Britain, affecting at least 10 per cent of the insured workforce every year between 1921 and 1938, with the exception of 1927 when the proportion fell to 9.7 per cent.[1] When uninsured workers were included, the total was higher and in 1932 3,400,000 persons, 17 per cent of the total workforce, were out of work.[2] Ken Roberts has noted that the lower economic groups, being the most vulnerable to unemployment, are the most affected by class inequalities in leisure.[3] This was historically the case as the concentration of unemployment in working-class areas intensified its social impacts. While areas of the midlands and south of England developed new industries and enjoyed a degree of prosperity with new opportunities for leisure through the welfare schemes of modernizing factories, regions in which the older staple industries were in economic decline experienced economic and social distress. In the north-east shipbuilding town of Jarrow, for example, over 80 per cent of workers were unemployed in 1932 while in the mining areas of South Wales the average rate was over 70 per cent. South Wales, Durham and Tyneside, West Cumberland and industrial Scotland were officially designated as depressed areas in 1934, but Lancashire, South Yorkshire and Merseyside were also badly affected by high and enduring unemployment.[4]

Unemployment challenged understanding of the work–leisure relationship and the idea of leisure as sphere for social change. Euphemistic terms were used to denote it but neither 'enforced leisure' nor 'spare time' was accurate. As Henry Durant understood, to have leisure alone was to have no leisure.[5] The durability of unemployment suggested it could become a permanent social condition, raising questions of what meaning leisure could have without work and whether leisure could replace work as the central life interest. The long-term unemployed, as Andrzej Olechnowicz has noted, were believed to be subject to a gradual regression from resignation to distress and finally apathy.[6] Being workless, the unemployed were excluded from much of the normal leisure life of the community by lack of money and loss of self-belief. Some critics, however, argued that the unemployed should not expect to share in leisure on an equal basis. Lawrence Pearsall Jacks, for example, was critical of unemployed Lancashire cotton operatives' perceived 'addiction' to greyhound racing and urged governmental restrictions on the leisure of those 'so liberally supported by the dole'.[7] In contrast, Labour councillors in South Wales supported the construction of greyhound tracks as a means of creating jobs.[8]

The government did little to address unemployment, being, as McKibbin suggests, content to keep the unemployed acquiescent.[9] The unemployed were consequently left, as Selina Todd notes, to help themselves.[10] In a widely reported meeting organized by the National Council of Social Service in the Albert Hall in January 1932, the Prince of Wales, describing the challenge of unemployment as a national opportunity for voluntary social service, appealed for assistance, following which hundreds of local schemes were formed to build centres and clubs for the unemployed.[11] In effect social service was asked to deal with the social implications of mass unemployment on behalf of a governing class. In November 1932 the Ministry of Labour engaged the NCSS to serve as a central advisory body for a national occupational club movement with a grant of £25,000 to organize voluntary schemes for the unemployed.[12] Through Community Service Clubs the NCSS encouraged the formation of new social groupings to give the unemployed scope for self-expression and a social life; as on the new estates it considered these clubs as an opportunity for experimentation in the use of leisure for the development of initiative and personality.[13]

Numerous schemes were devised to ameliorate the social effects of unemployment through a constructive use of time. The Ministry of Labour established Government Training Centres and Instructional Centres and voluntary occupational clubs were formed by a range of organizations, which included the Society of Friends' educational settlements at Maes-yr-Haf and Brynmawr in South Wales. The NCSS cited these interventions as exemplary successes in addressing the secondary effects of unemployment,[14] an assessment partly supported by recent research demonstrating that many of the unemployed, and their wives, found active occupational interests and conviviality in service clubs.[15] The Prince of Wales likened social service to kindliness, an assessment accepted uncritically by the NCSS at a time of growing unease within the social service movement about public perceptions of it as philanthropy and paternalism. By the political left, however, intervention in the leisure of the unemployed was constructed as surveillance and discipline.[16] Walter Hannington, communist leader of the National Unemployed Workers Movement condemned the NCSS alliance with the state as an attack on working-class interest, a belief shared by the large proportion of the unemployed who refused to join voluntary service clubs.[17] Interventions in unemployment reflected establishment concern about its potentially destabilizing socio-political effects; in 1925 for example, Baden Powell exhorted public schools, many of which had formed service clubs, to prepare more boys as scoutmasters and leaders in preparation for prolonged unemployment.[18] Leisure class interference through royal patronage and public school missions only added to disaffection, leading Hannington to dismiss service clubs as 'new temples of leisure' to contain the spare time of the unemployed.[19] Ellen Wilkinson, Labour MP for Jarrow, similarly argued that clubs for the unemployed emphasized their social dislocation and fuelled hatred amongst them of being organized for leisure.[20] However they were not universally rejected and, by 1935, 1,334 clubs had been established with a total membership of 142,210 men and 15,771 women.[21] Some reached into the wider community, a notable example being that established by Harry Goldthorpe, Secretary of the Bradford Unemployed Association. This provided a canteen, dance hall and billiards tables and also organized free meals and a week's holiday in Morecambe for the children of its 3,000 members.[22]

10.2 Unemployment, leisure and social capital

In 1933 the Pilgrim Trust, founded in 1930 by the American Edward Harkness to promote well-being, commissioned an investigation of unemployment under a committee led by William Temple, then Archbishop of York. Its task was to identify the effects of unemployment in terms of its duration, previous employment and attitudes to leisure. Its report, *Men Without Work*,[23] concluded that long-term unemployment presented dangers of moral decay and the creation of an unemployed class. This reflected a widely held fear. Beveridge had before the War written of the unemployable who, through defects of character – laziness, dishonesty, intemperance – constituted a degenerate human type with the potential to become a vagrant class.[24] In the early 1930s the Marienthal study in Austria similarly associated long-term unemployment with demoralization and apathy while a further study in Glasgow found connections between unemployment and psychoneurosis and psychosomatic illness.[25] These findings fed a wider sense of a crisis of civilization in the inter-war period[26] and heightened the importance of maintaining social cohesion to prevent the unemployed breaking away into a dislocated community.

The principal means of effecting this was the unemployed service club which placed an emphasis on membership, cohesion and community or, in twenty-first century terms, social capital. According to the Pilgrim Trust, the club helped the unemployed man to use his 'enforced leisure' profitably and compensated for the severance of relations with his fellow workers.[27] This was not wholly true; the degree of engagement with clubs varied considerably and neither did their members necessarily benefit from them. While some were formed spontaneously by the unemployed themselves,[28] the more usual means was intervention by what Henry Mess, Director of the Tyneside Council of Social Service, described as 'middle class persons anxious to be helpful.'[29] The NCSS, in receipt of government money, accentuated the positive aspects of clubs, describing one for unemployed women in Burnley as spacious and with cheerful rooms for keep fit classes, country dancing and social evenings.[30] Such claims did not address the concern that prolonged association with other unemployed men in service clubs could reconcile a man to unemployment and make it normative.[31] Furthermore, as Henry Durant observed, segregation could increase the consciousness of being a 'misfit.'[32] The object of service clubs thus became to use leisure as a field in which the unemployed could retain a sense of communal belonging through voluntary leisure association and civic engagement.

The Pilgrim Trust investigated the extent to which opportunities for the unemployed to develop leisure interests through social service clubs were taken and to what effect, and also the factors that enabled a club to serve the whole community and thus minimize social fragmentation. In essence it explored the policy question of whether leisure had the potential to sustain a socially and politically stable community in a world defined by a permanent absence of work. Two categories of unemployment were identified: industrial, which resulted directly from external sources such as laying off or workplace closure; and residual, which was internal and consequential on personal characteristics. This dichotomous categorization invoked a questioning of the connections between unemployment, social capital and character in the context of leisure. In towns where industrial unemployment was dominant the unemployed were drawn from a cross-section of the working class community and included what the Trust termed as the 'best' material as well as the 'poorer'. Under these conditions the unemployed club would be representative of the whole community rather than of the unemployed alone. Where unemployment was residual, however, the potential membership of a service club tended to be restricted to those with low employment value, the 'psychological misfits' of Beveridge's 'unemployables', and thus unrepresentative of the community.[33]

The investigation was conducted in six towns: Deptford, Leicester, Liverpool, Blackburn, Crook (in Durham) and the Urban District of Rhondda in South Wales. Case records of the unemployed were compiled, identifying individual household circumstances, employment and unemployment records and attitudes to social institutions, welfare schemes and leisure interests. The reports from Liverpool, Blackburn and the mining areas around Crook and the Rhondda revealed differences in the capacity of leisure to enable the unemployed to identify with the social community of the neighbourhood. Unemployment in Crook and the Rhondda resulted from industrial collapse. Crook, described by the Pilgrim Trust as an established English working-class civilization of social institutions, had a range of long-standing trade unions and co-operative societies that maintained vitality in social life and a degree of resilience to unemployment.[34] However, these mutual and membership organizations had not developed into community institutions and social life in Crook was constructed primarily around the family, an observation supported by Madeline Rooff who found little voluntary social service provision for leisure in Crook.[35] Through external intervention by the Tyneside Council of Social Service, Durham Community Service Council and adoption by the Ministry of Health Staff Social Service Association, Crook's Helmington Row Recreation Centre widened its appeal to both the employed and unemployed through social evenings, inter-centre games and exhibitions.[36] This suggested, as the Pilgrim Trust noted, the tentative growth of a communal culture through leisure association.[37]

In Rhondda too unemployment was almost entirely industrial. Chris Rojek has identified social capital and voluntary activity as key factors in maintaining the personal dignity and self-worth of those without work.[38] This was important in Rhondda, where high levels of social capital derived from long-standing voluntary leisure association in church choirs, bands, Workmen's Institutes, social clubs and chapel groups. A CUKT study of Pontypridd, for example, found 26 per cent of young men belonged to a Trade Union compared with a national average of 6 per cent.[39] The Pilgrim Trust described a self-managed club with 200 members, attributing its unusually high degree of control by the unemployed to this tradition.[40] South Wales Miners' Institutes in particular were important organizers of leisure, blending political and leisure cultures by hosting trade union and political meetings and providing reading and games rooms and even, in some cases, cinemas.[41] This culture of voluntarism was instrumental in the maintenance of the Maes-yr-Haf educational settlement, established at

Trealaw in 1927 by the Society of Friends under A.D. Lindsay, Master of Balliol College.[42] Maes-yr-Haf was one of several settlements established in the South Wales coalfield funded through the Pilgrim Trust and the state[43] and, like other educational settlements, it had adopted social and community objectives. Operating within an existing culture of communal leisure, it provided a holiday camp for the unemployed and functioned as an intermediary between the NCSS and unemployed clubs to procure funding for brass bands and playing field facilities. Through leisure it enabled the unemployed to remain within the social community; its holiday camp, for example, was available to their wives and families. Other settlements in South Wales organized clubs for unemployed girls in Merthyr Tydfil, Bargoed in the Rhymney Valley and the Oxford House settlement at Risca.[44] Additional service clubs were formed by existing community institutions as varied as Conservative Clubs, the Communist party and churches through which both the employed and unemployed shared in a communal leisure culture of brass bands and social dances.[45]

Blackburn presented a contrasting scenario as a cotton town with a dominant pattern of female employment and therefore a high proportion of unemployed women. Ninety-one per cent of Blackburn's unemployed were cotton workers. Characteristic attributes of Lancashire cotton operatives included personal independence and respectability, both of which served as a disincentive to join either of Blackburn's two main service clubs, Community House and the Gamecock Club, hosted by the YMCA. Priestley's account of Community House – a 'dismal hole in a dark back street' – presents a grim picture of an underfunded institution housed in a condemned elementary school building. Seventy-five per cent of its mainly male members were unskilled and nearly half were single. In addition to instruction in woodwork and cobbling, a club room provided rudimentary facilities for socials and table tennis in a 'hopeless atmosphere of disorder, shuffling and cadging'.[46] It failed to develop beyond a club for the unemployed and remained isolated from the wider community through a lack of active interest amongst its members and local perceptions that it represented a form of begging. The Gamecock Club, which, in keeping with the status of the YMCA as an organization for clerks and the better educated working-classes, also exhibited little inter-mixing of the employed and unemployed as employed YMCA members tended to avoid socialization with those of the Gamecock Club through perceived gradations of respectability.[47] Blackburn's clubs did not thus represent the community as they did in the Rhondda.

Liverpool was a different type of community as a port with a history of casual labour, a condition described by Beveridge as a limbo between sufficiency and destitution.[48] Unemployment exacerbated an already parlous condition, creating fear of the city becoming a 'derelict community'[49] with 140,000 persons estimated to be unemployed in 1932.[50] Unemployment was spatially distributed with a 30 per cent rate of unemployment in 'good working-class' areas but 70 per cent in slum districts.[51] The *Social Survey of Merseyside* found that, although the municipal provision of allotments and reduced fees for swimming baths and playing fields helped occupy time, the principal contribution was that made by voluntary social service organizations.[52] As a pioneering city in the co-ordination of voluntary action Liverpool had a mature framework of social service and the social centres for the unemployed provided through its Council of Voluntary Aid drew an average weekly attendance of 2,500 men. However, this represented a small fraction of the city's unemployed,[53] partly because Merseyside trade unions refused to support voluntary service clubs.

Service clubs in Norris Green and Everton were built by the unemployed and operated as family clubs where women could meet for social intercourse and recreation.[54] However many relied on philanthropic support, particularly in the form of adoption by external agencies.[55] Places were similarly adopted – Jarrow by Surrey and Redruth by Bath, for example.[56] The Dovecot Service Club built its own premises with wood supplied by the Liverpool Timber Trade Association; the Everton Valley Club was established with help from the British American Tobacco Company; other clubs were adopted by the Liverpool Steamship Owners' Association, the Liverpool Drapers and Allied Trades and the United Churches Movement.[57] However, adoption easily led to interference in club management and consequently undermined self-management; a CUKT investigation found examples in which it extended to the supervision of management committee meetings from which members and sometimes even the Warden were excluded.[58] The implication that unemployed men were unfitted to participate in the democratic management of their own club could therefore undermine the rationale of service clubs and increase suspicion of middle-class intervention as surveillance.

The Liverpool University Settlement David Lewis club provided a wide range of educational and leisure activities for the unemployed. Priestley found it a 'good place' with

> an amusing little theatre on the premises with a room below filled with bits of scenery, half-painted canvas cloths, odd 'props'. There are reading, chess and card rooms. I was told by one of the officials that the Club had a contract bridge team; this is the first time I have heard of working men playing contract bridge, to say nothing of playing in tournaments. ... It is a rather old-fashioned building and

needs some brighter decoration, but with its cosiness, recreations and companionship it must seem like heaven after those long dark slummy Liverpool streets.[59]

What Priestley did not remark was that these men were unusual merely by their presence. The most effective tool in the recruitment of young unemployed men to service clubs was sport; provision at Liverpool included a football competition with twenty-five teams from occupational centres, baseball and cricket leagues and physical training classes.[60] However, interest rarely extended beyond sport and did not lead to permanent relationships between clubs and the young unemployed. Provision for girls reflected contemporary gender roles with Junior Instruction Centres and a Domestic Training Centre placing an emphasis on domestic skills. Unemployed juveniles presented behavioural challenges, which made them prone to unemployment. The development of character to prevent their deterioration, as Beveridge suggested, was an important step to increasing their employability.[61] In Liverpool a substantial proportion of girls were considered 'thoroughly out of hand' but club leaders found keep-fit and dancing lessons, both popular contemporary leisure forms amongst women, appealed to them because they gave scope for creativity.[62] The National Council of Girls' Clubs also organized a national programme of physical training, which proved one of the few means to attract Lancashire mill girls.[63]

Many unemployed adults formed their own leisure associations that did not comply with social service definitions of a right use of leisure, leading the Pilgrim Trust to conclude that the concentration of long-term unemployment in Liverpool's over-crowded slum areas had created a segregated communal pattern of life in which the unemployed man had 'his corner, his friends, his library and his bookmaker'.[64] Claims of this nature re-ignited fears of Booth's 'social residuum'[65] and the formation of a socially detached community around the Labour Exchange and service club. However, for the majority of the unemployed the leisure of the service club was not part of their lives; instead, as an unemployed docker reported:

> I go round and meet a few of my friends and have a chat; then down to the Labour or Unemployment Assistance Board and have a talk or lounge about for a bit. Then I come back and have dinner. If anyone'll take me to the pictures in the afternoon I go there once a week or more; sometimes I go to a billiard hall and sit there. I don't do much reading except in the newspaper.... What I miss is having a few shillings extra to go across the water at weekends or to the football match. I often travelled to Manchester and beyond to watch the team playing.[66]

Gambling, the *bete noire* of social service, was virtually ubiquitous with betting on football pools, greyhounds and horses presenting a major obstacle to the engagement of the unemployed man in any other interest.[67] A Liverpool Council of Voluntary Aid investigation estimated approximately 50 to 70 per cent of men and 50 per cent of women to bet regularly.[68] Much gambling took place in the cellar and Irish clubs of the slums, which had created an alternative associational leisure and communal life.[69] Although indicating a capacity for community formation, these clubs only encouraged, as *Men Without Work* commented, the development of an unemployed community.[70] This social dislocation was interpreted in wider medical and eugenic discourse as an aspect of modernity with dangerous social implications. Leonard Lockhart, Medical Officer to the Boots Company, for example, linked unemployment to mental health problems and called for more education in the use of leisure to stave off degeneration into pathogenic idleness.[71] The report of a local survey by the University of Liverpool School of Social Sciences, published in the *Eugenics Review*, went further in linking the leisure of the unemployed to mental deficiency and degeneracy. Finding feeble mindedness in Liverpool to be a spatially distributed mental defect that manifested itself in 'pockets' of poverty and deprivation, David Caradog Jones, co-ordinator of the Social Survey of Merseyside and eugenist, identified the unemployed with the 'social problem group'.[72]

The Pilgrim Trust's *Men Without Work*, was important, as Todd notes, in demonstrating that the poor were not to blame for their poverty or unemployment.[73] It also highlighted the importance of a collective working-class culture of self-managed voluntary leisure associations to the maintenance of the community ties and affective bonds that external social service intervention could not reproduce. Other contemporary studies of the unemployed also reported a failure of voluntary social service to engage young adults in active leisure and training for social citizenship. Valentine Bell's report on Junior Instruction Centres found the young unemployed showed little ability to make a good use of leisure time with 80 per cent of boys not being members of a Lads' Club, Scouts, Boys' Brigade or any other voluntary organization.[74] A later report of 1943 presented similar evidence of difficulties experienced by the Clubs in attracting and retaining young adults.[75] Madeleine Rooff, however, found that where Junior Instruction Centres worked pro-actively with local clubs it was possible for unemployed girls to integrate with those employed and in some cases form their own social club.[76] Sometimes a change of name was sufficient; when the Liverpool Union of Girls' Clubs named its service clubs Afternoon Social Clubs they became well patronized. Nevertheless the difficulties experienced by voluntary youth organizations in appealing to the bulk of working-class young people remained insuperable and suspicions of service as charity proved durable.

The Pilgrim Trust report revealed the importance of associational leisure to community stability and active social citizenship, anticipating the New Labour interest in social capital. Where social capital existed, as for example in the Rhondda, it was not politically imposed through service clubs but had historically developed through local institutions of work, religion and civil society. Its importance to social cohesion in South Wales was also noted by the CUKT as a 'foundation on which to build a social consciousness of common purpose and interdependence' that had enabled service clubs in the coalfields to display a greater tendency to self-management than those in Liverpool.[77] *Men Without Work* exposed the deficit of an understanding of leisure without work; without economic security and its related material sources, much leisure was unaffordable and meaningless. Recent empirical work has supported this view; Kitae Sohn's analysis of testimonies of the unemployed reveals that leisure was not spare time but worrying and unsought idleness.[78] The Pilgrim Trust was, however, necessarily limited in its scope of investigation. Burnett, for example, quotes many examples of the unemployed occupying time constructively on allotments, forming bands or playing sport.[79] Outside social service provision, a wide range of left-wing and collective organizations, in co-operation with the unemployed, created an extended framework of sport and leisure association. In South Wales, for example, several unemployed sports teams were formed in the Rhondda through the National Unemployed Worker's Movement. Alternative welfare schemes were also formed for the unemployed with assistance from the Miners Welfare Fund leading, as Daryl Leeworthy notes, not only to an expression of Labour values through sport but to refuge and social intercourse.[80] Unlike service clubs these were not rejected by the unemployed or the labour movement but belonged to them; their assistance and support being not charitable philanthropy but collective solidarity.

Work-Based Leisure Communities

11.1 Work, leisure and community in inter-war Britain

The years immediately preceding the First World War were marked by significant industrial unrest with 40.9 million working days lost through strikes in 1912 alone[1] and trade union membership increasing to over four million by 1914.[2] A harmonious relationship between labour and capital was thus a major aim of post-war social reconstruction. Reformers and trade unions demanded shorter hours and a more equal distribution of leisure, both being resisted by employers. However, new Home Office guidelines on factory welfare[3] revived interest in the socialization of workers in factory-based leisure communities. Leisure became an important non-statutory component of welfare as a field for the creation of a social community out of the economic community of the workplace. Although employers construed the leisure of their welfare schemes as an economic and a social good, critics argued it to be a distraction from low wages and trade union activity. However, the welfare provision of leisure could also be interpreted as a moral act; Alfred Zimmern, for example, who had worked in the Ministry of Reconstruction, believed it countered the dehumanization of factory work[4] and Delisle Burns, reflecting the progressive liberal view that the factory was a social institution bound to the common good, suggested welfare could be both economically desirable and a moral good.[5] After the War, as scientific management and industrial psychology devised schemes to bind employees to the corporate identity of the firm, welfare was decreasingly an expression of the paternalism of an individual factory owner. The provision of work-based leisure schemes was voluntary as, in most cases, was the worker's decision to join them. Probably most were instigated by the employer, though it was not unknown for workers to develop their own factory social and leisure associations without intervention by management.[6]

11.2 The workplace as a social community

From the early nineteenth century the factory functioned as a social as well as an economic community as progressive employers adopted a paternal interest in the private lives of their employees. The provision of education and recreation was important from the beginning, with Robert Owen, a seminal figure in British socialism, setting a pioneering example. Owen described his New Lanark works as a community differentiated but not detached from wider society, a place where the worker was no longer a casual labourer but a 'vital machine' requiring maintenance and investment. The happiness of the worker depended upon the happiness of the factory community and Owen provided a range of amenities that included gardens and walks for summer use and rooms for amusements and 'rational recreation' in winter.[7] Other employers followed and by the early twentieth century the non-conformist Cadbury Brothers, Joseph Rowntree and William Lever were international leaders in their care for the social lives of their employees, providing model villages with recreational amenities and numerous leisure associations.[8] Nineteenth-century factory welfare was a personal effort by the employer to demonstrate a humane interest in his workers; he was, in Ruskin's estimation, fulfilling a paternal responsibility.[9]

As corporate scientific management superseded the personal management of the individual employer, welfare became a function of the new scientific management of Frederick Taylor, an American engineer who argued that a more co-operative relationship between management and workers and a simplification of jobs would increase productivity and profit. Taylor-inspired welfare capitalism, widely adopted in Britain in the inter-war period, was categorically different from Victorian industrial paternalism. Whereas the latter provided social benefits through the largesse of an owner-manager, typically support for a works band or sports team, welfare capitalism delivered social benefits through bureaucratic processes from which the personal relationship was absent.[10] The irony of this was, as Seebohm Rowntree observed, to widen the gulf between employer and workforce.[11] Although the family-owned factory had not disappeared by 1919, the trend was towards amalgamations and the replacement of skilled manual tasks by automated production lines, which made fewer mental demands on workers. The international trend from individual paternalism to corporate welfare in the early twentieth century was demonstrated in Mary Lathrop Goss' *Welfare Work in Corporations*, written to promote welfare as a moral fusion of business and religious duty.[12] The German steel firm of Krupps, for example, built a workers' housing colony with gymnasium, library and study-rooms while in 1896 the workers' colony of the Royal Hungarian Machine Factory of the State Railroad in Budapest included a reading-room, library and kindergarten. Service industries too provided welfare; the Bon Marche store in Paris had a women workers' rest-room with a library, piano and games. In America welfare provision was more extensive with firms, including the National Cash Register Company, Colorado Fuel and Iron Company and the International Harvester Company, providing libraries, games rooms, gymnasiums and facilities for meetings, lectures, film shows and dances.

Through welfare, employers sought to shape the leisure of their employees, promoting values and behaviours believed to increase production and profit. The idea of the factory as a community with a common interest, shared membership and reciprocity was a central tenet; as the president of the Harvester Company stated, welfare leisure brought together managers and factory floor workers between whom it was desirable to create a sense of membership of the firm.[13] By the 1920s scientific management had posited the industrial worker as a human machine requiring maintenance and adjustment for efficiency. It also increasingly informed British approaches to the management of industrial processes, aided by the formation of the National Institute of Industrial Psychology in 1919 by Charles Myers and John Henry Welch, which encouraged employers to conceptualize the human needs of the worker in terms of motivation and working conditions.[14] Informed by Le Bon's theories of the individual in the social group and McDougall's[15] advocacy of collective psychology and the group spirit, industrial psychologists sought to develop an *esprit de corps*, re-forming the artificial grouping of the factory workforce into an idealized and rational community.[16] As Robert Hyde, Director of the Industrial Welfare Society stated, leisure was a common ground on which the factory community could meet in social intercourse, rendering the gap between management and operatives obsolete by introducing a sense of fellowship and a better tone in the workplace.[17]

Although there was little disagreement that workers benefited from the provision of leisure amenities, the motivation of the employer became a controversial question in the years immediately after the War. Idealist-informed constructs of welfare posited the workplace not as an economic or even a social institution but an ethical place in which an employer had a moral duty to the quality of life of the worker.[18] Although this was the stated objective of many employers and progressive policy theorists, their respective philosophical rationales were fundamentally different. Nineteenth-century critiques of work by John Ruskin and William Morris posited a non-economic rationale for the provision of workplace social and cultural amenities. Morris argued that the factory system should nurture social life not as humane capitalism but as a collective and co-operative business culture; if labour could be made pleasant, work itself could be leisure.[19] Ruskin too believed the employer had social as well as economic obligations to his workers.[20] Whereas Morris' ideal was for happiness to arise through work, employers looked to welfare provision to make workers happy. Budgett Meakin, organizer of the Shaftesbury lectures on social issues concerning industry, argued the economic case for welfare to be its enabling of a community of interest between employer and employee, both of whom would benefit by the increased output produced through harmonious working and improved relations.[21] However, in *The Acquisitive Society*, published in 1920, Richard Tawney presented the ethical case that industry was primarily a service to society and only secondly to employers and shareholders;[22] John Hobson and Delisle Burns similarly argued industry to be a social service, being part of the whole social life of the community and not an economic community existing separately from it.[23] These ideas resonated with the new industrial conditions of post-First World War Britain; Seebohm Rowntree, a notably socially minded employer, conceded that if industry were in fact a service to the community, it was obligated to raise the living standard of workers who were simultaneously members of a factory community and citizens of the social community.[24] For Rowntree and the Cadbury Brothers too the progressive ideal of welfare was one of employers and workers co-operating as members of a community with civic and human responsibilities towards one another.[25] However, this argument never fully obscured the fact that the instrumental use of leisure to support a capitalist industrial system was incompatible with idealist and socialist constructs of leisure.

11.3 Model industrial villages and leisure

For all employers, the creation of a work-place community through welfare-based leisure was primarily an economic rather than a social undertaking. William Lever, Congregationalist, Liberal and self-proclaimed enlightened capitalist, was explicit on this, arguing that only through the self-interest of the employer could the best interests of employees be served.[26] Industrial model villages, notably Lever's Port Sunlight and the Cadburys' Bournville blurred private and social identities, being spatial communities that overlapped and interlocked with work-based leisure associations. The Cadbury Brothers pioneered the development of works sport provision in the late nineteenth century with teams in football, rugby, cricket, hockey, bowling, tennis and even water polo. The move to a new purpose-built estate at Bournville in 1879 expanded this provision and by 1912 the Bournville men's athletic club had 1,299 members with facilities for cricket, hockey, netball, tennis and croquet.[27] Sports grounds and buildings were managed by a Men's Works Committee through the works Athletic Club.[28] The Cadburys also established a custom of shared participation in sport and hobby clubs by managers and operatives and encouraged social citizenship, notably through the Bournville Women Workers' Social Service League, established in 1910 to improve women's working conditions in Birmingham's factories; in contrast to Lever's approach, this included help in trade union organization.[29]

Lever shared his surplus through Port Sunlight, a model village designed to instil a sense of community through housing, leisure amenities and civic and cultural buildings, notably the Gladstone Hall and the Lady Lever Art Gallery. Here Lever's 7,600 employees had access to 79 acres of playing fields, which included an open-air swimming bath, tennis lawns, bowling greens and a covered grandstand for 2,500 spectators. In addition there were allotment gardens, a library, museum, theatre, gymnasiums and a public house with limited sale of alcohol. Workers could join a range of clubs, which included a Girls' Institute, Junior Social Club and Men's Social Club.[30] To a contemporary observer its residents appeared well disciplined in leisure and, by residing in a model community, set to become model citizens;[31] their agency was however constrained by Lever's intrusive personal involvement in and oversight of the social life of the village, which ensured that Christian and normative social values were maintained.[32] This included retaining control of village organizations, for example the Men's Social Club, Dramatic Society and Scientific and Literary Society and the appointment of the village's social director as minister to the Port Sunlight Church.[33] The welfare provision of the Cadburys, Lever and Rowntree was replicated by several employers on a less grand scale but always in terms of a gift, identifying a commonality of interest and aiming to achieve the sense of an holistic factory community. This was, as Patrick Joyce notes, an emotional identification based on a deference in which the worker acquiesced;[34] after the War, it was increasingly challenged by industrial and social change. By the late nineteenth century British employers were moving from factory paternalism to an emphasis on loyalty to the firm; welfare provision, as Wray Vamplew comments, aided not only this end but could also distract workers' attention from a fast-expanding trade union movement.[35]

11.4 Leisure and industrial welfare in inter-war Britain

The state-regulated factory welfare provision of the War was adopted as a model for post-war industry and in 1919 the appointment of a person responsible for welfare in the workplace became a statutory requirement of the Home Office, which defined welfare work in economic terms as the provision by the management for the worker of the best conditions for employment conducive to maximum production.[36] The concept of the social factory was further promoted by the Whitley report on Industrial Councils, which recommended works welfare committees to engender a spirit of community and a sense of common interest.[37] An employers' Industrial Welfare Society was formed out of Robert Hyde's Boys' Welfare Association[38] and through the *Journal of Industrial Welfare* promoted the business advantages of welfare in restoring the human relationships lost in factory modernization, publicizing good practice in the organization of recreation, canteens and educational schemes.[39] The role of the British welfare supervisor was modelled on that of the American welfare secretary;[40] its purpose was, according to William Beardmore, the first chairman of the Society, to personalize the employer's recognition that the well-being of the workers was important by organizing games and recreations.[41]

Factory leisure provision boomed in inter-war Britain. By 1921 approximately 1,000 welfare supervisors had been appointed, organizing sports and social activities that were, according to Robert Hyde, widening social intercourse and creating better relationships in the factory.[42] By 1926 700 firms were represented in the Industrial Welfare Society, covering two million employees, mainly in the engineering, shipbuilding, iron, steel and food industries, with approximately 1,300 Welfare Supervisor posts.[43] The Cadburys continued to lead, expanding their provision with a Works Social Centre with lounge rooms, surgeons, dentists, library and reading rooms and a concert hall. This was, as the *Journal of Industrial Welfare* commented, a building of the kind that welfare workers dreamed of;[44] it also exceeded any level of municipal provision. When Priestley visited the factory he found this no idle claim; unlike new council estates with little provision for recreation, at Bournville it was everywhere. Its clubs and societies had a total membership of around 7,000 people, all of whom had joined voluntarily. Priestley was conscious of the ambivalent motivation for welfare but recognized that whatever critics might argue, it remained the case that Cadburys' workers enjoyed better conditions and more opportunities for leading a decent and happy life than most.[45] Welfare leisure spread beyond model villages; in 1923 the Liverpool shipping firm of Bibby's, for example, built a sports ground with extensive playing fields, tennis courts, a bowling green and a club house accommodating a Literary and Debating Society, drama, concerts and hobby clubs for its 2,000 employees.[46] A later survey of Merseyside found at least 45 firms to provide recreational facilities for 50,000 insured workers,[47] with sports teams representing, for example, Ogden's Imperial Tobacco Company, Lever's Port Sunlight and Crosfields & Son of Warrington, entering local leagues and competitions on a sub-regional basis.[48]

Welfare leisure provision often reached out into the wider community, compensating for the lack of state provision. A common complaint of voluntary youth workers in the inter-war period concerned the shortage of public playing fields and in many areas factory welfare schemes fulfilled this need. In Coventry, work-based leisure was an integral element of the town's social life with factory sports facilities, dance halls and concert rooms patronized by both workers and members of the local community.[49] Sport in particular aided the formation of local, regional and national leisure communities in banks, railway and insurance companies.[50] In Nottingham the Boot's company teams competed locally in cricket, football, tennis and rugby competitions; here sports events were important, as Simon Phillips notes, as family occasions and social gatherings.[51] A similar pattern prevailed in Bolton through the involvement of the wider social community in factory rounders competitions.[52] Through the corporate welfare systems of combinations and amalgamations, Lancashire cotton operatives developed a shared cultural identity at the level of factory, town and region; one combination scheme embraced 28,000 employees in thirty-eight associated firms with trained Welfare Supervisors working under the direction of a peripatetic Chief Supervisor.[53] The Amalgamated Cotton Mills Trust, for example, sponsored football and bowls leagues, physical culture classes, country dancing, excursions and social clubs as well as swimming, bowling and hockey clubs.[54] Welfare bound not only the factory but the south Lancashire cotton industry in a regional community of leisure. In 1922, for example, sixteen factory teams competed in the Bolton and District Sunday Schools Association rounders competition, with large numbers of spectators and extensive newspaper coverage.[55] In addition to sports, the Cotton Queen of Great Britain competition, initiated to promote an industry in economic decline, flourished throughout the 1930s with local heats and a final in Blackpool.[56]

Although welfare workers claimed that factory leisure cemented the relationship between capital and labour,[57] trade unionists saw it as a prop of capitalist production.[58] As a new professional sector, the meaning of welfare work was contested: was the primary duty of the welfare supervisor to the

Figure 9 Gibraltar Mill Rounders team, winners of Sir William Edge Shield 1926–28. The cotton mill was a site of leisure as well as work. In Bolton the popularity of the game of rounders was reflected in factory works teams and leagues and provided women with facilities and opportunities to play sport.

Source: © Bolton Council. From the Collection of Bolton Library and Museum Services.

individual worker or the employing organization? Initially welfare work aligned itself with social ideals and a primary responsibility to the worker as an individual.[59] More radically Margaret Bondfield, a trade union official who became Minister of Labour in 1924, claimed its function was to challenge capitalist psychology and business attitudes.[60] It was argued that welfare should focus on social citizenship to compensate for the neglect of social need within industry and campaign for more time for leisure and service to the community.[61] Employers, however, viewed welfare in economic terms, supported by the Industrial Welfare Society, which prioritized business objectives.[62] Employers had an economic interest in engaging with their local community; the *Journal of Industrial Welfare* regularly reported examples of increased production and lower absence levels where factory leisure extended to the wider community, and links with voluntary organizations such as boys' and girls' clubs, the YMCA and YWCA, British Drama League and English Folk Dance Society became important.[63] The use of leisure as a tool of scientific management was further advanced by the industrial hygiene movement through the influential Edgar

Figure 10 Rounders spectators. This Humphrey Spender image of spectators at a rounders match in Bolton shows how the boundaries between leisure and work could be blurred under welfare capitalism and illustrates the capacity of factory leisure to bind players, families and friends into an associational leisure community.

Source: © Bolton Council. From the Collection of Bolton Library and Museum Services.

Collis, Mansel Talbot Professor of Preventive Medicine, member of the Industrial Fatigue Research Board and later Director of Welfare and Health at the Ministry of Munitions. Industrial hygiene emerged as a sub-field of scientific management, advocating canteens, better ventilation and leisure amenities to gain more efficiency from the worker.[64] Hygiene became a cultural as well as a medical construct as employers increasingly viewed workers' leisure outside the factory in pathological terms.[65] This was not a novel phenomenon; Arthur Shadwell's pre-war study of workers' leisure patterns in England, Germany and America[66] had suggested that sport-obsessed English workers were excitable to a degree that was detrimental to industrial efficiency; German workers on the other hand were more emotionally stable with work, rather than leisure, being their preoccupation. Although unverifiable, it is easy to imagine how such claims might have concerned British employers. After the War some employers sought closure from commercial leisure with welfare schemes to isolate their employees from a perceived cultural contamination.[67] Welfare work thus became a conflicted field of professional practice; welfare supervisors, as Delisle Burns noted, were responsible to owners of capital but simultaneously morally responsible to workers and the community at large.[68] The struggle to establish welfare work as an idealist concept was unsuccessful and towards the close of the period it became more closely aligned to employer objectives and re-conceptualized as personnel management.

11.5 Co-operative and collective alternatives to welfare

Most workers did not belong to a factory welfare leisure scheme; Henry Durant estimated only around 25 per cent of manual workers had registered in works recreation schemes although this was based on a relatively limited survey.[69] Although trade unions, as we have seen, discouraged workers from engaging in welfare clubs, factory sport was not always incompatible with labour objectives; the factory with the best sports provision in Northampton was also that with the highest trade union activity.[70] Labour interest was pursued through alternative models of factory leisure based upon co-operation and mutuality rather than employer profit. Worker sport, as it became known, held more than an ideological appeal and, as Tony Collins notes, met a substantial demand for organized sport in working-class communities where no alternative provision existed.[71] In political terms it offered a non-capitalist alternative to commercial spectator sport and provided further evidence that Veblen's understanding of sport as the province of a leisure class was no longer viable. Veblen had argued that the self-reliance and good fellowship assumed essential to sport were valued by the leisure class only because they could be articulated in terms of cultural deficit and thus worthy of emulation.[72] This argument persuaded John Hobson that sport was futile and make-believe, a lower rather than higher form of self-realization.[73] However the popularity of sport in the inter-war years made it an ideal form of leisure through which to critique capitalism with a socialist alternative. Britain lagged behind other countries in this respect; worker sport groups had formed in several European countries before the First World War, including Finland (1887), France (1907) and Austria, where a Federation of Worker and Soldier Sports Clubs was established 1919.[74] By 1920 worker sport movements had also been formed in Germany (1,600,000 members) and Czechoslovakia (165,000).[75]

Worker sport promoted social change through socialism by living out co-operative and collective principles through leisure, emphasizing co-operation rather than competition and participation rather than performance. Strong connections between workers, sport and socialism were widely found in continental Europe; in Finland, for example, working-class associations had formed sport clubs as a vehicle for the promotion of socialism since 1903.[76] Between 1921 and 1937 worker sport Olympiads were held across Europe in Prague (1921), Frankfurt (1925), Moscow (1928), Vienna, (1931), Barcelona (1936) and (Antwerp 1937). These were designed to be fundamentally different in meaning from the so-called 'Bourgeois' Olympics and included other cultural forms of leisure, for example poetry, song, drama and political lectures. The International Worker Sports Festival in Vienna in 1931 drew 80,000 worker athletes from twenty-three countries and was hosted in a stadium constructed by the socialist Viennese government; its international ethos was marked by the athletes marching not under national symbols but a red flag.[77] In fascist Germany and Italy, worker sport organizations were taken over by Kraft durch Freude and the Dopolavoro organizations respectively. These assumed a comprehensive control of sport and leisure, the latter combining all athletic, sport societies, musical bands and choral societies in a national organization that worked through numerous regional and local committees, submitting leisure to political approval.[78]

Britain did not develop a similarly large movement; the British Workers' Sports Federation (BWSF), established in 1923 by Tom Groom with Clarion cyclists, trade unionists and labour sympathizers, never became a mass concern.[79] However it enabled sport to serve as a vehicle of socialist propaganda and community formation. Following the launch of the communist *Daily Worker* in 1930 the BWSF, by then affiliated to Red Sports International, changed its strategic priority of recruiting from existing sports clubs to the formation of worker sports clubs as a socialist alternative to employer-provided factory leisure.[80] The first issue of *The Worker Sportsman* in 1928 declared an intention to promote sport as a counter-attack on capitalist welfare provision.[81] In Bolton, for example, where employer leisure provision was well established, a Worker Sport Club for tram operatives was founded in the Bolton Socialist Club in the mid-1930s[82] while the Bolton Engineers Sports Club, formed in 1931 with tennis, hiking, boxing, football and swimming sections, gained a membership of almost 200 and became one of the most successful clubs associated with the BWSF.[83] Its objectives reached beyond sport to the support of workers on strike or locked-out by, for example, organizing fund-raising sports competitions and galas. Like many employer-provided clubs, it opened membership to all workers and organized public rambles and cycling trips.[84]

The outdoor movement was a further field of socialist activity with worker clarion clubs and rambling groups co-operating with external socialist organizations. The Manchester branch of the BWSF became a principal organizing agent of mass trespass rambles in protest against the private enclosure of northern upland for game shooting.[85] The Ramblers Association had ineffectively pursued legal means of securing access, being represented, as the BWSF was quick to point out, by Holford Knight, a member of the national government and supporter of the means test.[86] The mass trespass of Kinder Scout in 1932 led to the imprisonment of organizers but initiated a shift in public opinion, opening the route to the National Parks and Access to the Countryside Act of 1949. Although worker sport declined towards the close of the inter-war period it was important in terms of socialist leisure association and the consolidation of a sense of community grounded in alternative values to those of capitalist society. The Co-operative Wholesale Society, which incorporated mutuality and democratic accountability within its business philosophy, deployed welfare leisure to reinforce its own values in its workforce. In 1903 it established an experimental smoke and games room at its Balloon Street headquarters in Manchester,[87] and extended provision after the War with leisure schemes in its branches, for example, tennis and bowling clubs at the Worcester Co-operative[88] and a sports and social club at the Walden Society.[89] This expanded into a national network of co-operative sport provision through which both business aims and co-operative principles could be pursued. The first national Co-operative football competition was instituted in 1925; three years later the company announced through its works magazine *Ourselves* an affirmation of its commitment to greater goodwill between the Society and its staff through the channel of sport.[90] By the 1930s, for example, the Liverpool Co-operative Society Men's and Women's Guilds had 1,500 and two social institutes.[91]

The worker sport movement in Britain was not large but is historically important in terms of the moral dialogue of leisure. It flourished through a network of self-managed leisure associations in a fertile period of socialist activity and reached into working-class communities, corresponding with Burns' view that welfare should enable self-realization and social service.[92] Through leisure, it helped give an international dimension to socialism and is best understood in the context of what Stephen Jones referred to as a socialist totality in which leisure was harnessed to a critique of alienating work and production.[93]

11.6 Conclusion

Capitalist industry invested considerable human and economic resource in the provision of leisure through welfare systems in inter-war Britain. On the surface, the cornucopia of sports, outings, social clubs and cultural associations might seem to fulfil Morris' dream of the humanized factory in which machinery had provided more time for leisure. However, Ruskin's insistence that capitalism and co-operation were more than just different modes of business explains why this was not so. However lavish the provision, welfare leisure was part of a system that placed economic above social objectives. The worker, as Tawney argued, remained the servant of the shareholder and the leisure class.[94] Private welfare could never thus be primarily directed towards a common good in a capitalist economy. The Co-operative Society, on the other hand, reflected Morris' and Ruskin's vision more closely. While administered largely in accordance with contemporary patterns of business administration, its informing principle was the good of the whole, its welfare being much closer to Burns' ideal of improvement of workers' personalities rather than economic gain.[95]

Conclusions

By the end of the inter-war period both leisure and voluntary action had become established within social policy as constituent elements of a civilized society. In 1948 Beveridge identified leisure as a need in a social service state and a function of voluntary action being to promote its right use.[1] This was a far cry from Young England's philanthropic recreations and paternalist amusements. This book has attempted to explain the historical processes through which modern twentieth-century understandings of leisure and voluntary action were formed and has argued that the inter-relationships between them were shaped by a strand of social policy discourse that has not previously been accorded sufficient recognition. When contextualized in what Jose Harris termed as a structural transformation of welfare provision between the 1870s and 1940s,[2] leisure and voluntary action emerge as major elements of political, social and cultural debate and crucial adjuncts to a reformed society.

Leisure was not a mundane or residual construct but a vital element of social and civic life and central to nineteenth- and twentieth-century discourses of community, democracy and voluntary action. In his study of leisure in Victorian England Peter Bailey concluded that rational recreation failed to articulate a vision of a future society that would be improved by its success.[3] However, the current study suggests that as the meaning of leisure evolved from rational recreation to one formed by social science and social idealism, it was increasingly conceptualized and valued in terms of its potential contribution to a new and better society. Although the First World War was crucially important to the inter-war discourse of leisure, the beginnings of an intellectual shift from the philanthropy of rational recreation to a social conceptualization of leisure are discernible in the final two decades of the nineteenth century as social reform became increasingly concerned with the theory of the social community and the practicalities of its realization. There was no sharp break in thinking or practice; rational recreation approaches to leisure survived into the inter-war period but were increasingly less important as leisure came to be debated in terms of social philosophy and science.

The effectiveness of leisure and voluntary action in enabling social change is not easy to measure and it is of note that, despite Beveridge's validation of leisure and Adams' insistence that it was of equal importance to health and education, it has remained largely below the notice of historians of the NCSS and never became a social service in its own right.[4] Although leisure features in the historiography of voluntary action, this has often been in terms of its specific forms or of individual voluntary organizations and there has been less discussion of its changing meanings or its inclusion in the discourse of social policy and community building. Practical social interventions and developments in which leisure was crucial – university and social settlements, garden cities, the civic gospel, community centres and councils of voluntary aid – all emerged through a complex and slowly evolving debate in which the social meaning and function of leisure was debated, defined and re-defined. These developments, largely uncoordinated and in some cases having seemingly little in common, were manifestations of a gradual shift of emphasis in religious, philosophical and political belief towards the priority of the social good of the community as a whole. The cognitive shift from a discourse of recreation to one of leisure similarly marked a change from the moral and utilitarian framework of the mid-nineteenth century to the social and ethical understandings of leisure framed within the social sciences. It was primarily within the social domain that leisure was theorized and understood in terms of social change.

The links between theory, policy and practice were tenuous. Idealists were not noted for the formulation of practical schemes to implement their ideas, although it was important to these links that T.H. Green, the father of British social idealism, not only insisted that theory must be applied but was himself an active voluntary social worker. Mention of Green raises the extraordinary contribution of Balliol College to social idealist theory, and its application to social reforming effort in the use of leisure and to social citizenship has been noted at many points of this book. It also, however, reveals how an influential and relatively small coterie of intellectuals influenced the treatment of leisure in social service. Adams and Barker, for example, were almost single-handedly responsible for the differing theoretical and practical approaches to the village hall and new housing estate movements. However, the approach to social service, leisure and community in rural Britain provides ample evidence that idealism was not absolute in terms of policy implementation. A further important aspect of idealism is the legacy of Cecil Delisle Burns who has emerged as an outstanding and relatively ignored theorist of leisure in inter-war Britain.

Caution is necessary to avoid exaggeration of the impacts of idealism. Idealist theory failed to effect the changes in leisure and community articulated by its proponents. The declining political influence of liberalism contributed to this as did the failure of the state to ensure the positive freedoms necessary to a new leisure and a new model of community. Furthermore, theorists and practical reformers, for example the Barnetts, Bosanquets, Hadows, Tawney and Temple had little if any of the experience of working-class life that might have influenced their thinking on what should be done for or with working-class populations. How then might we evaluate the discourse of leisure and voluntarism described in the above chapters? In terms of voluntarism the shift from charitable philanthropy and the personal case work of the COS to the social and community focus of the NCSS was never total, but the former became less significant as the debate on social reform became ever more fixed on the community. Despite the frustration of reforming efforts through class antagonism, unemployment and economic depressions, there are grounds for suggesting that voluntary action in leisure exercised some positive influences on social change. If a rich voluntary communal life is a hallmark of a good society then the expansion of leisure association contributed significantly to this. In their landmark study of leisure after the Second World War, Rowntree and Lavers noted the continuing growth of the community centre and village hall movement of the inter-war years and, in a case study of High Wycombe, the existence of a thriving voluntary-based social leisure culture.[5] The establishment of a youth service also owed much to the numerous official reports on youth work undertaken in the 1930s. These are however external outcrops of deeper-lying cultural and social shifts that were more apparent in progressive social thinking and policy debate. In reality, practice occasionally drew directly from theory, often lagged behind, and in some cases ran contrary to it.

Assessing the contribution of leisure to social change, it is useful to return to Cecil Delisle Burns who understood the social and cultural significance of new behaviours and attitudes in leisure in inter-war Britain. Burns was interested in the question of whether modernity was a form of civilization. Leisure was a sphere in which characteristics of modernity were easily seen in new mass cultural forms, the social and political emancipation of women, the new housing programmes that replaced long-standing urban neighbourhoods and welfare capitalism. Modernity's characteristics were not however always positive; also associated with it were automation, fears of alienation, degeneration, a decline of civilization, passivity and totalitarianism. To Burns, however, modern civilization was not a product but a process and for him the question was not one concerned with the effects of modernity on leisure but with how a new leisure could be the basis for a civilization of modernity. For Burns this new leisure permeated the whole social life and culture.[6] Through fashion, new standards of living, the motor car, radio and cinema, leisure was more abundant, widening rather than narrowing cultural horizons. Burns believed leisure was important in enabling ordinary people to develop their own voluntary associations, describing community councils as signs of a common tendency towards the discovery of new uses of leisure.[7] Signs of more significant social change were seen in women's institutes, the worker sport movement, left-wing drama groups and trespassing ramblers, all of which in some way challenged cultural norms through voluntary leisure association. None effected immediate change and some were more successful than others but all contributed to movements for gradual change and reflect to varying degrees Jennifer Todd's 'inchoate cultural unease' with the values of a dominant social order. Leisure gave these groups and movements a collective identity, solidarity and visibility through shared activity, and nurtured new ideas and values that fed into the processes of material social and political change. More recent historical examples of this process might be seen in the normalization of women's participation in sports once considered to be exclusively male and the ornithological and wildlife groups that have shifted public opinion towards conservation measures now considered normative.

The capacity of associational leisure to effect social change depended in large part on social capacity for citizenship and democratic self-management. This inevitably involved considerations of social class. Having been a foundational theme in the historiography of leisure, class lost some of its status but has recently become of focal interest again.[8] The nature of voluntary intervention in leisure was, from the 1880s, grounded in the two conceptual foundations of idealism and socialism. Idealism valued the role of the state but emphasized the community service of the individual citizen at the local level whereas socialism valued the co-operative collective and believed the state was best positioned to effect radical social change.[9] Balliol College, the well-spring of thinking on social work and community, was the source not only of social idealism but also of a reformed social liberalism. Social work and social service were predominantly liberal concepts, informed by concepts of social ethics and democracy but never socialist; they focused on making the individual an active citizen as a means of improving an existing society. Working-class suspicions of middle-class intervention as paternalism or interference were never entirely allayed, arguably with some justification as public school missions, royal patronage and adoption remained in evidence even in the inter-war period. This is not to say that voluntary effort was wasteful or misguided; countless people benefited from and enjoyed the leisure of church societies, the scouts, guides and other youth brigades and indeed the sport and leisure complexes of welfare capitalism.

However, as Raymond Williams argued, social service tended to erase social class by a 'massing and simplifying of actual individuals' in reaction to social problems.[10] Service to the community was, he argued, a liberal concept, the outcome of a social conscience that sought to express solidarity with the poor by providing opportunities for educational and cultural betterment.[11] This seems very close to the idea of friendship that, with various modifications, prevailed throughout the period of this study. It was something of which inter-war social service was conscious; as Henry Mess lamented, it seemed impossible to disconnect social service from the idea of help given by the privileged, those with the leisure and means, to the unprivileged.[12] Alexander Lindsay, social worker and Master of Balliol College, interpreted this problem in terms of a tension between the working-class movement and voluntary social service.[13] John Hobson also picked up on this in noting that philanthropy had tended to focus on cultural rather than economic needs and arguing that, as aesthetic needs did not exist where survival needs remained unsatisfied, attempts to engage slum populations in middle-class cultural preferences were consequently futile.[14]

As Burns argued, voluntary association for social change could not be effective without an agreed vision of the public good.[15] Social idealism, Liberalism and socialism sought greater social and political democracy but disagreed on whether the route to this lay through the individual or the collective. This difference was also that between social service and the labour movement in that the former did not actively pursue the social and economic change necessary to address social conditions while the latter was collectivist, mutual and committed to socialist political aims. Socialism however, unconstrained by the liberal tradition of service from which social service emerged, was better able to shape leisure as an experimental space in which to promote and practise socialist and politically destabilizing values in a collective sphere. Socialist voluntary leisure associations such as the Clarion clubs, co-operative society clubs and worker sport clubs belonged to their members amongst whom their aims were shared; voluntary social service leisure associations, on the other hand, remained under the control of managers and leaders, seeking to provide some form of help to client groups while eschewing attempts to alter the underlying economic and social factors that determined their conditions of living. Although socialist interventions reached only a small portion of the population, and it is important to remember that it was not until 1924 that Britain had a Labour government, they resonated with a message that many people were prepared to hear.[16] In the Clarion, worker sport, co-operative and radical movements socialist values were embedded in leisure practice and leisure was consequently the expression of desire and action for social change.

The distinctions between the interests of non-socialist and socialist voluntary leisure associations outlined immediately above and in earlier chapters were important to the ideal community social reformers imagined. Both set out to address the social damage of nineteenth-century individualism and *laissez faire*. However, to return to Williams,[17] the community of social liberalism was essentially a community of service, inherited from a tradition of *noblesse oblige* and charitable philanthropy whereas that of socialism was one of solidarity and collective action. The former was that of social service, ethically informed, concerned with equality and social democracy and deploying leisure as a field of narrowing class differences and training in social citizenship. Its unifying achievement, as Williams notes, was to retain the status quo. Two aspects of this analysis are notable. The first was an insistence that the culture of the middle class should be shared by the working classes in order to 'raise' them from a perceived exclusion from culture. The second is that this view was widely shared by major co-ordinating and enabling bodies of voluntary intervention in leisure, notably the Juvenile Organizations Committees, National Council of Social Service, Rural Community Councils and the Carnegie United Kingdom Trust. These organizations had strong connections with, and in some cases received funding from, the state. It is worth repeating that much of their work was productive in enhancing the quality of life but this is not the same thing as social change. As Williams noted, the community of solidarity, in contrast, is that of a working-class culture not of proletarian painters or council estates but of collective social institutions and mutual responsibility and an antipathy to individualism. This type of community describes many of the mutual, co-operative and socialist leisure associations discussed in this book; unlike the leisure of service organizations that sought to inculcate a set of values, that of socialist organizations lived them out not only in leisure but in trade unions, co-operative societies and specifically socialist leisure-based movements.

A final important aspect of the contribution of leisure and voluntary action to social change was the development of an intellectual discourse of their meanings and policy significance. Through experimentation and participation in a moral dialogue,[18] understandings of charitable philanthropy and rational recreation were gradually re-cast in social terms of voluntary action and leisure. Both leisure and voluntarism were debated and shaped by ethical considerations. The right use of leisure was framed not just in terms of individual morality but of social ethics. The latter was contested; Christian religion, utilitarianism, socialism and idealism all had differing ethical priorities and competed in civil society to influence the social object of leisure. This made it possible to think about leisure and voluntarism in terms of the theorization of social change. In this new sense leisure meant active leisure and intellectual engagement; it did not include entertainment or relaxation but neither did its proponents necessarily deny these were also valuable ways of using spare time. They did not however lead to the highest levels of social or individual well-being. Civil society accommodated new thinking on the social nature and function of leisure, producing new understandings and fields of practice appropriate to a modernizing twentieth-century industrial society. It was within this moral dialogue that leisure and voluntary action underwent conceptual changes of meaning as existing understandings became inadequate to changing social contexts.

The first three decades of the twentieth century represented the high-water mark of the theorization of voluntary action through leisure. For a short period in the 1970s leisure enjoyed a high profile in social policy and practice following the local government reorganization of 1974 and the creation of municipal and publicly accountable Leisure Services Departments but these failed to survive the out-sourcing and privatization of Thatcher's Conservative administration. Perhaps this was inevitable; John Ruskin's belief that England had lost the sense of leisure as 'school' could not easily be remedied in a privatizing modern world of increased consumption and mass cultural forms that many people found benign and enjoyable and in which the idea of the social collective began to lose purchase.[19] Although the ideas of leisure described above were formed within the context of a mature industrial capitalist society, they are not obsolete. As twenty-first century technology ushers a new industrial revolution by reducing the need for work and full employment and raising the possibility of a post-work society, the discourse of leisure that flourished between 1880 and 1939 has much to offer to social policy debate.

Notes

Chapter 1

1 Rudy Koshar, 'Seeing, Traveling and Consuming: An Introduction', in *Histories of Leisure*, ed. R. Koshar (Oxford: Berg, 2007), 1–26.

2 Carolyn Taylor, 'Humanitarian Narrative: Bodies and Detail in Late-Victorian Social Work', *British Journal of Social Work* 38 (2008), 680–696.

3 Colin Rochester, *Rediscovering Voluntary Action. The Beat of a Different Drum* (Basingstoke: Palgrave Macmillan, 2013), 2.

4 Keith Thomas, 'Work and Leisure', *Past & Present* no. 29 (1964), 50–66; 'Work and Leisure in Industrial Society', *Past & Present* no. 30 (1965), 96–103.

5 Peter Bailey, *Leisure and Class in Victorian England: Rational Recreation and the Contest for Control, 1830–1885* (London: Methuen, 1987); Jeffrey Hill, *Sport, Leisure and Culture in Twentieth-Century Britain* (Basingstoke: Palgrave, 2002).

6 Maeve Cooke, *Re-presenting the Good Society* (London: MIT Press, 2006), 9–10.

7 Jennifer Todd, 'Social Transformation, Collective Categories, and Identity Change', *Theory and Society* 34, no. 4 (2005), 429–463.

8 Rochester, *Rediscovering Voluntary Action*, 16.

9 G.D.H. Cole 'Mutual Aid Movements in their Relation to Voluntary Social Service', in *Voluntary Social Services. Their Place in the Modern State*, ed. A.F.C. Bourdillon (London: Methuen, 1945), 118–134.

10 Robert Putnam, *Bowling Alone. The Collapse and Revival of American Community* (London: Simon and Schuster, 2001).

11 Jeffrey Hill, *Nelson: Politics, Economy, Community* (Edinburgh: Keele University Press, 1997).

12 Helen Meller, *Leisure and the Changing City, 1870–1914* (London: Routledge & Kegan Paul, 1976).

13 Jose Harris, *Private Lives, Public Spirit: Britain 1870–1914* (London: Penguin, 1994).

14 Helen McCarthy, 'Associational Voluntarism in Interwar Britain', in *The Ages of Voluntarism. How We Got to the Big Society*, ed. Matthew Hilton and James McKay (Oxford: Oxford University Press, 2011), 47–68.

15 Caitriona Beaumont, *Housewives and Citizens. Domesticity and the Women's Movement in England, 1928–64* (Manchester: Manchester University Press, 2013); 'Fighting for the "Privileges of Citizenship": the Young Women's Christian

Association, Feminism and the Women's Movement, 1928–1945', *Women's History Review* 23, no. 3 (2014), 463–479.

16 Helen McCarthy, 'Whose Democracy? Histories of British Political Culture between the Wars', *The Historical Journal* 55, no. 1 (2012), 221–238.

17 Robert Snape, 'Voluntary Action and Leisure: An Historical Perspective', *Voluntary Sector Review* 6, no. 2 (2015), 153–171.

18 J. Palisi and P.E. Jacobson, 'Dominant Statuses and Involvement in Types of Instrumental and Expressive Voluntary Associations', *Journal of Voluntary Action Research* 1, no. 6 (1977), 80–88; Rochester, *Rediscovering Voluntary Action*, 149–151.

19 Helen McCarthy, *The British People and the League of Nations. Democracy, Citizenship and Internationalism c.1914–48* (Manchester: Manchester University Press, 2011), 173.

20 Robert Tombs, *The English and their History* (London: Penguin, 2015), 512–513.

21 Zygmunt Bauman, *Community. Seeking Safety in an Insecure World* (Cambridge: Polity Press, 2001), 3.

22 William Morris, *News from Nowhere and Selected Writings and Designs* (Harmondsworth: Penguin, 1962).

23 Nick Abercrombie, Stephen Hill and Bryan S. Turner, *Penguin Dictionary of Sociology* 4th ed. (London: Penguin, 2000), 64.

24 Marilyn Taylor, *Public Policy in the Community* (Basingstoke: Palgrave, 2003), 34–35.

25 J. Bishop and P. Hoggett, *Organizing Around Enthusiasms: Patterns of Mutual Aid in Leisure* (London: Comedia, 1985).

26 G. Crow and G. Allan, *Community Life. An Introduction to Local Social Relations* (London: Harvester Wheatsheaf, 1994), 3.

27 Joanna Bourke, *Working-Class Cultures in Britain 1890–1960. Gender, Class and Ethnicity* (London: Routledge, 1994), 148–149.

28 Robert MacIver, *Community. A Sociological Study* (1917. 2nd ed. London: Macmillan, 1920).

29 Charles. A. Ellwood, 'Review: Community. A Sociological Study', *American Economic Review* 7, no. 3 (1917), 598–600.

30 MacIver, *Community*, 7.

31 MacIver, *Community*, 115.

32 MacIver, *Community*, 174.

33 William Beveridge, *Voluntary Action. A Report on Methods of Social Advance* (London: George Allen and Unwin, 1948), 8.

34 Amitai Etzioni, 'Creating Good Communities and Good Societies', *Contemporary Sociology* 29, no. 1 (2000), 188–195.

35 Nick Stevenson, 'Cultural Citizenship, Education and Democracy: Redefining the Good Society', *Citizenship Studies* 14, no. 3 (2010), 275–291.

36 Gerard Delanty, *Social Theory in a Changing World: Conceptions of Modernity* (Cambridge: Polity Press, 1999), 11.

37 M.J.D. Roberts, *Making English Morals. Voluntary Association and Moral Reform in England, 1787–1886* (Cambridge: Cambridge University Press, 2004), 280.

38 Like leisure, social work is a term with historically changing meanings. There are varying accounts of its origins. Canon Barnett used it in a paper delivered at St. John's College, Oxford in 1883. Here it is used as defined by Henry Mess as any activity undertaken through personal relationships, without consideration for profit, to increase the welfare of those unable to reach the desired social standard, *Voluntary Social Services since 1918* (London: Kegan Paul, Trench, Trubner, 1947), 228.

39 Gerard Delanty, *Community* (London: Routledge, 2010), 5.

40 John Garrard, *Democratisation in Britain. Elites, Civil Society and Reform since 1800* (Basingstoke: Palgrave, 2002), 125.

41 Sandra Dawson, 'Working-Class Consumers and the Campaign for Holidays with Pay', *Twentieth Century British History* 18, no. 3 (2007), 277–305.

42 H.K Anheier, *Civil Society, Measurement, Evaluation, Policy* (London: Earthscan, 2004); S. Khilnani, 'The Development of Civil Society', in *Civil Society: History and Possibilities*, ed. S. Kaviraj and S. Khilnani (Cambridge: Cambridge University Press, 2001), 11–32; T. Janoski, *Citizenship and Civil Society* (Cambridge: Cambridge University Press, 1998), 12.

43 Jose Harris, 'From Richard Hooker to Harold Laski: Changing Perceptions of Civil Society in British Political Thought, Late Sixteenth to Early Twentieth Centuries', in *Civil Society in British History: Ideas, Identities, Institutions*, ed. Jose Harris (Oxford: Oxford University Press, 2003), 13–37.

44 Jose Harris, 'Political Thought and the Welfare State 1870–1940: An Intellectual Framework for British Social Policy', *Past and Present* 135 (1992), 116–141.

45 Michael Edwards, *Civil Society* (Cambridge: Polity Press, 2004).

46 R. Rodger and R. Colls, 'Civil Society and British Cities', in *Cities of Ideas: Civil Society and Urban Governance in Britain, 1800–2000*, ed. R. Colls and R. Rodger (Aldershot: Ashgate, 2004), 1–20.

47 See R.J. Morris, 'Civil Society and the Nature of Urbanism: Britain, 1750–1850', *Urban History* 25, no. 3 (1998), 289–301. DOI: 10.1017/S096392680001292X

48 R.J. Morris, 'Structure, Culture and Society in British Towns', in *The Cambridge Urban History of Britain Volume Three, 1840–1950*, ed. Martin Daunton (Cambridge: Cambridge University Press, 2000), 410.

49 Frank Prochaska, *Schools of Citizenship: Charity and Civic Virtue* (London: Institute for the Study of Civil Society, 2002), 4.

50 Raymond Williams, *The Long Revolution* (Harmondsworth, Penguin, 1961), 339.

51 Hugh Cunningham, 'Leisure and Culture', in *The Cambridge Social History of Britain, Volume 2. People and their Environment*, ed. F.M.L. Thompson (Cambridge: Cambridge University Press, 1990), 279–340.

52 Harris, *Private Lives, Public Spirit*, 250.

53 B. Kohler-Koch and C. Quittkat, 'What is "Civil" Society and Who Represents It?', in *The New Politics of European Civil Society*, ed. B. Kohler-Koch and Hans-Jorg Trenz (Abingdon: Routledge, 2011), 19–39.

54 Karl Spracklen, *The Meaning and Purpose of Leisure. Habermas and Leisure at the End of Modernity* (Basingstoke: Palgrave Macmillan, 2009), 48–49.

55 F.M.L. Thompson, *The Rise of Respectable Society. A Social History of Victorian Britain 1830–1900* (London: Fontana, 1988), 13.

Chapter 2

1 Pat Thane, *Foundations of the Welfare State*, 2nd ed. (London: Longman, 1996).

2 Derek Fraser, *The Evolution of the British Welfare State: A History of British Social Policy since the Industrial Revolution*, 4th ed. (Basingstoke: Palgrave Macmillan, 2009).

3 Roberts, *Making English Morals*.

4 Arnold Toynbee, *Lectures on the Industrial Revolution of the Eighteenth Century in England* (London: Longmans, Green, 1913), 51, 158–159, 243.

5 Jose Harris, *Community and Civil Society/Ferdinand Tonnies* (Cambridge: Cambridge University Press, 2001).

6 Eamon Duffy, *The Stripping of the Altars: Traditional Religion in England 1400–1580* (London, Yale University Press, 1992), 14.

7 John A. Hobson, *The Evolution of Modern Capitalism. A Study of Machine Production* (London: Walter Scott, 1895), 325.

8 See for example Frederick Engels, *The Condition of the Working Class in England* (1844; London: Panther, 1969), 157–159. Engels found in Manchester an 'unbridled thirst for pleasure' amongst the working class, together with 'contempt for the existing social order'.

9 Asa Briggs, *Victorian Cities* (London: Pelican, 1968), 88–138.

10 Peter Gaskell, *Artisans and Machinery: The Moral and Physical Condition of the Manufacturing Population* (1836; London: Frank Cass, 1968).

11 Engels, *Condition of the Working Class in England*, 157–158.

12 Leon Faucher, *Manchester in 1844; Its Present Condition and Future Prospects* (London: Simpkin Marshall, 1844).

13 Emma Griffin, *England's Revelry. A History of Popular Sports and Pastimes 1660–1830* (Oxford: Oxford University Press, 2005).

14 Robert Poole, *Popular Leisure and the Music Hall in Nineteenth-Century Bolton* (Lancaster: Centre for North-West Regional Studies, University of Lancaster, 1982).

15 William Cooke Taylor, *Notes of a Tour in the Manufacturing Districts of Lancashire.* 3rd ed. (1842; London: Frank Cass, 1968), 132–134.

16 Hannah More, *Thoughts on the Importance of the Manners of the Great to Society* (1789; London: T. Cadell, 1818), 18–19, 79.

17 Alexis de Tocqueville, 'Last Impressions of England', in *Alexis de Tocqueville, Journeys to England and Ireland,* ed. J.P. Mayer (New York: Doubleday, 1968), 51–59.

18 John Morrow, *Young England: The New Generation* (London: Leicester University Press, 1999).

19 John Manners, 'Speech on Field-Garden Allotments, Bingley, 11th October 1844', in Morrow, *Young England,* 67–68. Although not a member of Young England, Robert Slaney, Liberal MP for Shrewsbury and an active enthusiast for a paternalist philanthropic provision of leisure amenities also argued the benefits of socially mixed cricket: Robert A. Slaney, *Essay on the Beneficial Direction of Rural Expenditure* (London, 1824).

20 Bailey, *Leisure and Class,* 35.

21 George J. Romanes, 'Recreation', *Nineteenth Century* 6, no. 31 (1879), 401–424.

22 John Stuart Mill, 'Utilitarianism', in *J.S. Mill and Jeremy Bentham, Utilitarianism and Other Essays,* ed. A. Ryan (Harmondsworth: Penguin, 1987), 272–338.

23 Stuart Mill, 'Utilitarianism', 284.

24 Engels, *Condition of the Working Class,* 154.

25 Simon Gunn, 'Translating Bourdieu: Cultural Capital and the English Middle Class in Historical Perspective', *British Journal of Sociology* 56, no.1 (2005), 49–64.

26 Thomas Wright, 'On a Possible Popular Culture', *Contemporary Review* 40, (1881), 25–44.

27 Delanty, *Community,* 24–31.

28 E.P. Thompson, *The Making of the English Working Class* (London: Pelican, 1968), 463.

29 Thompson, *The Making of the English Working Class,* 451.

30 Kenneth Good, 'The Drive for Participatory Democracy in Nineteenth Century Britain', *Commonwealth & Comparative Politics* 47, no. 3, (2009), 231–247.

31 See Engels, *Condition of the Working Class in England,* 156–157.

32 Bernard Harris, 'Voluntary Action and the State in Historical Perspective', *Voluntary Sector Review* 1, no. 1 (2010), 25–40.

33 Good, 'The Drive for Participatory Democracy'.

34 Alexis de Tocqueville, *Journeys to England and Ireland* (1835; New York: Doubleday, 1968), 74.

35 Martin Gorsky, 'The Growth and Distribution of English Friendly Societies in the Early Nineteenth Century', *Economic History Review* New Series, 51, no. 3 (1998), 489–511.

36 Simon Cordery, *British Friendly Societies, 1750–1914* (Basingstoke: Palgrave Macmillan, 2003), 33–34; Bernard Harris, *Origins of the British Welfare State*, 79.

37 Martin Gorsky, 'Mutual Aid and Civil Society: Friendly Societies in Nineteenth Century Bristol', *Urban History* 25, no. 3 (1998), 302, 322.

38 Good, 'The Drive for Participatory Democracy'.

39 Elizabeth Gaskell, *Mary Barton* (1848; London: Dent, 1996), 38.

40 James Hole, *An Essay on the History and Management of Literary, Scientific and Mechanics' Institutions* (London: Longmans, 1853), 74–77. Hole was Honorary Secretary of the Yorkshire Union of Mechanics' Institutes.

41 Thomas Kelly, *A History of Adult Education in Great Britain* (Liverpool: Liverpool University Press, 1992), 189.

42 Charles Williams, *Accrington Mechanics' Institution 1845–1895: A Story of Fifty Years Jubilee Booklet* (Accrington: Broadley, 1895).

43 Judith Flanders, *Consuming Passions: Leisure and Pleasure in Victorian Britain* (London: Harper Press, 2006), 31–32.

44 Samuel Couling, *A History of the Temperance Movement in Great Britain and Ireland* (London: William Tweedie, 1862), 19–39.

45 Couling, *History of the Temperance Movement*, 43.

46 J.S. Blocker, D.M. Fahey and I.R. Tyrell (eds) *Alcohol and Temperance in Modern History: An International Encyclopaedia, Volume One* (Oxford: ABC-Clio, 2003), 547.

47 Simon Morgan, *A Victorian Woman's Place: Public Culture in the Nineteenth Century* (London: I.B. Tauris, 2007), 96–97.

48 Couling, *History of the Temperance Movement*, 58.

49 Couling, *History of the Temperance Movement*, 62.

50 'Temperance Recreation', *Manchester Times and Gazette* 14 March 1840; 'Temperance', *Manchester Times and Gazette* 4 April 1840.

51 Peter Taylor, *Popular Politics in Early Industrial Britain: Bolton 1825–1850* (Keele University: Ryburn Publishing, 1995).

52 Roberts, *Making English Morals*, 151.

53 *The Star of Temperance, A Weekly Publication for the Diffusion of Temperance Information*, ed. Rev. F. Beardsall (Manchester) and Rev. J. Baker (Chester) no. 8, 20 February, 1836.

54 Erika Rappaport, 'Sacred and Useful Pleasures: "The Temperance Tea Party and the Creation of a Sober Consumer Culture in Early Industrial Britain", *Journal of British Studies* 52, no. 4 (2013), 990–1016.

55 Couling, *History of the Temperance Movement*, 130–132.

56 'Whelan and Co's Directory, 1853, Bolton', in *Four Bolton Directories* (Manchester: Neil Richardson, 1982), 52–106.

57 Annemarie McAllister, 'Picturing the Demon Drink: How Children were Shown Temperance Principles in the Band of Hope', *Visual Resources* 28, no. 4 (2012), 309–323.

58 Stephanie Olsen, *Juvenile Nation. Youth, Emotions and the Making of the Modern British Citizen* (London: Bloomsbury, 2014), 31.

59 See Gareth Stedman Jones, 'Class Expression versus Social Control? A Critique of Recent Trends in the Social History of Leisure', *History Workshop* 4, (1977), 162–170.

60 Couling, *History of the Temperance Movement*, 242.

61 Henry Solly, *Working Men's Social Clubs and Educational Institutes* (London: Working Men's Club and Institute Union, 1867), 13.

62 Solly, *Working Men's Social Clubs*, 19.

63 B.T. Hall, *Our Sixty Years: The Story of the Working Men's Club and Institute Union*, (London: WMCIU, 1922), 286–298; Solly, *Working Men's Social Clubs*, 36.

64 Williams, *The Long Revolution*, 102.

65 Solly, *Working Men's Social Clubs*, 55–56.

66 Solly, *Working Men's Social Clubs*, 73–79.

67 Hall, *Our Sixty Years*, 211.

68 Solly, *Working Men's Social Clubs*, 128.

69 Ambrose G. Barker, *Seventy Years a Club, being a Brief History of the Formation and Events in the Life of the Walthamstow Working Men's Club and Institute* (Privately Published, 1932), 133.

70 Robert Archey Woods, *English Social Movements* (London: Swann Sonnenschein 2nd ed. 1895), 26–27.

71 Stanton Coit, *Neighbourhood Guilds* (London: Swan Sonnenschein, 2nd ed. 1892), 81.

72 Henry Solly, *Working Men's Clubs and Alcoholic Drinks: Is the Prohibitory Policy Necessary or Expedient?* (London: Palmer, 1872), 2.

73 Jonathan Rose, *The Intellectual Life of the British Working Classes* (London: Yale University Press, 2001).

74 Solly, *Working Men's Social Clubs*, 233.

75 Solly, *Working Men's Social Clubs*, 36.

76 Solly, *Working Men's Social Clubs*, 29–30.

77 Fraser, *The Evolution of the British Welfare State*, 128–129.

78 Roberts, *Making English Morals*, 294.

79 MacIver, *Community*, 41, 99.

Chapter 3

1 Callum G. Brown, *The Death of Christian Britain: Understanding Secularization 1800–2000* (London: Routledge, 2009).

2 Thane, *Foundations of the Welfare State*, 21.

3   See Gerald Parsons (ed.) *Religion in Victorian Britain Volume One, Traditions* (Manchester: Manchester University Press, 1988).

4   Alison Twells, *The Civilising Mission and the English Middle-Class, 1792–1850* (Basingstoke: Palgrave Macmillan, 2009), 5.

5   Duffy, *Stripping of the Altars*, 136. See also J.F. Merritt, 'Religion and the English Parish'. In *The Oxford History of Anglicanism, Volume One*, ed. Anthony Milton, 122–124 (Oxford: Oxford University Press, 2017).

6   John Atherton, *Christianity and the Market. Christian Social Thought for our Times* (London: Society for the Promotion of Christian Knowledge, 1992), 144.

7   For example the Christian Socialist Society, Christian Socialist League, Christian Social Brotherhood and Free Church Socialist League.

8   Philip Blond and James Noyes, *Holistic Mission: Social Action and the Church of England* (Lincoln: ResPublica, 2013), 14.

9   Anne Holt, *A Ministry to the Poor: Being the History of the Liverpool Domestic Mission Society 1836–1936* (Liverpool: Henry Young, 1936). The Manchester and Salford Wesleyan Mission and the Liverpool Central Mission offered a similar social provision; see William H. Crawford, *The Church and the Slum. A Study of English Wesleyan Mission Halls* (New York: Eaton and Mains, 1908).

10 Good, 'Participatory Democracy in Nineteenth Century Britain', 243.

11 Charles Deane Little, *The History and Romance of our Mother Sunday School: 150 Years of Methodism in Bolton* (London: Epworth Press, 1935).

12 Bailey, *Leisure and Class*, 57; Poole, *Popular Leisure and the Music Hall*, 19.

13 Doreen Rosman, *The Evolution of the English Churches 1500–2000* (Cambridge: Cambridge University Press, 2003), 214, 301.

14 Paul O'Leary, 'Networking Respectability: Class, Gender and Ethnicity among the Irish in South Wales, 1845–1914', *Immigrants & Minorities* 23, no. 2–3 (2005), 255–275.

15 Robert Snape, *Leisure and the Rise of the Public Library* (London: Library Association Publishing, 1995).

16 Parsons, 'From Dissenters to Free Churchmen: The Transitions of Victorian Non-Conformity', in *Religion in Victorian Britain, Volume One, Traditions*, ed. G. Parsons, 67–116, 80 (Manchester: Manchester University Press, 1988).

17 'What Attitude Should Christian Churches Take in Relation to Amusements?' *The Congregationalist* (1879), 547–556 and 650–665.

18 Douglas A. Reid, 'Playing and Praying', in *The Cambridge Urban History of Britain, Volume Three 1849–1950* ed. Martin Daunton (Cambridge: Cambridge University Press, 2000), 745–807.

19 Rosman, *The Evolution of the English Churches*, 299.

20 D.W. Bebbington, *Evangelicalism in Modern Britain. A History from the 1730s to the 1980s* (London, Routledge, 1989), 128.

21 Stephen Orchard, 'The Free Churches and their Nation', in *Free Churches and Society. The Nonconformist Contribution to Social Welfare 1800–2010*, ed. Lesley Husselbee and Paul Ballard (London: Continuum, 2012), 5–21.

22 Thompson, *The Rise of Respectable Society*, 252.

23 Meller, *Leisure and the Changing City*, 123–146.

24 Bebbington, *Evangelicalism in Modern Britain*, 127–128.

25 Albert Fried, and Richard M. Elman (eds) *Charles Booth's London* (London: Pelican, 1971), 234–254.

26 Rosman, *The Evolution of the English Churches*.

27 Harris, *Private Lives, Public Spirit*, 157.

28 Meller, *Leisure and the Changing City*, 144–146.

29 Christopher P. Hosgood, 'Negotiating Lower-Middle-Class Masculinity in Britain: The Leicester Young Men's Christian Association, 1870–1914', *Canadian Journal of History* 37, no. 2 (2002), 253–273.

30 Geoff Spurr, 'Lower-Middle-Class Masculinity and the Young Men's Christian Association 1844–1880', *Social History* 47, no. 5 (2014), 547–576.

31 Emily Kinnaird, *Reminiscences* (London, John Murray, 1925), 65.

32 Brian Harrison, 'For Church, Queen and Family: The Girls' Friendly Society 1874–1920', *Past & Present* no. 61 (1973), 107–138.

33 Charles E.B. Russell and Lilian M. Russell, *Lads' Clubs. Their History, Organisation and Management* (London: Black, 1932), 14–17.

34 Robert Baden Powell, *Scouting for Boys*, 3rd ed. (London: C. Arthur Pearson, c. 1910), 227–228.

35 Callum Brown, *The Death of Christian Britain*.

36 Jeremy Morris, 'The Strange Death of Christian Britain: Another Look at the Secularization Debate', *Historical Journal* 46, no. 4 (2003), 963–976.

37 J. Carvell-Williams, 'Nonconformity in the Nineteenth Century', in *Congregational Yearbook* (London: Jackson and Walford, 1899), 34–39.

38 J. Morlais Jones, 'Wanting is What' in *Congregational Yearbook* (London: Jackson and Walford, 1897), 16–35.

39 Dominic Erdozain, *The Problem of Pleasure: Sport, Recreation and the Crisis of Victorian Religion* (Woodbridge: Boydell Press, 2010), 230–231.

40 Helen M.F. Jones, 'Darning, Doylies and Dancing: The Work of the Leeds Association of Girls' Clubs (1904–1913)', *Women's History Review* 20, no. 3 (2011), 369–388, DOI: 10.1080/09612025.2011.567053

41 Graham Bowpitt, 'Evangelical Christianity, Secular Humanism and the Genesis of British Social Work', *British Journal of Social Work* 28, no. 5 (1998), 675–693.

42 Bebbington, *Evangelicalism in Modern Britain*, 132.

43 John Lewis Paton, *John Brown Paton: A Biography* (London: Hodder and Stoughton, 1914), 186–199.

44 See E.P. Hennock, *Fit and Proper Persons. Ideal and Reality in Nineteenth Century Urban Government* (London: Edward Arnold, 1973), 168.

45 John Brown Paton, *A Plea for Recreative Evening Schools and for the Secondary Education of our Industrial Classes* (London: James Clarke, c. 1885); J.B. Paton, *Recreative Instruction of Young People* (London: James Clarke, 1886).

46 Paton, *John Brown Paton*, 207.

47 Alexander Hadden, *A Short Note on the Work of the Ancoats Recreation Committee, 1878–1898* (Manchester: Ancoats Recreation Committee).

48 National Home Reading Union, *Annual Report* 1896–7.

49 National Home Reading Union, *Notes, Reports and Announcements* 1894.

50 National Home Reading Union, *General Magazine* 14, no. 4 (1905).

51 Robert Snape, 'The National Home Reading Union', *Journal of Victorian Culture* 7, no. 1 (2002), 86–110.

52 E.P. Hennock, *The Origin of the Welfare State in England and Germany 1850–1914: Social Policies Compared* (Cambridge: Cambridge University Press, 2007).

53 John Brown Paton, *The Inner Mission: Four Addresses* (London: Isbister, 1888).

54 John Brown Paton, 'Christianity and the Well-being of the People', in *Inner Mission Leaflets* (London: J. Clarke, n.d.).

55 In 1893 Paton helped Leonard found the Co-operative Holidays Association.

56 Paton, *John Brown Paton*, 216; 'A Social Institute in Every Board School' *The Review of Reviews* (1898), 299. Leonard later formed and managed both the Co-operative Holidays Association and the Holiday Fellowship.

57 William Sinclair and Henry G. Rawson, 'The Social Institutes' Union', *Times* [London] 29 November 1901, 6. *The Times Digital Archive*. Accessed 14 April 2017.

58 Paton, *John Brown Paton*, 217.

59 'Popular Education', *Reynold's Newspaper*, 6 October 1895.

60 'Education Report for England and Wales', *Times* [London] 27 September 1898, 4. *The Times Digital Archive*. Accessed 13 April 2017.

61 Madeline Rooff, *A Survey of Girls Organisations in England and Wales* (Edinburgh: Carnegie United Kingdom Trust, 1935), 188.

62 John Brown Paton, 'The Inner Mission of Germany and its Lesson to Us', in *Inner Mission Leaflets*, 1–44, (London: J. Clarke, n.d.).

63 Percy Dearmer, 'Art and Life'. In *A Lent in London* (London: Longmans Green, 1895), 155–168. Dearmer was Secretary of the London branch of the Christian Social Union 1891–1912.

64 Michael Freeden (ed.) *Minutes of the Rainbow Circle, 1894–1924* (London: Offices of the Royal Historical Society, 1989).

65 Keith Laybourn, 'The Guild of Help and the Changing Face of Edwardian Philanthropy', *Urban History* 20, no. 1 (1993), 43–60.

66 John Brown Paton, *Applied Christianity: A Civic League – Social and Educational – for Our Cities and Towns* (London: James Clarke, 1905).

67 The date of its foundation has been published variously as 1905 and 1906. 1904 is taken from one of its own publications. It was modelled on the American Institute of Social Service whose President, Josiah Strong visited Britain in support; see 'Institutes Of Social Service – A Reception'. *Times* [London] 6 July 1904, 5. *The Times Digital Archive.* Accessed 14 April 2017.

Chapter 4

1 Andrew Mearns, *The Bitter Cry of Outcast London* (London: James Clarke, 1883). Mearns was Secretary of the London Congregational Union.

2 The 'slum' had varying meanings; here it refers to inner-urban areas with high levels of poverty, poor health, housing, education and over-crowding whose populations lay largely beyond the reach of middle-class philanthropic intervention.

3 Rosalind Williams, *Notes on the Underground. An Essay on Technology, Society and the Imagination* (London: MIT Press, 1990), 151–185.

4 Helen Dendy, 'The Industrial Residuum', in *Aspects of the Social Problem* ed. Bernard Bosanquet (London: Macmillan, 1895), 82–102.

5 Alan Mayne, *The Imagined Slum: Newspaper Representation in Three Cities, 1870–1914* (Leicester: Leicester University Press, 1993).

6 Beveridge, *Voluntary Action*, 130.

7 John Gorst, 'Settlements in England and America', in *The Universities and the Social Problem*, ed. John Knapp (London: Rivington, Percival, 1895), 1–30.

8 Stephen A. Webb, 'The Comfort of Strangers: Social Work, Modernity and Late Victorian England – Part I', *European Journal of Social Work* 10, no. 1 (2007), 39–54. DOI: 10.1080/13691450601143625

9 David Boucher and Andrew Vincent, *British Idealism and Political Theory* (Edinburgh: Edinburgh University Press, 2000), 28.

10 See for example Sandra Den Otter, *British Idealism and Social Explanation: A Study in Late Victorian Thought* (Oxford: Clarendon Press, 1996); M. Carter, *T.H. Green and the Development of Ethical Socialism* (Exeter: Imprint Academic, 2003).

11 Andrew Vincent, 'Green, Thomas Hill (1836–1882)', *Oxford Dictionary of National Biography*, Oxford University Press, 2004; online ed., January 2012 (http://www.oxforddnb.com/view/article/11404, accessed 28 April 2016).

12 Bernard Bosanquet, 'The Meaning of Social Work', *International Journal of Ethics* 11, no. 3 (1901), 291–306.

13 Den Otter, *British Idealism*, 208.

14 Fraser, *The Evolution of the British Welfare State*, 162.

15 Henrietta Barnett, 'Passionless Reformers', in Rev. and Mrs. Samuel A. Barnett, *Practicable Socialism: Essays on Social Reform* (London: Longmans Green, 1888), 51.

16 Universities Settlements Association, *Sixth Annual Report 1890*, 4.

17 Chris Waters, *British Socialists and Politics of Popular Culture* (Manchester: Manchester University Press, 1990), 1, 101.

18 Ashley, 'University Settlements in Great Britain'. See also Kate Bradley, *Poverty, Philanthropy and the State: Charities and the Working Classes in London, 1918-79* (Manchester: Manchester University Press, 2009), 100.

19 'A Co-operative Settlement', *The Wheatsheaf* 7, no. 1 (1902), 98–99.

20 W. Francis Aiken, *Canon Barnett, Warden of Toynbee Hall* (London: S.W. Partridge, 1902), 50.

21 Edward Cummings, 'University Settlements', *Quarterly Journal of Economics* 6, no. 3 (1892), 257–279.

22 *Sixth Annual Report of the Universities Settlement in East London*, 1890.

23 Henrietta Barnett, 'What Has the Charity Organisation Society to Do with Social Reform'? in Samuel Augustus Barnett and Henrietta Barnett, *Practicable Socialism: Essays in Social Reform*, (London: Longmans, Green, 1888), 157–172.

24 *Sixth Annual Report of the Universities Settlement*, 1890, 37.

25 Fried and Elman (eds) *Charles Booth's London*, 262–265.

26 Percy Ashley, 'University Settlements in Great Britain', *The Harvard Theological Review* 4, no. 2 (1911), 175–203.

27 Samuel Barnett, 'The Recreation of the People', in *Practicable Socialism: Essays in Social Reform*, New Series, (London: Longmans, Green, 1915), 53–69.

28 Samuel Barnett, 'Twenty One Years of University Settlements', in *Practicable Socialism*, New Series, 121–131.

29 Henrietta Barnett, 'The Hopes of the Hosts', in *Practicable Socialism*, New Series, 70–73.

30 Samuel Barnett, 'University Settlements' in *Practicable Socialism*, 1st ed., 96–108.

31 Samuel Barnett, 'Relief Funds and the Poor' in *Practicable Socialism*, 1st ed., 22–47.

32 Robert Archey Woods, 'The University Settlements', in *English Social Movements* (New York: Scribner's Sons, 1891), 79–118.

33 Henrietta Barnett, 'The Children's Country Holiday Fun', in *Practicable Socialism*, New Series, 41–52.

34 First published in 1888 with a New Series in 1915. The latter includes a larger number of chapters dealing with leisure.

35 Samuel Barnett 'Relief Funds and the Poor' in *Practicable Socialism*, 1st ed., 22–47.

36 Barnett, 'University Settlements', 125.

37 Barnett, 'The Recreation of the People'.

38 Barnett, 'The Recreation of the People'.

39 Barnett and Barnett, *Practicable Socialism*.

40 Samuel Barnett, 'Poverty, its Cause and Cure', in *Practicable Socialism*, New Series, 143–149.

41 Henrietta Barnett, 'The Hopes of the Hosts'.

42 Lucinda Matthews-Jones, '"I Still Remain One of the Old Settlement Boys": Cross-Class Friendship in the First World War. Letters of Cardiff University Settlement Lads' Club', *Cultural and Social History* 13, no. 2 (2016), 195–211, DOI: 10.1080/14780038.2016.1202011

43 Samuel Barnett, 'University Settlements', in *Practicable Socialism*, 1st ed., 96–108.

44 Henrietta Barnett, 'The Poverty of the Poor', in *Practicable Socialism*, 1st ed., 1–21.

45 Stephen A. Webb, 'The Comfort of Strangers: Social Work, Modernity and Late Victorian England – Part II', *European Journal of Social Work* 10, no. 2 (2007), 193–207.

46 Henrietta Barnett, '"At Home" to the Poor', in *Practicable Socialism*, 1st ed., 77.

47 Henrietta Barnett, '"At Home" to the Poor'.

48 Snape, 'The National Home Reading Union'.

49 Ashley, 'University Settlements in Great Britain'.

50 Samuel Barnett 'Settlements or Missions', in Samuel and Henrietta Barnett *Towards Social Reform* (London: T. Fisher Unwin, 1909), 271–288; Thomas Hancock Nunn, 'The Universities' Settlement in Whitechapel', *Economic Review* 2, no. 4 (1892), 478–495.

51 Peter Clark, *British Clubs and Societies 1580–1800* (Oxford: Clarendon Press, 2000), 470.

52 Georgina Brewis, *A Social History of Student Volunteering: Britain and Beyond 1880–1980* (New York: Palgrave Macmillan, 2014), 23.

53 F. Arnold, 'Oxford House and Toynbee Hall' *Leisure Hour* (April 1888), 274–279.

54 John A. R. Pimlott, *Toynbee Hall: Fifty Years of Social Progress 1884–1934* (London: Dent, 1935), 78.

55 Toynbee Hall, *Annual Report of the Universities Settlement in East London*, 1890, 25.

56 *Toynbee Record*, 2, no. 9 (June 1890), 100.

57 'Lolesworth Club', *Toynbee Record* 6, no. 8 (1894), 116.

58 Joan D. Browne, 'The Toynbee Travellers' Club', *History of Education* 15, no. 1 (1986), 11–17, DOI: 10.1080/0046760860150102

59 The average working man's weekly wage in Whitechapel was between fifteen and twenty-five shillings. (Quoted in Francis Eardley, 'A Workman's Club in the East End' *Good Words*, December 1895, 227–229.) The Barnetts later claimed that the Club had been instituted primarily for the settlement workers. See Mrs S.A. Barnett, *Canon Barnett: His Life, Work and Friends, Vol. One* (London: John Murray, 1918), 359.

60 'The Toynbee Travellers' Club in Embryo', *Review of Reviews* 5, no. 30 (June 1892), 619–621; Cummings, 'University Settlements', 257–279.

61 Booth's survey reported some of the worst streets in Bethnal Green to be in this parish: London School of Economics, 'Charles Booth's London',

http://booth.lse.ac.uk/notebooks. Oxford House later became formally associated with St. Matthew's parish in Bethnal Green.

62 Ruth Louise Cherrington, 'The Development of Working Men's Clubs: A Case Study of Implicit Cultural Policy', *International Journal of Cultural Policy* 15, no. 2 (2009), 187–199.

63 A.F. Winnington Ingram, 'Working Men's Clubs'. In *The Universities and the Social Problem: An Account of the University Settlements in East London*, ed. John M. Knapp (London: Rivington Percival & Co., 1895), 33–50.

64 *The Oxford House in Bethnal Green* (London: T. Brakell, 1948), 12.

65 A.F. Winnington Ingram, 'Working Men's Clubs'.

66 Francis Eardley, 'A Workman's Club in the East End', *Good Words*, December 1895, 227–231.

67 Anne Pimlott Baker, 'Boulton, Sir Harold Edwin, Second Baronet (1859–1935)', *Oxford Dictionary of National Biography*, Oxford University Press, 2004 (http://www.oxforddnb.com/view/article/47750, accessed 26 October 2016).

68 Will Reason, *University and Social Settlements* (London: Methuen, 1898), 81.

69 Winnington Ingram, 'Working Men's Clubs', *Leisure Hour* (October 1903), 274–279.

70 T.C. Collings, 'The Settlements of London' *Leisure Hour* (July 1895), 600–606.

71 Kate Bradley, 'Juvenile Delinquency, the Juvenile Courts and the Settlement Movement 1908–1950: Basil Henriques and Toynbee Hall', *Twentieth Century British History* 19, no. 2, (2008), 133–155; Trevor Harris, 'Anti-social City: Science and Crime in Late Victorian Britain', in *Anti-Social Behaviour in Britain. Victorian and Contemporary Perspectives*, ed. Sarah Pickard (Basingstoke: Palgrave Macmillan, 2014), 18–19.

72 Roberts, *Making English Morals*, 280.

73 Olsen, *Juvenile Nation*.

74 Stefan Collini, 'Hobhouse, Bosanquet and the State: Philosophical Idealism and Political Argument in England 1880–1918', *Past and Present* 72, (1976), 86–111.

75 Quoted in Ashley, 'University Settlements', 185.

76 Ashley, 'University Settlements', 186.

77 W.R. Anson, 'The Oxford House in Bethnal Green', *Economic Review* (1893), 10–22.

78 Neil Skinner and Matthew Taylor, '"It's Nice to Belong", Boxing, Heritage and Community in London', in *Sport, History and Heritage. Studies in Public Representation*, eds Jeffrey Hill, Kevin Moore and Jason Wood (Woodbridge: Boydell Press, 2012), 59–76.

79 Georgina Brewis, 'From Working Parties to Social Work: Middle-class Girls' Education and Social Service 1890–1914', *History of Education* 38, no. 6 (2009), 761–777.

80 Nigel Scotland, *Squires in the Slums. Settlements and Missions in Late-Victorian London* (London: I.B. Tauris, 2007), 101–112.

81 *The Oxford House in Bethnal Green* (London: T. Brakell, 1948), 42.

82 Brewis, 'From Working Parties to Social Work'.

83 *University Hall* Pamphlet, March 1890 (Mary Ward Archive, LMA).

84 John Rodgers, *Mary Ward Settlement. A History 1891–1931* Passmore Edwards Research Series No.1 (London: Mary Ward Settlement, 1931), 3.

85 Rodgers, *Mary Ward Settlement*, 6.

86 Rodgers, *Mary Ward Settlement*, 5.

87 John Sutherland, *Mrs Humphry Ward: Eminent Victorian and Pre-Eminent Edwardian* (Oxford: Oxford University Press, 1991), 220–222.

88 Passmore Edwards Settlement, *Annual Report, 1898–99*.

89 Jane Lewis, *Women and Social Action in Victorian and Edwardian England* (Aldershot: Edward Elgar, 1991), 214.

90 Victoria Women's Settlement, *1st Annual Report 1898*.

91 Margaret Simey, *Charity Re-discovered: A Study of Philanthropic Effort in Nineteenth Century Liverpool* (Liverpool: Liverpool University Press, 1992), 132.

92 Victoria Women's Settlement, *2nd Annual Report 1899*.

93 ibid.

94 Bebbington, *Evangelicalism in Modern Britain*, 118.

95 Frank Prochaska, *Christianity and Social Service in Modern Britain. The Disinherited Spirit* (Oxford: Oxford University Press, 2006), 68.

96 Victoria Women's Settlement, *7th Annual Report 1904*.

97 Simey, *Charity Rediscovered*, 130–135.

98 Liverpool University Settlement, *Annual Report 1906*.

99 Margaret Simey, 'D'Aeth, Frederic George (1875–1940)', *Oxford Dictionary of National Biography*, Oxford University Press, 2004; online ed., May 2014 (http://www.oxforddnb.com/view/article/54584, accessed 26 May 2016). D'Aeth was a major figure in the development of social service in the early twentieth century, being instrumental in the formation of the pioneering Liverpool Council of Voluntary Aid in 1909 and the National Council of Social Service in 1919.

100 Susan Pedersen, 'Macadam, Elizabeth (1871–1948)', *Oxford Dictionary of National Biography*, Oxford University Press, 2004 (http://www.oxforddnb.com/view/article/53582, accessed 19 May 2016).

101 Earl of Woolton, *Memoirs* (London: Cassell, 1959), 14–16.

102 Liverpool University Settlement, *Annual Report 1911*.

103 F.J. Marquis and S.E.F. Ogden, *Palaces for the People: A Suggestion for the Recreation of the Poorest People* (Liverpool: Liverpool University Settlement, 1912), 19–20.

104 Marquis and Ogden, *Palaces for the People*, 19.

105 Marquis and Ogden, *Palaces for the People*, 27.

106 Ashley, 'University Settlements', 186.

107 Brewis, *Social History of Student Volunteering*, 25.

108 Bernard Bosanquet, *Aspects of the Social Problem* (London: Macmillan, 1895), 26.

109 William A. Bailward, *The Slippery Slope* (London: John Murray, 1920), 101.

110 Samuel Barnett, 'Principles of Recreation', in *Towards Social Reform*, 289–298.

111 'A Social Settlement', *Gloucester Journal*, 19 February 1898, 5.

112 Ernest Duckerschoff, *How the English Workman Lives* (London: P.S. King, 1899), 55–73.

113 Bill Luckin, 'Revisiting the Slums in Manchester and Salford in the 1930s', in *Urban Politics and Space in the Nineteenth and Twentieth Centuries* ed. Barry Doyle (Newcastle: Cambridge Scholars Publishing, 2007), 134–147.

114 Andy Croll and Martin Johnes, 'A Heart of Darkness? Leisure, Respectability and the Aesthetics of Vice in Victorian Wales', in *Disreputable Pleasures. Less Virtuous Victorians at Play*, ed. Mike Huggins and J.A. Mangan (London: Frank Cass, 2004), 153–171.

115 Hancock Nunn, 'The Universities' Settlement in Whitechapel'.

116 Webb, 'The Comfort of Strangers' Part II.

117 Arnold, 'Oxford House and Toynbee Hall'.

118 Anson, 'The Oxford House in Bethnal Green'.

119 Toynbee Hall, *Annual Report* 1891, 18; Woods, *English Social Movements*, 90.

120 Arnold 'Oxford House and Toynbee Hall'.

121 Webb, 'The Comfort of Strangers: Social Work Part 1'.

Chapter 5

1 Thomas More, *Utopia* (London: Penguin, 2012), 64–65.

2 Dorothea Hollins (ed.), *Utopian Papers* (London: Masters & Co., 1908).

3 See Dennis Hardy, *Utopian England: Community Experiments 1900–1945* (London: Routledge, 2000); Harvey Taylor, *A Claim on the Countryside: A History of the British Outdoor Movement* (Edinburgh: Keele University Press, 1997).

4 Ebenezer Howard, *Garden Cities of Tomorrow* (London: Swan Sonnenschein, 1902), 18.

5 Sarah Rutherford, *Garden Cities* (Oxford: Shire Publications, 2014).

6 Howard, *Garden Cities*, 133.

7 W.R. Hughes, *New Town* (London: Dent, 1919), 132–133.

8 Abigail Beach and Nick Tiratsoo, 'The Planners and the Public', in *The Cambridge Urban History of Britain Volume Three, 1840–1950*, ed. Martin Daunton (Cambridge: Cambridge University Press, 2000), 525–550.

9 C.S. Bremner, 'Garden City, The Housing Experiment at Letchworth', *Fortnightly Review* 88, (1910), 512–526.

10 Rutherford, *Garden Cities*, 70–71.

11 Rutherford, *Garden Cities*, 57.

12 'The Art of Living Together', *Times* (London), Friday, 27 August 1920; p. 8; Issue 42500.

13 Hughes, *New Town*, 132.

14 Hughes, *New Town*, 134.

15 Andrew J. Davies, *To Build a New Jerusalem: The British Labour Movement from the 1880s to the 1990s* (London: Michael Joseph, 1992), 60.

16 Mark Bevir, *The Making of British Socialism* (Oxford: Princeton University Press, 2011), 185.

17 Davies, *To Build a New Jerusalem*, 48.

18 Carol Jenkins, 'Foley, Alice (1891–1974)', *Oxford Dictionary of National Biography*, Oxford University Press, 2004 (http://www.oxforddnb.com/view/article/71614, accessed 16 March 2017).

19 Malcolm Chase, *Chartism: A New History* (Manchester: Manchester University Press, 2007), 142–144.

20 Paul Salveson, *Socialism with a Northern Accent, Radical Traditions for Modern Times* (London: Lawrence and Wishart, 2012), 63.

21 Tony Judge, *Gardens of Eden. British Socialists in the Open Air 1890–1939* (London: Alpha House, 2014).

22 Elizabeth Baigent, '"God's Earth will be Sacred": Religion, Theology, and the Open Space Movement in Victorian England', *Rural History* 22, no. 1 (2011), 31–58

23 Henrietta Barnett, 'Passionless Reformers', in *Practicable Socialism*, 1st ed., 48–61.

24 Charles F. Harford, *The Keswick Convention. Its Message, Its Method and Its Men* (London: Marshall Brothers, 1907), 4.

25 David Matless, *Landscape and Englishness.* 2nd ed. (London: Reaktion Books, 2016), 335.

26 T.A. Leonard, 'Labour: its Rights and Duties', *Colne Times*, 4 August 1892.

27 T.A. Leonard, 'The Philosophy of Holiday-making', *Colne Times*, 7 August 1891, 6.

28 John Lewis Paton, *John Brown Paton*.

29 'An Ideal Holiday. A Week of Co-operative Holiday Making', *Young Oxford* (1897), 423–425.

30 William Morris, 'How I Became a Socialist', in *Collected Works of William Morris, Vol. 23* (London: Longman, 1915), 277–281.

31 John Ruskin, 'The Moral of Landscape', in *Modern Painters Volume 3* (London: Smith, Elder & Co., 1856), 286–314.

32 Douglas Hope, 'The Democratisation of Tourism in the English Lake District: The Role of the Co-operative Holidays Association and the Holiday Fellowship', *Journal of Tourism History* 8, no. 2 (2016), 105–126. DOI: 10.1080/1755182X.2016.1187207

33 Robert Snape, 'The Co-operative Holidays Association and the Cultural Formation of Countryside Leisure Practice', *Leisure Studies*, 23, no. 2 (2004), 143–158. DOI: 10.1080/0261436042000226345

34 *Comradeship* 4 (1) September 1910.

35 *People's Friend*, 16 May 1904, p. 416 (Scrapbook CHA Archive).

36 *Comradeship* 2 (3) February 1909.

37 Hope, 'The Democratisation of Tourism'.

38 *Comradeship* 4 (1) September 1910.

39 *Comradeship* 1 (1) October 1907.

40 Huddersfield CHA Rambling and Reading Club *Minute Book* 1911.

41 Hagen Schulze, *Germany: A New History*. Trans. Deborah Lucas Schneider (London: Harvard University Press, 1998), 181–182.

42 *Comradeship* 7(4) March 1914.

43 Snape, 'The Co-operative Holidays Association'.

44 Cooke, *Re-presenting the Good Society*, 25.

45 Mary Davis, *Comrade or Brother? A History of the British Labour Movement* 2nd ed., (London: Pluto Press, 2009), 285.

46 John Ruskin, 'Co-operation', in *Time and Tide* (London: Smith Elder, 1872), 1–5.

47 Blatchford helped form the Manchester Fabian Society and that city's branch of the Independent Labour Party.

48 June Hannam and Karen Hunt, *Socialist Women. Britain, 1880s to 1920s* (London: Routledge, 2002), 90.

49 C.F.G. Masterman, *The Condition of England* 3rd ed., (London: Methuen, 1909), 149.

50 Krishan Kumar, *The Making of English National Identity* (Cambridge: Cambridge University Press, 2003), 215.

51 Robert Blatchford, *Merrie England* (London: Walter Scott, 1894), 50, 149.

52 Blatchford, *Merrie England*, 129.

53 Blatchford, *Merrie England*, 145.

54 Henry Hyndman, *Further Reminiscences* (London: Macmillan, 1912), 363.

55 Davies, *To Build a New Jerusalem*, 66; Denis Pye, *Fellowship is Life. The National Clarion Cycling Club 1895–1995* (Bolton: Clarion Publishing, 1995), 48–53.

56 Stephen G. Jones, *Sport, Politics and the Working Class: Organised Labour and Sport in Interwar Britain* (Manchester: Manchester University Press, 1988), 32.

57 Pye, 'Bolton Socialist Party and Club', 8.

58 Flanders, *Consuming Passions*, 455.

59 Tom Groom, 'The Fifty-Year Story of the Club' *Jubilee Souvenir* (Halifax: Alex Taylor/ National Clarion Cycling Club, 1944).

60 Pye, *Fellowship is Life*, 88–89.

61 Percy Dearmer, *Christian Socialism. Practical Christianity*, Clarion Pamphlet No. 19 (London: Clarion Newspaper Company, 1897).

62 Pye, *Fellowship is Life*, 9.

63 David Prynn, 'The Clarion Clubs, Rambling and the Holiday Associations in Britain since the 1890s'. *Journal of Contemporary History* 11, nos. 2/3 (1976), 65–77.

64 Alice Foley, *A Bolton Childhood* (Manchester: Manchester University Extra-Mural Department, 1973), 72.

65 Melanie Tebbutt, 'Rambling and Manly Identity in Derbyshire's Dark Peak, 1880s–1920s', *Historical Journal* 49, no. 4 (2006), 1125–1153.

66 Salveson, *Socialism with a Northern Accent*, 12–15.

67 Cecil Delisle Burns, 'Ideals of Democracy in England', *International Journal of Ethics* 27, no. 4 (July 1917), 432–445.

68 Hill, *Nelson*, 10–44.

69 Stan Iveson and Roger Brown, *A Monument to a Movement* (Preston: Independent Labour Party Publications, 1987), 8.

70 Hill, *Nelson*, 50; Stan Iveson and Roger Brown, A *Monument to a Movement*, 17.

71 Zoe Lawson, 'Wheels within Wheels – the Lancashire Cycling Clubs of the 1880s and 90s', in *Lancashire Local Studies in Honour of Diana Winterbotham*, ed. Alan G. Crosby (Preston: Carnegie, 1993), 123–145.

72 *ILP Clarion House Jubilee Year 1912–1962* (National Labour Party, 1962).

73 Lawson 'Wheels', 139.

74 Pye, *Fellowship is Life*, 42–45.

75 *Nelson ILP Clarion House History* http://www.clarionhouse.org.uk/history.htm

76 Iveson and Brown, *A Monument to a Movement*.

77 Iveson and Brown, *A Monument to a Movement*, 24; *Ribble Valley Clarion Club House & Environs* [pamphlet] pamphlet c. 1914; Ribble Valley Clarion Club House, *Complete Amendment of Rules, October 1915* [pamphlet].

78 James Johnston, 'The Work of an Educational Department in a Co-operative Society', *Manchester and Salford Equitable Co-operative Society's Monthly Herald* 86 (1896), 8–10.

79 Owen Balmforth, *The Huddersfield Industrial Society: History of Fifty Years' Progress 1870–1910* (Manchester: Co-operative Wholesale Society, n.d.), 214–227.

80 Salveson, *Socialism with a Northern Accent*, 50.

81 Denis Pye, 'Bolton Socialist Party and Club: 100 Years at Wood Street, 1905–2005', *North West Labour History* 30 (2005), 8–11.

82 Bolton Social Democratic Foundation Minute Book, 14 April 1896–23 April 1901.

83 Foley, *A Bolton Childhood*, 69.

84 Ernest Barker, *Political Thought in England 1848–1914* (London: Oxford University Press, 1928).

85 MacIver, *Community*, 112.

Chapter 6

1 Cecil Delisle Burns, *Leisure in the Modern World* (London: Allen and Unwin, 1932), 71.

2   See for example F.R. Leavis, *Mass Civilisation and Minority Culture* (Cambridge: Minority Press, 1930); Q.D. Leavis, *Fiction and the Reading Public* (London: Chatto and Windus, 1932).

3   John Stevenson, *British Society 1914–45* (Harmondsworth: Penguin, 1984), 381.

4   London School of Economics, *New Survey of London Life and Labour, Volume Nine Life and Leisure* (London, P.S. King, 1935), 1–5.

5   Mass Observation Worktown Collection, Box 1-C 'Draft Articles about the Worktown Project'.

6   *A Short History of the Working Men's Club and Institute Union* (London: WMCIU, 1927), 78.

7   *New Survey of London, Volume Nine*, 125, 133–135.

8   Ross McKibbin, *Classes and Cultures in England 1918–1951* (Oxford: Oxford University Press, 1998), 419.

9   D. Caradog Jones, *The Social Survey of Merseyside Volume Three* (London: Hodder and Stoughton, 1934), 279.

10 Mass Observation Worktown Collection, Box 35 'Cinema-Going Survey'; Box 36 'Cinema Observations'.

11 Hill, *Sport, Leisure and Culture*; Jones, *Social Survey of Merseyside Volume Three*, 279.

12 London School of Economics, *New Survey of London Life and Labour Volume One 'Forty years of change'* (London: P.S. King, 1935), 279. See also Peter Swain, '"Bolton against All England for a Cool Hundred": Crown Green Bowls in South Lancashire, 1787–1914', *Sport in History* 33, no. 2 (2013), 146–168.

13 'Synthetic Sport', *Social Service Bulletin* 9, no. 1 (1928), 6–7.

14 McKibbin, *Classes and Cultures*, 362–365.

15 John Nauright and Charles Parrish (eds), *Sports Around the World: History, Culture, and Practice, Volume Two* (Santa Barbara: ABC-CLIO, 2012), 9.

16 Robert Snape, 'All-in Wrestling in Inter-War Britain: Science and Spectacle in Mass Observation's "Worktown"', *International Journal of the History of Sport* 30, no. 2 (2013), 1418–1435, DOI: 10.1080/09523367.2013.804812

17 Mass Observation *The Pub and the People* (London: The Cresset Library, 1987), 217, 271–312.

18 Gambling remained a social evil to the 1924 Conference on Christian Politics, Economics and Citizenship and even the football pools were the topic of a sermon delivered in Bolton in the late 1930s. *Report on the Conference on Christian Politics, Economics and Citizenship* (London: Longmans Green, 1924), 65–81; Mass Observation Worktown Collection Box 4F 'Gambling'.

19 Jack Williams, 'Recreational Cricket in the Bolton Area Between the Wars', in *Sport and the Working Class in Modern Britain*, ed. Richard Holt (Manchester: Manchester University Press, 1990), 101–120.

20 Martin Pugh, *State and Society. A Social and Political History of Britain since 1870* 5th ed., (London: Bloomsbury, 2017), 292–293.

21 Dawson, 'Working Class Consumers and the Campaign for Holidays with Pay', 277–305.

22 Annebella Pollen, *The Kindred of the Kibbo Kift: Intellectual Barbarians* (London: Donlan Books, 2015); David Fowler, *Youth Culture in Modern Britain, c. 1920–c. 1970* (Basingstoke: Palgrave Macmillan, 2008), 46–50.

Chapter 7

1 J. Davis, *A History of Britain 1885–1939* (Basingstoke: Macmillan, 1999), 137; Tombs, *The English and their History*, 656–658.

2 Arthur Marwick, *The Deluge. British Society and the First World War*, 2nd ed. (Basingstoke: Macmillan, 1991), 279–280.

3 George Orwell, 'Inside the Whale', in *Essays*, ed. John Carey (London: Everyman, 2002), 211–248.

4 Demos, *The Meaning of Reconstruction* (London: The Atheneaum Literature Department, 1918), 5.

5 Labour Party, *Labour and the New Social Order: A Report on Reconstruction* (London: Labour Party, 1918).

6 H. Babbington-Smith, 'Reconstruction in Britain Following the War', *Scientific Monthly* 8, no. 4 (1919), 298–305.

7 'The King's Speech' *Times* [London] 12 February 1919, 11. *The Times Digital Archive*. Accessed 8 August 2016.

8 'Labour Policy Declared' *Times* [London] 26 October 1922, 14. *The Times Digital Archive*. Accessed 8 August 2016.

9 'Workmen and Employers' *Times* [London] 17 February 1919, 11+. *The Times Digital Archive*. Accessed 8 August 2016.

10 A.G. Johnson, *Leisure for Workmen and National Wealth* (London: P.S. King, 1908); G. Cross, *A Quest for Time. The Reduction of Work in Britain and France, 1840–1940* (London: University of California Press, 1989), 131–132.

11 William Lever, 1st Viscount Leverhulme. *The Six Hour Day and other Industrial Questions*, 2nd ed. (London: George Allen and Unwin, 1919).

12 L.T. Hobhouse, *The Labour Movement* (London: Fisher Unwin, 1906), 8.

13 Liberal Party, *Liberal Policy in the Task of Political and Social Reconstruction* (London: Liberal Party, 1918), 71.

14 Dawson, 'Working Class Consumers and the Campaign for Holidays with Pay', 277–305.

15 S. Webb and H. Cox, *The Eight Hours Day* (London: Walter Scott, 1891), 71.

16 John A. Hobson, *Work and Wealth: A Human Valuation* (London: Macmillan, 1914), 236, 248–249.

17 Great Britain. Committee on Adult Education. *Industrial and Social Conditions in Relation to Adult Education* (London: HMSO, 1918).

18 Hugh Cunningham, *Time, Work and Leisure: Life Changes in England since 1700*, (Manchester: Manchester University Press, 2014), 100–101; Labour Party, *Labour and the New Social Order*.

19 Cecil Delisle Burns, *Industry and Civilization* (London: Allen and Unwin, 1925), 111–112; *Modern Civilization on Trial* (London: George Allen & Unwin, 1931), 226–227; Paul Greenhalgh, 'Education, Entertainment and Politics: Lessons from the Great International Exhibitions', in *The New Museology*, ed. Peter Vero (London: Reaktion Books, 1989), 74–98.

20 London School of Economics, *New Survey of London Life and Labour, Volume Nine. Life and Leisure.*

21 France, for example had a Minister of Leisure and Sports; see Cristina Fusetti, 'Social Capital and Sport Governance in France', in *Social Capital and Sport Governance in Europe*, eds Margaret Groeneveld and Barrie Houlihan (Abingdon: Routledge, 2011), 108–129.

22 Harris, 'Political Thought and the Welfare State 1870–1940'.

23 Euan McArthur, *Scotland, CEMA and the Arts Council 1919–1967* (Abingdon: Routledge, 2016).

24 Carter, *T.H. Green and the Development of Ethical Socialism*; Marc Stears, *Progressives, Pluralists and the Problems of the State. Ideologies of Reform in the United States and Britain 1906–1926* (Oxford: Oxford University Press, 2002), 44, notes that Sidney Webb also recognized twentieth-century socialism's debt to the philosophy of T.H. Green.

25 For further detail on social idealism and its influence on the new liberalism see Michael Freeden, *The New Liberalism: An Ideology of Social Reform* (Oxford: Clarendon Press, 1978) and 'Civil Society and the Good Citizen: Competing Conceptions of Citizenship in Twentieth-century Britain', in *Civil Society in British History. Ideas, Identities, Institutions,* ed. Jose Harris (Oxford: Oxford University Press, 2004), 275–291; W.J. Mander, *British Idealism: A History* (Oxford: Oxford University Press, 2011); Harris, 'Political Thought and the Welfare State 1870–1940', 116–141; Tom Hulme, 'Putting the City Back into Citizenship: Civics Education and Local Government in Britain, 1918–45', *Twentieth Century British History* 26, no. 1 (2015), 26–51.

26 T.H. Green, *Lectures on the Principles of Political Obligation* (1882; London: Longmans, Green, 1941), 244.

27 Green, *Lectures on the Principles of Political Obligation*, 244.

28 Green, *Lectures on the Principles of Political Obligation*, 246.

29 Henry Stead and Edith Hall (eds), *Greek and Roman Classics in the British Struggle for Social Reform* (London: Bloomsbury, 2015).

30 Eugenia Low 'The Concept of Citizenship in Twentieth Century Britain: Analysing Contexts of Development', in P. Catterall, W. Kaiser and U. Walton-Jordan (eds), *Reforming the Constitution. Debates in Twentieth-century Britain* (London: Frank Cass, 2000), 179–200.

31 Freeden, *The New Liberalism*, 113–114.

32 Melvin Richter, *The Politics of Conscience. T.H. Green and His Age* (London: Weidenfeld and Nicolson, 1964), 295–296.

33 Harris, *Private Lives, Public Spirit*, 228.

34 Richter, *The Politics of Conscience*, 153.

35 Freeden, *The New Liberalism*, 57.

36 Edward Caird, *Lay Sermons and Addresses delivered in the Hall of Balliol College, Oxford* (Glasgow: James Maclehose, 1907).

37 Harris, 'Political Thought and the Welfare State 1870–1940', 138.

38 Appointed lecturers to the South Place Ethical Society included several figures featured here, amongst them Cecil Delisle Burns, John A. Hobson and Bertrand Russell. The *International Journal of Ethics* was founded in America and enabled transatlantic discussion of idealism.

39 Clement Attlee, *The Social Worker* (London, G. Bell, 1920), 16.

40 Richard Alston, 'The Space of Politics. Classics, Utopia and the Defence of Order', in *Greek and Roman Classics in the British Struggle for Social Reform*, eds Henry Stead and Edith Hall (London: Bloomsbury, 2015), 183–196.

41 Peter Womack, 'Dialogue and Leisure at the Fin de Siecle', *Cambridge Quarterly* 24, no. 1 (2013), 134–156.

42 Bernard Bosanquet, 'The Place of Leisure in Life', *International Journal of Ethics* 21, no. 2 (1911), 153–165.

43 Aristotle, *The Nichomachean Ethics, Book Six, Intellectual Virtue* (Oxford: Oxford University Press, 1980), 1140b.

44 Bosanquet, 'The Place of Leisure in Life'.

45 George Sabine, 'The Social Origin of Absolute Idealism', *Journal of Philosophy, Psychology and Scientific Methods* 12, no. 7 (1915), 169–177.

46 Den Otter, *British Idealism and Social Explanation*, 4, 208.

47 Cecil Delisle Burns, 'Poverty and Reconstruction', *International Journal of Ethics* 28, no. 3 (1918), 393–405; Alfred Hopkinson, *Rebuilding Britain: A Survey of Problems of Reconstruction After the War* (London: Cassell, 1918).

48 Charles A. Ellwood, 'The Social Problem and the Present', *Sociological Review* 8, no. 1 (1915), 1–14.

49 MacIver, *Community*, 217.

50 H.A.L Fisher, *The Common Weal* (Oxford: Clarendon Press, 1924), 22.

51 Bertrand Russell, *Principles of Social Reconstruction* (London: George Allen & Unwin, 1916), 94, 240.

52 Thanassis Samaras, 'Leisure in Classical Greek Society', in *The Palgrave Handbook of Leisure Theory*, eds Karl Spracklen, Brett Lashua, Erin Sharpe and Spencer Swain (London: Palgrave Macmillan, 2017), 229–247.

53 Aristotle, *The Nichomachean Ethics. Book 1, The Good for Man*, 3–22.

54 Melissa Lane, *Greek and Roman Political Ideas* (London: Penguin, 2014), 192–213.

55 Aristotle *Politics*, Book 1, The Political Association and its Relation to other Associations, Chapter 2, 1252b8. In *The Politics of Aristotle*, ed. E. Barker (Oxford, Clarendon Press, 1946), 4–5.

56 Aristotle, *Politics*, Book 7, Political Ideals and Educational Principles, Chapter 3, 1325b10. In Barker, *Politics of Aristotle*, 288–289.

57 Aristotle, *Politics*, Book 8, The Training of Youth, Chapter 1, 1337b. In Barker, *Politics of Aristotle*, 332–336.

58 Benjamin Kline Hunnicutt, 'Plato on Leisure, Play, and Learning', *Leisure Sciences* 12, no. 2 (1990), 211–227.

59 London School of Economics, *New Survey of London Life and Labour, Volume Nine, Life and Leisure*, 6.

60 Ernest Barker, *The Uses of Leisure* (London: World Association for Adult Education, 1936).

61 Veronica Huta, 'Eudaimonia', in *The Oxford Handbook of Happiness*, eds Susan A. David, Ilona Bonniwell and Amanda Conley Ayers (Oxford: Oxford University Press, 2013), 201–213.

62 Harris, 'Political Thought and the Welfare State 1870–1940', 127.

63 Bernard Bosanquet, 'The Duties of Citizenship', in *Aspects of the Social Problem*, ed. B. Bosanquet (London: Macmillan, 1895), 1–27, 16.

64 Harold Laski, 'The Pluralistic State', *Philosophical Review* 28, no. 6 (1919), 562–575, 572.

65 Ernest Barker, *The Political Thought of Plato and Aristotle* (London: Methuen, 1906), 226–228; *The Uses of Leisure*, 6.

66 Fisher, *The Common Weal*, 19.

67 Discussion of modern leisure in terms of Aristotle and Plato is hampered by semantics and translation; a useful guide is Hunnicutt 'Plato on Leisure, Play, and Learning'.

68 The title of Chapter 12 of Burns' *Leisure in the Modern World*.

69 Thorstein Veblen, *The Theory of the Leisure Class: An Economic Study in the Evolution of Institutions* (New York: Macmillan, 1899); John A. Hobson, *The Social Problem, Life and Work* (London: James Nisbet, 1902); *Work and Wealth*, 141.

70 Masterman, *The Condition of England*, 40–42, 50.

71 W.D. Rubinstein, 'Britain's elites in the Inter-War period 1918–39', *Contemporary British History* 12, no.1 (1998), 1–18.

72 George Orwell, 'The Lion and the Unicorn', in *The Penguin Essays of George Orwell*, ed. Michael Crick (London: Penguin, 1984), 138–187.

73 Robert Graves and Alan Hodge, *The Long Weekend: A Social History of Great Britain 1918-1939* (1940; London: Sphere Books, 1991), 124; McKibbin, *Classes and Cultures*, 22–23.

74 McKibbin, *Classes and Cultures*, 106.

75 John A. Hobson, *John Ruskin Social Reformer*, 3rd ed. (London: James Nisbet, 1904).

76 John Ruskin, 'Essays on Political Economy', in *Unto this Last and Other Essays* (London: Dent, 1907), 197–207.

77 John Ruskin, 'Unto this Last', in *Unto this Last and Other Essays* (London: Dent, 1907), 107–193.

78 Hobson, *The Social Problem*, 80.

79 Hobson, *Work and Wealth*, 228.

80 Lawrence Goldman, *The Life of R.H. Tawney. Socialism and History* (London: Bloomsbury, 2014), 311.

81 R.H. Tawney, *Equality* (1931; London: George Allen & Unwin, 1952), 57.

82 R.H. Tawney, *The Acquisitive Society* (1920; New York: Dover, 2004), 130–137.

83 Hobson, *Work and Wealth*, 156.

84 Hobson, *Work and Wealth*, 236.

85 Hobson, *Work and Wealth*, 249.

86 Hobson, *Work and Wealth*, 7.

87 John A. Hobson, *Problems of a New World* (London: G. Allen and Unwin, 1921), 54.

88 G.V. Kracht, 'Social Ideals and Social Progress', *International Journal of Ethics* 27, no. 4 (1917), 472–484.

89 *Report on the Conference on Christian Politics, Economics and Citizenship. Report on Leisure* (London: Longmans Green, 1924), 19–20.

90 Storm Jameson, *The Soul of Man in the Age of Leisure* (London: Stanley Nott, 1935), Pamphlets on the New Economics no. 17, 25–26.

91 Henry Durant, *The Problem of Leisure* (London: Routledge, 1938), 44–45.

92 'Dr. C. Delisle Burns, Labour Thinker and Lecturer' *Times*, 23 January 1942, p. 7, col. E.

93 The essence of social idealism was neatly captured in the inscription to the copy of *Industry and Civilization* Burns presented to B.S Rowntree, which reads 'in the hope that theory may be practically useful'; author's personal copy.

94 C. Delisle Burns, 'The Moral Effects of War and Peace', *International Journal of Ethics* 25, no. 3 (1915), 317–327; 'When Peace Breaks Out', *International Journal of Ethics* 26, no. 1 (1915), 82–91; 'Productivity and Reconstruction', *International Journal of Ethics* 28, no. 3 (1918), 393–405.

95 Delisle Burns, *Leisure in the Modern World*.

96 Delisle Burns, *Modern Civilization on Trial*.

97   C. Delisle Burns, *Democracy: Its Defects and Advantages* (London: George Allen & Unwin, 1929).

98   Delisle Burns, *Industry and Civilization*.

99   Delisle Burns, *Leisure in the Modern World*, 14.

100 Tawney, *Equality*, 153.

101 Delisle Burns, *Leisure in the Modern World*, 163.

102 Cecil Delisle Burns, 'Art and Understanding', *Social Service Review* 11, no. 8 (1930), 165–170.

103 Alexandra Harris, *Romantic Moderns: English Writers, Artists and the Imagination from Virginia Woolf to John Piper* (London: Thames Hudson, 2010), 169–192.

104 C. Delisle Burns, *Democracy*, 248.

105 Delisle Burns, *Leisure in the Modern World*, passim.

106 Todd, 'Social Transformation'.

107 See for example A.E. Zimmern, 'The Control of Industry after the War', in *The Re-organization of Industry* (Oxford: Ruskin College, 1916); R.S. Lynd, and H.M. Lynd, *Middletown: A Study in American Culture* (New York: Harcourt Brace, 1929), 271; Delisle Burns, *Industry and Civilization*; Durant, *Problem of Leisure*, 26; Paul T. Frankl, *Machine-Made Leisure* (London: Harper, 1932), 169; B. Seebohm Rowntree, *Poverty and Progress: A Second Social Survey of York* (London: Longmans, Green & Co. 1941), 477. Further American works include G.A. Lundberg, M. Komarovsky and M.A. McInerny, *Leisure: A Suburban Study* (New York: Columbia University Press, 1934) and M. Neumeyer and E. Neumeyer, *Leisure and Recreation: A Study of Leisure and Recreation in their Sociological Aspects* (New York: Barnes & Co., 1936).

108 E.M. Forster, 'The Machine Stops', in *Collected Short Stories of E.M. Forster* (London: Sidgwick and Jackson, 1965), 115–158.

109 Hartley Burr Alexander, 'The Fear of Machines', *International Journal of Ethics* 28, no. 1 (October 1917), 80–93.

110 *New Survey of London Volume Nine*, 9.

111 Durant, *Problem of Leisure*, 17–22.

112 Jameson, *The Soul of Man in the Age of Leisure*, 14.

113 *New Survey of London Volume Nine*, 10.

114 Durant, *Problem of Leisure*, 141.

115 Fisher, *Common Weal*, 94.

116 C.E. Clift, 'The Leisure Occupation of Young People', in *Reconstruction and Social Service: Report of a Conference called by the National Council of Social Service* (London: P.S. King, 1920), 127–136. See also Brad Beaven 'Going to the Cinema: Mass Commercial Leisure and Working-class Cultures in 1930s Britain', in *Leisure and Cultural Conflict in Twentieth-Century Britain*, ed. Brett Bebber (Manchester: Manchester University Press, 2012), 63–83.

117 Mary Ward Settlement, *Annual Report* 1923, 4.

118 CUKT, *The Film in National Life* (London: George Allen and Unwin, 1932), 39, 83.

119 Rooff, *Youth and Leisure*, 38, 79.

120 F.R. Leavis, *Mass Civilization and Minority Culture*.

121 Q.D. Leavis, *Fiction and the Reading Public*, 209.

122 Clive Bell, *Civilization: An Essay* (London: Chatto and Windus, 1929), 205–231.

123 Orwell, 'The Lion and the Unicorn'.

124 Mass Observation, *The Pub and the People* (1943, London: The Cresset Library, 1987), 76–79.

125 John Ruskin, *Time and Tide*, 17.

126 Arthur Clutton Brock, in NCSS *Report on the National Conference on the Leisure of the People* (Manchester, 1919); Durant, *Problem of Leisure*, 1.

127 William Morris, 'How We Live and How We Might Live', in *News from Nowhere and Selected Writings and Designs*, ed. Asa Briggs (1888; Harmondsworth: Penguin, 1962), 158–180.

128 Morris, *News from Nowhere*.

129 William Morris, 'Useful Work versus Useless Toil', in *News from Nowhere*, 117–136.

130 Morris, 'How We Live', 176.

131 Morris, 'How We Live', 173.

132 Hobson, *The Social Problem*, vi.

133 Hobson, *Work and Wealth*, 234–235.

134 Constance Harris, *The Use of Leisure in Bethnal Green: A Survey of Social Conditions in the Borough 1925 to 1926* (London: The Lindsey Press, 1927), 39, 54.

135 National Institute of Industrial Psychology, *Leisure Pursuits Outside the Factory. An Account of an Investigation into the Leisure Pursuits Outside the Family Circle in a County Town, a Rural District and in a Holiday Camp* (London: National Institute of Industrial Psychology, 1939); Walter Greenwood, *How the Other Man Lives* (London: Labour Book Service, n.d.), 198.

136 Lewis Mumford, *Technics and Civilization* (1934. London: Routledge and Kegan Paul, 1955), 303.

137 Frankl, *Machine-made Leisure*, 169–170.

138 Delisle Burns, *Modern Civilization on Trial*, 207.

139 Delisle Burns, *Modern Civilization on Trial*, 114.

140 Chris Hilliard, 'Producers by Hand and Brain: Working-Class Writers and Left-Wing Publishers in 1930s Britain', *Journal of Modern History* 78, no. 1 (2006), 37–64.

141 *Unity Theatre Handbook*, Warwick Modern Records, Archive of Union of Communication Workers, MRC MSS. 148/UCW/6/13/42/9.

142 *The Red Stage. Organ of the Workers' Theatre Movement*, no. 1 (1931), 4. MRC MSS. 212/X/3/4.

143 Ruth and Edmund Frow, 'The Workers' Theatre Movement in Manchester and Salford, 1931–1940', *North West Labour History* 17 (1992–93), 66–71.

144 Delisle Burns, *Leisure in the Modern World*, 160.

145 Lynd and Lynd, *Middletown*, 269.

146 John Russell, *Man and the Machine. Essex Hall Lecture, 1931* (London: Lindsey Press, 1931), 25. The Essex Hall Lectures were presented under the auspices of the General Assembly of Unitarian and Free Christian Churches.

147 Waters, *British Socialists and the Politics of Popular Culture*, 187–188.

148 Delisle Burns, *Leisure in the Modern World*, 70–71.

149 Delisle Burns, *Modern Civilization on Trial*, 287.

150 Chris Rojek, '"Leisure" in the writings of Walter Benjamin', *Leisure Studies* 16, no. 3 (1997), 155–171.

151 Delisle Burns, *Modern Civilization on Trial*, 194–195.

152 Mass Observation Archive Worktown Papers Box 40B, Mill Work.

153 See Rooff, *Youth and Leisure*, 78.

154 D. Le Mahieu, *A Culture for Democracy: Mass Communication and the Cultivated Mind in Britain between the Wars* (Oxford: Oxford University Press, 1998), 322–323; See also McKibbin, *Classes and Cultures*, 527–536; Hill, *Sport, Leisure and Culture in Twentieth Century Britain*; Stevenson, *British Society 1914–45*.

Chapter 8

1 Peter Grant, 'Voluntarism and the Impact of the First World War', in *The Ages of Voluntarism: How We Got to the Big Society*, ed. M. Hilton and J. McKay (Oxford: British Academy, 2011), 27–46.

2 Demos, *The Meaning of Reconstruction*.

3 J.M. Heighton, *The Place of the Voluntary Worker in Civic Life and Social Work* (London: Simpkin Marshall, 1918), 29, 33–34.

4 A.J.P. Taylor, *English History 1914–1945* (Oxford: Oxford University Press, 1992), 175. See also Rochester, *Rediscovering Voluntary Action*, 69–84; G. Finlayson, 'A Moving Frontier: Voluntarism and the State in British Social Welfare, 1911–1949', *Twentieth Century British History* 1, no. 2 (1990), 183–206.

5 George Orwell, 'The Lion and the Unicorn', in *Essays*, ed. John Carey (London: Everyman, 2002), 291–348.

6 'Training in Social Service', *Times*, 28 December 1915, 3; B. Wollenberg, *Christian Social Thought in Great Britain between the Wars* (London: University Press of America, 1997), 28.

7 See for example Nick Hayes, 'Counting Civil Society: Deconstructing Elite Participation in the English Provincial City 1900-1950', *Urban History* 40, no. 22

(2013), 287–314; Laura Balderstone, 'Semi-detached Britain? Reviewing Suburban Engagement in Twentieth-century Society', *Urban History* 41, no. 1 (2014), 141–160.

8 Rooff, *Youth and Leisure.*

9 Gertrude Williams, 'The Training and Recruitment of Social Workers', in *Voluntary Social Services since 1918*, ed. Henry Mess (London: Kegan Paul, Trench, Trubner, 1947), 214–246.

10 Victor Branford and Patrick Geddes, *The Making of the Future: Our Social Inheritance* (London: Williams and Norgate, 1919), 379. Civic Societies were further evidence of the continuing influence of Green's social philosophy in the post-First World War years; see Hulme, 'Putting the City Back into Citizenship'.

11 Arthur Greenwood, *The Education of the Citizen* (London: National Adult School Union, 1920), 25.

12 Paton, *Applied Christianity: A Civic League.*

13 Lucy Hewitt, *A Brief History of the Civic Society Movement* (Canterbury: Civic Voice, 2014).

14 Lucy Hewitt, 'Associational Culture and the Shaping of Urban Space: Civic Societies in Britain before 1960', *Urban History* 39, no. 4 (2012), 590–606.

15 Sybella Branford, 'Citizenship and the Civic Association', *Sociological Review* 13, no. 4 (1921), 228–234. Sybella Branford worked with Henrietta Barnett in the planning of Hampstead Garden Suburb and on various co-operative housing schemes.

16 Branford, 'Citizenship and the Civic Association'; A. Collins, 'The Organization of Voluntary Social Service in Relation to the Work of Statutory Authorities', in *Reconstruction and Social Service: Report of a Conference called by the National Council of Social Service*, ed. in National Council of Social Service (London: P.S. King, 1920), 151–165.

17 J.B. Priestley, *English Journey* (London: Heinemann, 1934), 197–198.

18 Helen McCarthy, 'Parties, Voluntary Associations and Democratic Politics in Inter-War Britain', *Historical Journal* 50, no. 4 (2007), 891–912.

19 Beaumont, *Housewives and Citizens.*

20 Helen McCarthy, 'Service Clubs, Citizenship and Equality: Gender Relations and Middle-Class Associations in Britain between the Wars', *Historical Research* 81, no. 213 (2008), 531–552.

21 Goldman, *The Life of R.H. Tawney*, 110.

22 COPEC, *Report on The Social Function of the Church*, 197–198.

23 COPEC, *Report on Leisure* in *COPEC Commission Reports Volume 4* (London. Longmans, Green, 1924). The committee responsible for this report was chaired by the Rev. T. Pym, Head of Cambridge House and included James Adderley, former Head of Oxford House, Reginald Kennedy-Cox, Warden of the Dockland

Settlements and C.M.L. Wickham, Warden of the Bishop Creighton Settlement in Fulham.

24 COPEC *Report on Leisure*, 24.

25 Bolton Public Library Oral History Project, Tape Catalogue 155a Ab/SS/1B/004.

26 COPEC, *Report on Leisure*, 15.

27 Charlotte Wildman, 'Religious Selfhoods and the City in Inter-war Manchester', *Urban History* 38, no. 1 (2011), 103–123.

28 Coit, *Neighbourhood Guilds*, 96.

29 Margaret Brasnett, *Voluntary Social Action: A History of the National Council of Social Service 1919–1969* (London: National Council of Social Service, 1969), 22–24.

30 Brasnett, *Voluntary Social Action*, 27.

31 National Council of Social Service, *Reconstruction and Social Service* (London: P.S. King, 1920).

32 Margaret Simey, *Charity Re-Discovered*, 143–145.

33 *Manchester Guardian*, 'Co-ordinating Social Agencies', 7 April, 1920, 8; C.E. Clift, 'The Leisure Occupation of Young People', 127–137; Arthur Collins, 'The Organization of Voluntary Social Service', 151–165.

34 Collins, 'The Organization of Voluntary Social Service'.

35 Brasnett, *Voluntary Social Action*, 41.

36 *Manchester Guardian*, 'The People's Leisure: A Forthcoming Manchester Conference' October 15 1919, p. 3.

37 NCSS *Report on the National Conference on the Leisure of the People*.

38 G.D.H Cole, 'A Retrospect of the History of Voluntary Social Service', in *Voluntary Social Services*, ed. Bourdillon, 11–30, 24.

39 NCSS *Monthly Bulletin* Series 1, no. 1 (1920), 1. See also Jeremy Burchardt, *Paradise Lost. Rural Idyll and Social Change in England since 1800* (London: I.B. Tauris, 2002), 144–7.

40 NCSS *Monthly Bulletin* Series. 1, no. 4 (October 1920), 66.

41 NCSS *Monthly Bulletin* Series. 1, no. 4 (October 1920), 66.

42 Victor Branford and Patrick Geddes, *The Coming Polity. A Study in Reconstruction* (London: Williams and Norgate, 1917), 18.

43 Liverpool Council of Voluntary Aid, *Report on the Uses of Leisure in Liverpool* (Liverpool, 1923).

44 Harris, *The Use of Leisure in Bethnal Green*.

45 *New Survey of London Life and Labour Volume One*, 'Forty years of Change', 279.

46 Jones, *Social Survey of Merseyside Volume Three*, 265, 309.

47 Church of England, *The Church and Social Service* (London: Society for the Promotion of Christian Knowledge, 1920), 20, 25.

48 Liverpool Council of Voluntary Aid, *Report on the Uses of Leisure in Liverpool* (Liverpool, 1923).

49 Jones, *Social Survey of Merseyside Volume Three*, 305–306.

50 Harold Perkin, *The Rise of Professional Society: England since 1800* (London: Routledge, 1989), 356.

51 *The Equipment of the Workers: An Enquiry by the St. Philip's Settlement [YMCA Sheffield] Education and Research Society into the Adequacy of the Adult Manual Workers for the Discharge of their Responsibilities as Heads of Households, Producers and Citizens* (London: George Allen and Unwin, 1919); see also Brad Beaven and John Griffiths, 'Creating the Exemplary Citizen: The Changing Notion of Citizenship in Britain 1870–1939', *Contemporary British History* 22, no. 2 (2008), 203–225. DOI: 10.1080/13619460701189559

52 The enhancement of social capital became a major objective of social policy under the New Labour Government of 1997; it was concerned with the capacity of a neighbourhood community to function without external intervention and thus with social citizenship.

53 See Jeremy Burchardt, 'Reconstructing the Rural Community: Village Halls and the National Council of Social Service 1919 to 1939', *Rural History* 10, no. 2 (1999), 193–216. DOI: http://dx.doi.org/10.1017/S0956793300001783; 'State and Society in the English Countryside: The Rural Community Movement 1918–39', *Rural History* 23, no. 1 (2012), 81–106; 'Agricultural History, Rural History or Countryside History' *Historical Journal* 50, 2 (2007), 465–481; P. Brassley, J. Burchardt and P. Thompson, P. (eds), *The English Countryside between the Wars: Regeneration or Decline?* (Woodbridge: Boydell, 2006); T. Wild, *Village England: A Social History of the Countryside* (London: I.B. Tauris, 2004).

54 John Stevenson, 'The Countryside, Planning, and Civil Society in Britain, 1926–1947', in *Civil Society in British History*, ed. Jose Harris, 191–211.

55 Matless, *Landscape and Englishness*, 276.

56 Burchardt, *Paradise Lost*, 140–144.

57 A.W. Ashby, *The Rural Problem. Social Reconstruction Pamphlets No. 1* (London: The Athenaeum, 1917). Ashby completed a diploma in Economics and Political Science at Ruskin College in 1911 and founded the Institute for Research in Agricultural Economics at Oxford. From 1917–1919 he worked in the Board of Agriculture and Fisheries. As an economist his recognition of the need for more leisure and voluntary social service indicates their wider importance to social reconstruction during the war.

58 'Village Clubs. Fight against Rural Snobbery', *Times*, 19 November 1921, 5.

59 Burchardt, 'Reconstructing the Rural Community'.

60 Henry W. Wolff, *Rural Reconstruction* (London: Selwyn and Blount, 1921), 16.

61 'Idea of Village Hall', *Times*, September 9, 1921, 4; 'Happy Village – Village Clubs Association', *Times*, May 18 1922, 17.

62 Henry A. Mess, and Constance Braithwaite, 'The Great Philanthropic Trusts', in
    H. Mess, *Voluntary Social Services since 1918*, ed. Gertrude Williams. London: Kegan
    Paul, Trench, Trubner, 1947, 172–187.

63 Teresa Smith, 'Grace Hadow', *Dictionary of National Biography*.

64 Howard Edwin Bracey, *English Rural Life. Village Activities, Organisations and
    Institutions* (London: Routledge & Kegan Paul, 1959), 126.

65 Jeremy Burchardt, 'Rethinking the Rural Idyll'. *Cultural and Social History* 8, no. 1
    (2011), 73–94; A.F.C. Bourdillon, 'Voluntary Organizations to Facilitate Co-operation
    and Co-ordination', in *Voluntary Social Services*, ed. Bourdillon, 162–193.

66 Bourdillon, *Voluntary Social Services*, 182–183.

67 Thomas Kelly, *History of Public Libraries in Great Britain 1845–1975* (London: The
    Library Association, 1977), 211–212.

68 CUKT *Annual Report and Minutes*, 1918.

69 Bill Luckin, *Death and Survival in Urban Britain: Disease, Pollution and Environment
    1800–1950* (London: I.B. Tauris, 2015), 142.

70 Carole King, 'The Rise and Decline of Village Reading Rooms', *Rural History* 20, no. 2
    (2009), 163–186. doi:10.1017/S0956793309990033

71 Lawrence Weaver, *Village Clubs and Halls* (London: George Newnes, 1920).

72 Bourdillon, 'Voluntary Organizations to Facilitate Co-operation and
    Co-ordination'.

73 Brasnett, *Voluntary Social Action*, 50. This committee included W.G.S Adams,
    S. Bostock, ex-Chairman of the Agricultural Organisation Society, Lady Denman,
    President of the National Federation of Women's Institutes and R. Hart Synnot of the
    Horace Plunkett Foundation.

74 Mess, *Voluntary Social Services*, 103.

75 Burchardt, 'Reconstructing the Rural Community'.

76 Ashby, *The Rural Problem*, 36.

77 F.R. Leavis and Denys Thompson, *Culture and Environment: the Training of Critical
    Awareness* (1933; London: Chatto and Windus, 1959), 1–2.

78 C. Osborn, 'Women's Village Councils', *Charity Organisation Society Review*, no. 256
    (1918), 139–144. The first was formed at Findon, Sussex, in 1917.

79 Brasnett, *Voluntary Social Action*, 32–33.

80 Bracey, *English Rural Life, Village Activities*, 144.

81 Beaumont, *Housewives and Citizens*, 26.

82 Rooff, *Youth and Leisure*, 72.

83 W.E. Williams 'Adult Education', in Henry Mess, *Voluntary Social Services since 1918*,
    edited by Gertrude Williams, 146–171. London: Kegan Paul, Trench, Trubner, 1947.

84 Nicola Verdon, 'The Modern Countrywoman: Farm Women, Domesticity and Social
    Change in Interwar Britain', *History Workshop Journal* 70, (2010), 86–107.

85 NCSS, *Annual Report* 1924, 15.

86 Mess, *Voluntary Social Services*, 102; NCSS *Annual Report*, 1924; CUKT, *Annual Report and Minutes*, 1927. The presentation of music in villages was not a new development; Oxford University Musical Club had provided penny concerts in North Oxfordshire Villages before the First World War, with performances attracting mostly working-class audiences of up to 150 people; see Rose, *The Intellectual Life of the British Working Classes*, 198.

87 National Council of Social Service, 'A Rural Community Council', in *The Reconstruction of Country Life, being Notes on a Conference of Rural Community Councils held at Oxford in 1925* (London: National Council of Social Service, 1925), 39–43.

88 NCSS, *Village Halls. Their Construction and Management* (London: National Council of Social Service, n.d.), 12.

89 CUKT *Annual Report* 1920, 6.

90 William Henry Hadow, *Report Upon the History and Prospects of Music in the United Kingdom* (Dunfermline: Carnegie United Kingdom Trust, 1921).

91 Hadow, *British Music*, 6, 8, 13.

92 Luckin, *Death and Survival in Urban Britain*, 143.

93 CUKT *Annual Report and Minutes* 1923; Robert Snape, 'Continuity, Change and Performativity in Leisure: English Folk Dance and Modernity 1900–1939', *Leisure Studies* 28, no. 3 (2009), 297–311. DOI: 10.1080/0261436090304623.

94 'Folk Songs and Dances', *Progress. Civic, Social, Industrial. The Organ of the British Institute of Social Service* 3, no. 3 (1908), 208–209.

95 Cecil Sharp, *The Country Dance Book, Part 1* (1911; London: Novello, 1927). Five further volumes were published. Others were involved in the field collection of folk song, notably the Rev. Sabine Baring-Gould and the composer Ralph Vaughan Williams; it was Sharp, however, who was most active in driving the folk revival.

96 Sutherland, *Mrs. Humphry Ward*, 224.

97 Mary Neal, *The Esperance Morris Book. A Manual of Morris Dances, Folk-Songs and Singing Games* (London: J. Curwen, 1910). The first performance of the Esperance Guild of Morris Dancers was at a Christmas party at the Passmore Edwards settlement in St. Pancras. For further detail on the origins and growth of the Esperance Club see Frank Kidson and Mary Neal, *English Folk-Song and Dance*, (Cambridge: Cambridge University Press, 1915). According to the Mary Neal Project website the Esperance Club was based in Somerstown near Kings Cross, opening four nights each week, the girls being taught English folk song and dance by traditional musicians and dancers who travelled from towns and rural villages to London. http://www.maryneal.org/about/1101/about-mary-neal/ [retrieved 20 November 2015].

98 Sharp, *The Country Dance Book; Part 1*, 11.

99 English Folk Dance and Song Society, *Annual Report 1931–32*.

100 Kumar, *The Making of English National Identity*, 232–233.

101 Cecil Sharp, *The Dance: An Historical Survey of Dancing in Europe* (London: Halton and Truscott Smith, 1924), 32.

102 Douglas Kennedy, 'The Folk Dance Revival in England', *Folk Dance: the Journal of the English Folk Dance and Song Society* 2, no. 1 (1935), 72.

103 Simon Dentith, *Society and Cultural Forms in Nineteenth Century England* (Basingstoke: Macmillan, 1998), 85. In *Lark Rise to Candleford* Flora Thompson recorded how music hall songs had become part of the repertoire of the singers of the village public house by the 1880s.

104 A.D. Hall, 'The Revival of Country Life', *Social Service Bulletin* 8, no. 5 (1927), 67–69.

105 Griffin, *England's Revelry*, 254.

106 Burchardt, 'State and Society in the English Countryside'.

107 Jane Robinson, *A Force to be Reckoned With. A History of the Women's Institute* (London: Virago, 2011), 116–117.

108 Beveridge, *Voluntary Action*, 135.

109 Elizabeth Peretz, 'The Forgotten Survey: Social Services in the Oxford District: 1935–40', *Twentieth Century British History* 22, no. 1 (2011), 103–113.

110 NCSS, National Conference on the Leisure of the People, 91.

111 Martin Pugh, *'We Danced All Night'. A Social History of Britain between the Wars* (London: Bodley Head, 2008), 275; Nick Mansfield, 'Paternalistic Consumer Co-operatives in Rural England, 1870–1930', *Rural History* 23, no. 2 (2012), 205–211.

112 C.L. Mowat, *Britain Between the Wars 1918–1940* (London: Methuen, 1956), 256.

113 Robert Colls, *Identity of England* (Oxford: Oxford University Press, 2002), 301.

114 James Nott, *Music for the People. Popular Music and Dance in Interwar Britain* (Oxford: Oxford University Press, 2002), 148–149.

115 Beaumont, *Housewives and Citizens*, 148–149.

116 Juliet Gardiner, *The Thirties: An Intimate History* (London: Harper Press, 2010), 273.

117 John Burnett, *A Social History of Housing 1815–1970* (London: Methuen, 1980), 218–219.

118 Alison Ravetz, *Council Housing and Culture. The History of a Social Experiment* (London: Routledge, 2001), 50.

119 Mark Clapson, *Invincible Green Suburbs, Brave New Towns: Social Change and Urban Dispersal in Post-war England* (Manchester: Manchester University Press, 1998), 121; Mark Clapson, 'Working-Class Women's Experiences of Moving to New Housing Estates in England since 1919', *Twentieth Century British History* 10, no. 3 (1999), 345–365.

120 Brad Beaven, *Leisure, Citizenship and Working-Class Men in Britain, 1850–1945* (Manchester: Manchester University Press, 2005), 133.

121 *Liverpool Daily Post*, 2 January 1929, 'Drift Back to the Slums'. Letter from Eleanor F. Rathbone, Liverpool University Archive.

122 Richard Alston, 'The Space of Politics', 183–196.

123 Rooff, *Youth and Leisure*, 133.

124 Jones, *Social Survey of Merseyside, Volume Three*, 262–264.

125 Mass Observation Worktown Collection Box 44A Social Conditions and Housing.

126 See Darrin Bayliss, 'Revisiting the Cottage Council Estates: England, 1919–39', *Planning Perspectives* 16 (2001), 169–200.

127 Darrin Bayliss, 'Building Better Communities: Social Life on London's Cottage Council Estates 1919–1939', *Journal of Historical Geography* 29, no. 3 (2003), 376–395.

128 NCSS *Annual Report*, 1930–31, 30.

129 NCSS Community Centres and Associations Committee of the National Council of Social Service *New Housing Estates and their Social Problems*, 4th ed. 1937, 3.

130 Morris 'How We Live'.

131 Barker's adoption of a Greek understanding of leisure in the context of the modern world is not dissimilar to that of Delisle Burns. Along with Burns he was a contributor to Marvin's influential *The Unity of Western Civilization* published in 1915. This was an edited collection of lectures given at a summer school at the Woodbrooke Settlement near Birmingham in 1915, and suggests that Barker and Burns would have been familiar with each other's work.

132 Ernest Barker, 'New Housing Estates – The Problem', *Social Service Review* 12, no. 3 (1931), 47–50.

133 Ernest Barker, *Reflections on Leisure* (London: NCSS, 1947), 15.

134 Barker, 'New Housing Estates'.

135 Henry A. Mess and Harold King, 'Community Centres and Community Associations', in *Voluntary Social Services since 1918*, ed. H. Mess, 69–98.

136 Ernest Barker, 'Community Centres and the Uses of Leisure', in *Adult Education* (London: National Institute of Adult Education, 1938).

137 J.H. Bingham, 'The Greeks Had a Word for It', *Adult Education* 11, no. 1 (1938), 24–30.

138 Ernest Barker, *Greek Political Theory: Plato and his Predecessors* (1918; London: Methuen, 1960), 21.

139 Barker, *Reflections on Leisure*, 18–19.

140 'New Estates Conference', *Social Service Review* 13, no. 4 (1932), 59–72.

141 Hilda Jennings, 'Voluntary Social Services in Urban Areas', in *Voluntary Social Services since 1918*, ed. Henry Mess, 28–39 (London: Kegan Paul, Trench, Trubner, 1947).

142 NCSS *Social Service Review* 14, no. 7 (1933), 123.

143 Ruth Durant, *'Watling': A Survey of Social life on a New Housing Estate* (London: P.S. King, 1939), 2, 7.

144 Durant, *Watling*, 28–31.

145 'Community Centres on Housing Estates' *NCSS Social Service Review* 14, no. 7 (1933), 123.

146 Durant, *Watling*, 91–92.

147 Durant, *Watling*, 26, 108.

148 Durant, *Watling*, 55.

149 Durant, *Watling*, 61.

150 Derrick Deakin, *Wythenshawe: The Story of a Garden City* (Chichester: Phillimore, 1989), 81–86.

151 NCSS, *A Brief Account of the Work of the National Council of Social Service*, 28–32.

152 English Folk Dance and Song Society Manchester Branch, *Minutes*, 26 January 1931.

153 NCSS, *New Housing Estates*, 6.

154 Durant, *Watling*, 117.

155 E.W. Woodhead, 'Community Centres and the Local Authority', *Adult Education* 11, no. 1 (1938), 11–17.

156 Durant, *Watling*, 18–20.

157 Elizabeth Roberts, *A Woman's Place. An Oral History of Working-Class Women 1890–1940* (Oxford: Blackwell, 1995), 184–185.

158 Terence Young, *Becontree and Dagenham. A Report made for the Pilgrim Trust* (London: Sidders & Son, 1934), 78.

159 Young, *Becontree and Dagenham*, 84–85.

160 Andrzej Olechnowicz, *Working-class Housing in England between the Wars: The Becontree Estate* (Oxford: Clarendon Press, 1997).

161 W. Mabane, 'The Present Condition of University and Social Settlements in Great Britain', *Sociological Review* 15, no. 1 (1923), 29–34.

162 Branford and Geddes, *The Coming Polity*, 232–233.

163 Mark Freeman, '"No Finer School than a Settlement": The Development of the Educational Settlement Movement', *History of Education* 31, no. 3 (2002), 245–262, DOI: 10.1080/00467600210122612

164 CUKT, Minutes of the Annual General Meeting, 1930.

165 Olechnowicz, *Working-class Housing in England*, 181–182.

166 Young, *Becontree and Dagenham*, 90.

167 Young, *Becontree and Dagenham*, 222.

168 Beaumont, *Housewives and Citizens*, 52–53.

169 Young, *Becontree and Dagenham*, 186.

170 Young, *Becontree and Dagenham*, 72.

171 Young, *Becontree and Dagenham*, 222–223.

172 Young, *Becontree and Dagenham*, 224–225.

173 Young, *Becontree and Dagenham*, 210.

174 Young, *Becontree and Dagenham*, 225.

175 National Council of Social Service. Community Centres and Associations
     Committee, *New Housing Estates and their Social Problems*, 4th ed. (1937), 19.

176 Barker, *New Housing Estates*, 14.

Chapter 9

1   Arthur H. Norris, *Report on the National Conference on the Leisure of the People*
    (Manchester, 1919), 45.

2   B.A. Campbell, 'Boys' Clubs' in *Report on the National Conference on the Leisure of
    the People* (Manchester, 1919), 49.

3   Mike Brake, *Comparative Youth Culture. The Sociology of Youth Cultures and Youth
    Sub-Cultures in America, Britain and Canada* (London: Routledge, 2003), 23.

4   Pearl Jephcott, 'Work Among Boys and Girls', in *Voluntary Services since 1918*, edited
    by Henry A. Mess (London: Kegan Paul, Trench, Trubner, 1947), 129–145.

5   Great Britain. Board of Education, *The Service of Youth. Circular to Local Education
    Authorities for Higher Education* (27 November 1939).

6   Trevor May, *An Economic and Social History of Britain 1760–1990* (Harlow:
    Longman, 1996), 335.

7   Henriette R. Walter, *Munition Workers in England and France* (New York: Division of
    Industrial Studies, Russell Sage Foundation, 1917), 15–16; Great Britain, Ministry of
    Munitions Health of Munitions Workers Committee, *Final Report: Industrial Health
    and Efficiency* (London: HMSO, 1918) Cd. 9065.

8   Dorothea E. Proud, *Welfare Work. Employers' Experiments for Improving Working
    Conditions in Factories* (London: G. Bell, 1916). Proud, a Spence Scholar in Sociology
    at the University of Adelaide, was awarded a Doctorate of Science by the London
    School of Economics for her study of industrial welfare in Britain.

9   Proud, *Welfare Work*, 186–188. Lloyd George stated this in his foreword to the
    book.

10 Great Britain, Ministry of Munitions Health of Munitions Workers Committee, *Final
    Report: Industrial Health and Efficiency* (London: HMSO, 1918) Cd. 9065, 6.

11 Great Britain. Ministry of Munitions. Health of Munition Workers Committee, *Final
    Report. Industrial Health and Efficiency* (London: HMSO, 1918), 117–118.

12 Russell and Russell, *Lads' Clubs*, 4.

13 A Scottish National Council of Juvenile Organisations was formed by the Secretary
    for Scotland in 1919.

14 Great Britain, *Education Act, 1921*, 53. See also Robert Snape, 'Industrial Welfare, Sport and Leisure in post-First World War Social Reconstruction' in D. Day (ed.), *Sport and Leisure on the Eve of the First World War* (Crewe: Manchester Metropolitan University, 2016), 1–21.

15 Bradford Council of Social Service, *The Texture of Welfare. A Survey of Social Service in Bradford* (London: P.S. King, 1923), 60–61.

16 Great Britain. Juvenile Organisations Committee, *Notes on Work and Progress of Local Committees* (London: Board of Education, 1920).

17 'Bristol and Recreation', *Western Daily Press*, 29 October 1919, 7.

18 *Bristol Juvenile Organizations Committee Handbook* (Bristol: E.S.A. Robinson, 1920).

19 Katharine C. Dewar, *The Girl* (London: G. Bell, 1921), 99.

20 Rooff, *Youth and Leisure*, 7–29.

21 Rooff, *Youth and Leisure*, 7–10.

22 Rooff, *Youth and Leisure*, 133.

23 R. Fabes and A. Skinner, 'The Girls' Friendly Society and the Development of Rural Youth Work', in *Essays in the History of Community and Youth Work*, edited by R. Gilchrist, T. Jeffs and J. Spence (Leicester: Youth Work Press, 2001), 185–190.

24 Barry Doyle 'The Structure of Elite Power in the Early Twentieth Century City: Norwich 1900–35', *Urban History*, 24 (1997), 179–199.

25 Rooff, *Youth and Leisure*, 141.

26 Bill Luckin, 'Revisiting the Slums', 134–147.

27 Robert Gunn Davis, 'Slum Environment and Social Causation', *Westminster Review* 166, no. 3 (1906), 249–257 and 'The Social Question: A Plea for More Scientific Methods', *Westminster Review* 165, no. 3 (1906), 265–268.

28 Helen Dendy, 'Marriage in East London', in *Aspects of the Social Problem*, ed. B. Bosanquet (London, Macmillan, 1895), 75–81.

29 Maude Stanley, *Clubs for Working Girls* (London: Macmillan, 1890), 23–41. The prevention of early marriage was also a function of boys' clubs; according to A.F. Winnington Ingram, 'Workingmen's Clubs', a boy who dropped out between the boys' club and the men's club was almost invariably married at nineteen or twenty.

30 Fred Marquis, 'The Settlement's Problem'. Reprint from *The Optimist*, October 1913, Liverpool University Settlement Archive, D7/5/5/1.

31 G. Stanley Hall, *Adolescence, Volume One* (London: Appleton, 1914), 318–320.

32 Stefan Collini, *Public Moralists. Political Thought and Intellectual Life in Britain* (Oxford: Oxford University Press, 1991), 116–117.

33 Clift, 'The Leisure Occupation of Young People', 127–137.

34 Collini, *Public Moralists*, 274.

35 Lawrence Pearsall Jacks, *Constructive Citizenship* (London: Hodder and Stoughton, c. 1927), 161.

36 P.J.O. Self, 'Voluntary Organizations in Bethnal Green', in Bourdillon ed., *Voluntary Social Services*, 235–262.

37 Rob Boddice, 'In Loco Parentis? Public-school Authority, Cricket and Manly Character, 1855–62', *Gender and Education* 21, no. 2 (2009), 159–172.

38 'Work of Boys' Clubs', *Times* [London] 17 January 1934, 9. *The Times Digital Archive* [accessed 6 October 2016].

39 'Clubs for Boys', *Times* [London] 27 March 1929, 11. *The Times Digital Archive* [accessed 6 October 2016].

40 Durant, *Problem of Leisure*, 203.

41 York House, *Annual Report*, 1932–33 (Liverpool: Liverpool University Settlement).

42 *Character* (Liverpool: Liverpool University Settlement New Building Series Booklet no. 5, c.1930).

43 *The Settlement and Liverpool College. A 'Public School' Club* (Liverpool University Settlement, New Building Series, Booklet no. 2. Liverpool, c. 1925).

44 'Public School Boys' Tour of East London'. *Times* [London] 2 May 1928, 1. *The Times Digital Archive* [accessed 6 October 2016].

45 See P. Williamson, 'The Monarchy and Public Values, 1900–1953', in *The Monarchy and the British Nation, 1780 to the Present* ed. Andrzej Olechnowicz (Cambridge: Cambridge University Press, 2007), 223–257.

46 See David Fowler, *The First Teenagers. The Lifestyle of Young Wage-earners in Interwar Britain* (London: Woburn Press, 1995); Melanie Tebbutt, *Being Boys. Youth, Leisure and Identity in the Inter-War Years* (Manchester: Manchester University Press, 2012); Selina Todd, *Young Women, Work and Family in England 1918–1950* (Oxford: Oxford University Press, 2005); 'Young Women, Work and Leisure in Inter-war England', *Historical Journal* 48, no. 3 (2005), 789–809; Fiona Skillen, 'Woman and the Sport Fetish: Modernity, Consumerism and Sports Participation in Interwar Britain', *International Journal of the History of Sport* 29, no. 15 (2012), 750–765; Penny Tinkler, 'Feminine Modernity in Interwar Britain and North America: Corsets, Cars and Cigarettes'. *Journal of Women's History* 20, no. 3 (2008), 113–143.

47 Clift, 'The Leisure Occupation of Young People', 127–136.

48 Katharine C. Dewar, *The Girl* (London: G. Bell, 1921), 22.

49 Harris, *The Use of Leisure in Bethnal Green*, 51.

50 Edith Neville 'Warden's Report', *Mary Ward Settlement Annual Report*, 1923.

51 John Springhall, *Youth, Empire and Society. British Youth Movements, 1883–1940* (London: Croom Helm 1977).

52 J.A. Mangan, 'Games Field and Battlefield: A Romantic Alliance in Verse and the Creation of Militaristic Masculinity', *International Journal of the History of Sport* 27, nos. 1 & 2 (2010), 190–204.

53 Michael J. Foster, *The History of the British Boy Scouts 1909–1987: An Early Breakaway Movement* (Aylesbury: Brotherhood of British Scouts, 1987), 2.

54 Roger T. Stearn, 'Vane, Sir Francis Patrick Fletcher, Fifth Baronet (1861–1934)', *Oxford Dictionary of National Biography*, Oxford University Press, 2004; online edn., May 2006, http://www.oxforddnb.com/view/article/77196 [accessed 27 September 2016].

55 Foster, *History of the British Boy Scouts*, 3.

56 Rhys Jones, Peter Merriman and Sarah Mills, 'Youth Organizations and the Reproduction of Nationalism in Britain: The Role of Urdd Gobaith Cymru', *Social and Cultural Geography* 17, no. 5 (2016), 714–734.

57 Sarah Mills, 'Geographies of Education, Volunteering and the Lifecourse: The Woodcraft Folk in Britain (1925–75)' *Cultural Geographies* 23, no. 1 (2014), 103–119.

58 Mary Davis, *Fashioning a New World: A History of the Woodcraft Folk* (Loughborough: Holyoake Books, 2000), 19–21.

59 Davis, *Fashioning a New World*, 21

60 Jon Savage, *Teenage. The Creation of Youth Culture* (London: Pimlico, 2008), 109–112.

61 The origins of the phrase have been attributed to England, Scotland and most recently Cheshire (see Pollen, *Kindred of the Kibbo Kift*, 11).

62 Pollen, *Kindred of the Kibbo Kift*, 34.

63 Davis, *Fashioning a New World*, 22–24.

64 Leslie Paul, *Angry Young Man* (London: Faber & Faber, 1951), 55–56.

65 *The Mark* 1, no. 10 (1923), 129.

66 John Hargrave, *The Confession of the Kibbo Kift. A Declaration and General Exposition of the Work of the Kindred* (London: Duckworth, 1927), 133–135.

67 Hargrave, *The Confession of the Kibbo Kift*, 56.

68 David Fowler, *Youth Culture in Modern Britain*, 30–58.

69 Pollen, *Kindred of the Kibbo Kift*, 11.

70 Pollen, *Kindred of the Kibbo Kift*, 11.

71 Paul, *Angry Young Man*, 54–55.

72 Margaret A. Ormrod, '"For as Many as Will"; Some Notes on Folk Dancing', *The Mark* 1, no. 3 (August 1922), 37–38; Neal, *Esperance Morris Book Volume One*, 8.

73 Paul, *Angry Young Man*, 62.

74 David Prynn, 'The Woodcraft Folk and the Labour Movement 1925–70', *Journal of Contemporary History* 1, no. 18 (1983), 79–95.

75 Paul, *Angry Young Man*, 17, 71.

76 Paul, *Angry Young Man*, 55.

77 Leslie Paul, Talk about the beginning and the early history of the Woodcraft Folk. Filmed at the Co-operative History Workshop, County Hall, London 9 March 1985. Internet Archive https://archive.org/details/WoodcraftFolkHistory

78 Rooff, *Youth and Leisure*, 15.

79 Rooff, *Youth and Leisure*, 137.

80 Iveson and Brown, *Monument to a Movement*.

81 Rooff, *Youth and Leisure*, 152.

82 Sarah Mills, 'Geographies of Education', 103–119.

83 Paul, *Angry Young Man*, 63.

84 See for example Hester Barron's account of the Children's Country Holiday Fund, 'Changing Conceptions of the Poor Child: The Children's Country Holiday Fund 1918–1939' *Journal of the History of Childhood and Youth* 9, no. 1 (2016), 29–47.

Chapter 10

1 May, *An Economic and Social History of Britain 1760–1990*, 373.

2 John Burnett, *Idle Hands. The Experience of Unemployment 1790–1990* (London: Routledge, 1994), 205.

3 Ken Roberts, 'Social Class and Leisure during Recent Recessions in Britain', *Leisure Studies* 34, no. 2 (2015), 131–149.

4 Burnett, *Idle Hands*, 209–210.

5 Durant, *The Problem of Leisure*, 98.

6 Andrzej Olechnowicz, 'Unemployed Workers, "Enforced Leisure" and Education for "The Right Use of Leisure" in Britain in the 1930s', *Labour History Review* 70 (2005), 27–52.

7 Lawrence Pearsall Jacks, *The Education of the Whole Man: A Plea for a New Spirit in Education* (London: London University Press, 1931), 106,137.

8 Daryl Leeworthy, 'A Diversion from the New Leisure: Greyhound Racing, Working-Class Culture, and the Politics of Unemployment in Inter-war South Wales', *Sport in History*, 32, no. 1 (2012), 53–73.

9 Ross McKibbin, *Parties and People England 1914–1951*. Oxford, Oxford University Press, 2011, 102.

10 Selina Todd, *The People. The Rise and Fall of the Working Class 1910–2010* (London: John Murray, 2014), 65.

11 'The Prince's Lead', *Social Service Review* 13, no. 2 (1932), 21–22.

12 CUKT *Annual Report and Minutes*, 1932, 21.

13 NCSS, *Annual Report 1933–34*, 14.

14 A.F.C. Bourdillon, 'Voluntary Organizations to Facilitate Co-operation and Co-ordination', 164–193; Henry Mess, 'Social Service with the Unemployed', in *Voluntary Social Services since 1918* ed. Henry Mess (London: Kegan Paul, Trench Trubner, 1947), 40–54, 18.

15 Neil Penlington, 'Masculinity and Domesticity in 1930s South Wales: Did Unemployment Change the Domestic Division of Labour?', *Twentieth Century British History* 21, no. 3 (2010), 281–299.

16 Burnett, *Idle Hands*, 218–9.

17 Walter Hannington, *The Problem of the Distressed Areas* (London: Gollancz, 1937), 204.

18 'Unemployed Boys and Scouting', *Times* (London), Thursday, 25 May 1933, 13, issue 46453.

19 Hannington, *The Problem of the Distressed Areas*, 196.

20 Ellen Wilkinson, *The Town that was Murdered: The Life-Story of Jarrow* (London: Gollancz Left Book Club, 1939), 232–234.

21 National Council of Social Service, *Unemployment and Community Service* (London: NCSS, 1936).

22 Burnett, *Idle Hands*, 242.

23 Pilgrim Trust, *Men without Work* (Cambridge: Cambridge University Press, 1938), 195.

24 William Beveridge, *Unemployment. A Problem of Industry* (London: Longmans, Green, 2nd ed., 1930), 134–138.

25 Burnett, *Idle Hands*, 227–230.

26 Stephen Spender, *Forward from Liberalism* (London: Gollancz, 1937), 65; Richard Overy, *The Morbid Age: Britain and the Crisis of Civilization, 1919*–1939 (London: Penguin, 2010); James Klugmann, 'The Crisis of the Thirties: A View from the Left' in *Culture and Crisis in Britain in the Thirties*, edited by Jon Clark, Margot Heinemann, David Margolies and Carole Snee (London: Lawrence and Wishart, 1979), 13–36.

27 Pilgrim Trust, *Men Without Work*, 354.

28 Burnett, *Idle Hands*, 241–243 lists the WEA and miners' lodges as organizers of clubs.

29 Mess, 'Social Service with the Unemployed', 40–54.

30 NCSS, *Annual Report* 1933–34, 45.

31 Pilgrim Trust, *Men Without Work*, 176, 394.

32 Durant, *The Problem of Leisure*, 106.

33 The terminology is that used by the Pilgrim Trust and resonates with that adopted in the St. Phillip's Settlement Report discussed in Chapter 8.

34 Pilgrim Trust, *Men Without Work*, 278.

35 Rooff, *Youth and Leisure*, 144.

36 Pilgrim Trust, *Men Without Work*, 315–318.

37 Pilgrim Trust, *Men Without Work*, 318, 378–379.

38 Chris Rojek, *Leisure Theory. Principles and Practices* (Basingstoke: Palgrave Macmillan, 2005), 210–213.

39 CUKT, *Disinherited Youth: A Survey 1936–1939*. Edinburgh: Constable, 1943.

40 Pilgrim Trust, *Men Without Work*, 113.

41 Robert James, "'A Very Profitable Enterprise": South Wales Miners' Institute Cinemas in the 1930s', *Historical Journal of Film, Radio and Television* 27, no. 1 (2007), 27–61.

42 Brasnett, *Voluntary Social Action*, 67.

43 Freeman, 'No Finer School than a Settlement'.

44 Rooff, *Youth and Leisure*, 229.

45 Pilgrim Trust, *Men Without Work*, 298–311.

46 Priestley, *English Journey*, 282–285.

47 Pilgrim Trust, *Men Without Work*, 321–323.

48 Beveridge, *Unemployment*, 143.

49 Beveridge, *Unemployment*, 89.

50 D. Caradog Jones, *The Social Survey of Merseyside Volume Two* (London: Hodder and Stoughton, 1934), 366.

51 CUKT, *Disinherited Youth*, 53.

52 Jones, *Social Survey of Merseyside Volume Three*, 314.

53 Liverpool Council of Social Service, *Annual Report*, 1933.

54 ibid.

55 Examples include the adoption of the Jarrow club by the staff of the Board of Admiralty, the Gateshead club by the BBC staff club.

56 Mess, 'Social Service with the Unemployed', 50.

57 NCSS, *Annual Report 1933–34*, 24.

58 CUKT, *Disinherited Youth*, 112–114.

59 Priestley, *English Journey*, 245–246.

60 Pilgrim Trust, *Men Without Work*, 342.

61 Beveridge, *Unemployment*, 138.

62 Pilgrim Trust, *Men Without Work*, 256–257.

63 Rooff, *Youth and Leisure*, 6.

64 Pilgrim Trust, *Men Without Work*, 90–91.

65 John Welshman, 'The Concept of the Unemployable', *Economic History Review* 59, no. 3 (2006), 578–606.

66 Pilgrim Trust, *Men Without Work*, 158.

67 Pilgrim Trust, *Men Without Work*, 98.

68 Liverpool Council of Voluntary Aid, *Report on Betting*, 7.

69 Pilgrim Trust, *Men Without Work*, 97.

70 Pilgrim Trust, *Men Without Work*, 384.

71 Leonard Lockhart, 'Industrial Problems from the Standpoint of General Practice', *British Medical Journal* 2, no. 3682 (1931), 179–182.

72 David Caradog Jones, 'Mental Deficiency on Merseyside. Its Connection with the Social Problem Group', *Eugenics Review* 24, no. 2 (1932), 97–105.

73 Todd, *The People*, 75.

74 Valentine Bell, *Junior Instruction Centres and their Future. A Report to the Carnegie United Kingdom Trust* (Edinburgh: Constable, 1934), 62.

75 CUKT, *Disinherited Youth.*

76 Rooff, *Youth and Leisure*, 55.

77 CUKT, *Disinherited Youth*, 112–113.

78 Kitae Sohn, 'Did Unemployed Workers Choose not to Work in Interwar Britain? Evidence from the voices of unemployed workers', *Labor History* 54, no. 4 (2013), 377–392, DOI: 10.1080/0023656X.2013.807097

79 Burnett, *Idle Hands*, 236–240.

80 Daryl Leeworthy, 'Partisan Players: Sport, Working-Class Culture, and the Labour Movement in South Wales 1920–1939', *Labor History* 55, no. 5 (2014), 580–593.

Chapter 11

1 Rosemary Rees, *Britain 1890–1939* (London: Heinemann, 2003), 59–61.

2 Pugh, *State and Society*, 189.

3 Great Britain. Home Office, *Welfare and Welfare Supervision in Factories and Workshops* (London: HMSO, 1919).

4 Zimmern, 'The Control of Industry after the War', 61–85.

5 Burns, *Industry and Civilization*, 118.

6 Paul Thompson and David McHugh, *Work Organisations: A Critical Approach* (Basingstoke: Palgrave Macmillan, 2009), 164.

7 Robert Owen, *A New View of Society* (London: Penguin, 1991), 40–42.

8 Helen Jones, 'Employers' Welfare Schemes and Industrial Relations in Inter-War Britain', *Business History* 25, no. 1 (1983), 61–75. DOI: 10.1080/00076798300000005; E. Robertson, E. Korczynski and M. Pickering (2007), 'Harmonious Relations? Music at Work in the Rowntree and Cadbury Factories', *Business History* 49, no. 2 (2007), 211–234. DOI: 10.1080/00076790601170355

9 John Ruskin, *Unto this Last and Other Essays* (1850; London: Dent, 1907), 129–130.

10 Bob Morris and Jim Smyth, 'Paternalism as an Employer Strategy, 1800–1960', in *Employer Strategy in the Labour Market*, eds Jill Rubery and Frank Wilkinson (Oxford: Oxford University Press, 1994), 195–225.

11 Seebohm Rowntree, 'The Aims and Principles of Welfare Work', *Welfare Work* 1, no. 1 January (1920), 5.

12 Mary Lathrop Goss, *Welfare Work in Corporations* (Philadelphia: American Baptist Publication Society, 1911), 36.

13 Goss, *Welfare Work in Corporations*, 5–8, 15–25.

14 R.B. Lawson, J.E. Graham and K.M. Baker, A *History of Psychology: Globalization, Ideas and Applications* (Hove: Routledge, 2016), 209.

15 William McDougall, *The Group Mind* (Cambridge: Cambridge University Press, 1927).

16 J. Drever, 'The Human Factor in Industrial Relations', in *Industrial Psychology*, ed. C.S. Myers (London: Thornton Butterworth, 1929), 18–88.

17 Robert Hyde, 'Organisation of Welfare Schemes', *Journal of the Royal Society for the Promotion of Health*, 42 (1921), 175–179.

18 Burns, 'Productivity and Reconstruction', 393–405. The point was made as early as 1894 by Ashbee in *Workshop Reconstruction*.

19 William Morris, 'Useful Work versus Useless Toil', in *News from Nowhere and Selected Writings and Designs* (Harmondsworth: Penguin, 1962), 117–136.

20 Ruskin, *Unto This Last and Other Essays*, 129–130.

21 Budgett Meakin, *Model Factories and Villages: Ideal Conditions of Labour and Housing* (London: Fisher Unwin, 1905), 23. Meakin was a co-founder, with John Brown Paton, of the British Institute of Social Service, which presented the Shaftesbury Lectures. S.E. Fryer, 'Meakin, James Edward Budgett (1866–1906)', rev. Mark Pottle, *Oxford Dictionary of National Biography*, Oxford University Press, 2004, http://www.oxforddnb.com/view/article/34970 [accessed 29 January 2016].

22 R.H. Tawney, *The Acquisitive Society* (1920; New York; Dover Publications, 2004).

23 Hobson, *Work and Wealth*, 241–248; Burns, *Industry and Civilization*, 234.

24 B. Seebohm Rowntree, Paper given to meeting of Industrial Welfare Society, 21 November 1929. Borthwick Institute Rowntree Papers, ART/17/15.

25 B. Seebohm Rowntree, *The Human Factor in Business* (London: Longmans Green, 1921), 156; Edward Cadbury, *Experiments in Industrial Organization* (London: Longmans Green, 1912).

26 Lever, *The Six Hour Day and other Industrial Questions*, 90.

27 Cadbury, *Experiments in Industrial Organization*, 221.

28 Cadbury, *Experiments in Industrial Organization*, 206.

29 Cadbury, *Experiments in Industrial Organization*, 233–234.

30 William Lever, *The Buildings Erected at Port Sunlight and Thornton Hough. Paper presented to Meeting of the Architectural Association, March 1st 1902*; Jones, *Social Survey of Merseyside Volume Three*, 310.

31 Walter L. George, *Labour and Housing at Port Sunlight* (London: Alston Rivers, 1900), 178.

32 J. Kay, '"Maintaining the Traditions of British Sport?" The Private Sports Club in the Twentieth Century', *International Journal of the History of Sport* 30, no. 4 (2013), 1655–1666; W.P. Jolly, *Lord Leverhulme: A Biography* (London: Constable, 1976), 79.

33 David J. Jeremy, 'The Enlightened Paternalist in Action: William Hesketh Lever at Port Sunlight before 1914', *Business History* 33, no. 1 (1991), 58–81.

34 Patrick Joyce, *Work, Society and Politics: the Culture of the Factory in later Victorian England* (London: Methuen, 1982), 90.

35 Wray Vamplew, 'Sport, Industry and Industrial Sport in Britain before 1914: Review and Revision', *International Journal of the History of Sport* 19, no. 3 (2015), 340–355.

36 Great Britain. Home Office, *Welfare and Welfare Supervision in Factories and Workshops* (London: HMSO, 1919).

37 Industrial Council Plan in Great Britain. *Report of the Whitley Committee on Relations between Employers and Employed of the Ministry of Reconstruction* (Washington: Bureau of Industrial Research, 1919), 90–91.

38 Hyde, who had been warden of the Hoxton Settlement, was asked by Seebohm Rowntree to supervise boys' welfare in the Ministry of Munitions in 1916.

39 'Editorial', *Journal of Industrial Welfare* 2, no. 1 (1920).

40 Lindy Biggs, *The Rational Factory: Architecture, Technology and Work in America's Age of Mass Production* (London: Johns Hopkins University Press, 1996), 65–69.

41 William Beardmore, 'Welfare as a Business Asset', *Journal of Industrial Welfare* 2, no. 1 (1920), 29–30.

42 Hyde, 'Organisation of Welfare Schemes', 175–179.

43 Great Britain Committee on Industry and Trade, *Survey of Industrial Relations* (London: HMSO, 1926), 192.

44 'Bournville's New Social Centre', *Journal of Industrial Welfare* 9, no. 99 (1927), 94–95.

45 Priestley, *English Journey*, 100.

46 Liverpool Council of Voluntary Aid, *Report on the Uses of Leisure in Liverpool*, 8.

47 Jones, *Social Survey of Merseyside Volume Three*, 310.

48 Kay, 'Maintaining the Traditions of British Sport?'

49 A. Smith, 'Cars, Cricket, and Alf Smith: The Place of Works based Sports and Social Clubs in the Life of Mid-Twentieth-Century Coventry', *International Journal of the History of Sport* 19, no. 1 (2002), 137–150, DOI: 10.1080/714001702

50 Michael Heller, 'Sport, Bureaucracies and London Clerks 1880–1939', *International Journal of the History of Sport* 25, no. 5 (2008), 579–614, DOI: 10.1080/09523360701875541

51 Simon Phillips, '"Fellowship in Recreation, Fellowship in Ideals": Sport, Leisure and Culture at Boots Pure Drug Company, Nottingham c. 1883–1945', *Midland History* 29, no. 1 (2004), 107–123.

52 Robert Snape, 'Everyday Leisure and Northernness in Mass Observation's Worktown 1937–1939', *Journal for Cultural Research* 20, no. 1 (2016), 31–44.

53 Great Britain Committee on Industry and Trade, *Survey of Industrial Relations*, 191.

54 Stephen. G. Jones, 'Work, Leisure and the Political Economy of the Cotton Districts Between the Wars', *Textile History* 18, no. 1 (1987), 33–58; T. Griffiths, *The Lancashire Working Classes c. 1880–1930* (Oxford: Clarendon Press, 2001), 163.

55 L. Oliver, '"No Hard-Brimmed Hats Please" Bolton Women Cotton-Workers and the Game of Rounders, 1911–39', *Oral History* 25 (1995), 40–45.

56 Rebecca Conway, 'Making the Mill Girl Modern? Beauty, Industry, and the Popular Newspaper in 1930s' England', *Twentieth Century British History* 24, no. 4 (2013), 518–541.

57 'Obstacles to Welfare Work: Fear and Ignorance' (*Observer*, 15 September 1929), 21. This comment was made by the Welfare Supervisor of Messrs J. Lyons and Co. at a conference of the Industrial Welfare Society.

58 C.J. Hunt, 'Sex versus Class in Two British Trade Unions in the Early Twentieth Century', *Journal of Women's History*, 24 no. 1 (2012), 86–110.

59 Eleanor T. Kelly, *Welfare Work in Industry* (London: Pitman, 1925), 19. This commitment to social ideals did not survive; the Welfare Workers' Association, formed in 1913, became the Institute of Labour Management in 1931 and the Institute of Personnel Management in 1946.

60 'Industry as a Social Service'. Paper at conference by Miss Bondfield, *Welfare Work* 3, no. 26 (1922), 27.

61 Eleanor T. Kelly, 'The Relation of Industry to the Welfare of the Community', *Welfare Work* 4, no. 43 (July 1923), 123–124.

62 Jones, 'Employers' Welfare Schemes and Industrial Relations', 67.

63 J.G. Paterson, 'Industry and Leisure. Fitness', *Industrial Welfare and Personnel Management*, 16 (1934), 18–25.

64 Edgar L. Collis, 'Efficiency and Fatigue', *Journal of Industrial Welfare* 2, no. 8 (1920); 'Industrial Efficiency and Fatigue', *Journal of the Royal Society for the Promotion of Health* 41 (1920), 235–241.

65 Biggs, *The Rational Factory*, 69.

66 Arthur Shadwell, *Industrial Efficiency. A Comparative Study of Industrial Life in England, Germany and America* (London: Longmans, Green, 1906), 259–266.

67 Biggs, *The Rational Factory*, 69.

68 Burns, *Industry and Civilization*, 12.

69 Durant, *The Problem of Leisure*, 240–241.

70 'Trade Union Sport' *Manchester Guardian* (February, 1926), 16.

71 Tony Collins, *Sport in Capitalist Society: A Short History* (London: Routledge, 2013), 18.

72 Thorstein Veblen, *The Theory of the Leisure Class* (1899. New York: Dover, 1994), 161.

73 Hobson, *Work and Wealth*, 146–151.

74 Arnd Kruger and James Riordan, *The Story of Worker Sport* (Champaign: Human Kinetics, 1996).

75 George W. Sinfield, 'The Worker's Sport Movement', *Labour Monthly* 12, no. 2 (March 1930), 167–171.

76 Lauri Keskinen, 'Working-class Sports Clubs as Agents of Political Socialisation in Finland, 1903–1923', *International Journal of the History of Sport* 28, no. 6 (2011), 853–875.

77 James Riordan, 'The Worker Sport Movement', in *The International Politics of Sport in the Twentieth Century*, eds J. Riordan and A. Kruger (London: Routledge, 1999), 105–120.

78 'International Leisure Conference', *Journal of Industrial Welfare* 17 (1935), 16–26; Gaetano Salvemini, *Under the Axe of Fascism* (London: Victor Gollancz, 1936), 362–370.

79 Jones, *Sport, Politics and the Working Class*, 75.

80 Sinfield, 'The Worker's Sport Movement'.

81 *The Worker Sportsman*, 1 (1928), 1, 4. MRC, TUC Archive MSS 292/807.12/5.

82 Mass Observation Worktown Collection, Box 7H Irish Labour Club and Socialist Club.

83 *Daily Worker*, 5 August 1931. Andrew Thorpe in 'The Membership of the Communist Party of Great Britain', *Historical Journal* 43, no. 3 (2000), 777–800 quotes Samuel Raphael's observation that engineers were a dominant section within the party.

84 *Bolton Evening News 'Buff' Sports Edition*, 10 August 1931.

85 Jones, *Sport, Politics and the Working Class*, 142–143.

86 *The Worker Sportsman*, 1, no. 3 (1932), 9.

87 *The Worker Sportsman*, 7 no. 11 (1903), 171.

88 *The Worker Sportsman*, 23 (1923), 27.

89 *The Wheatsheaf* 'A People's Co-operative Club' (September 1923), 138.

90 'Sport and Goodwill. The C.W.S and its Employees', *Ourselves* 4, no. 2 (1928), 1.

91 Jones, *Social Survey of Merseyside Volume Three*, 308.

92 Burns, *Industry and Civilization*, 117.

93 Jones, *Sport, Politics and the Working Class*, 116.

94 Tawney, *Acquisitive Society*, 136–137.

95 Burns, *Industry and Civilization*, 117.

Chapter 12

1 Beveridge, *Voluntary Action*, 268.

2 Harris, 'Political Thought'.

3 Bailey, *Leisure and Class*, 175.

4 Beveridge, *Voluntary Action*, 222.

5 B. Seebohm Rowntree and G.R. Lavers, *English Life and Leisure. A Social Study* (London: Longmans, Green, 1951).

6 Burns, *Leisure in the Modern World*, 15.

7   Burns, *Leisure in the Modern World*, 201.

8   Todd, *The People*.

9   Stears, *Progressives, Pluralists*, 34–43.

10 Raymond Williams, *Culture and Society 1780–1950* (Harmondsworth: Penguin, 1961), 126.

11 Williams, *Culture and Society*, 316–317.

12 Mess, *Voluntary Social Services*, 2.

13 A.D. Lindsay, 'Conclusion' in Bourdillon (ed.) *Voluntary Social Services*, 298–306.

14 Hobson, *The Social Problem*, 82–83.

15 Burns, *Modern Civilization on Trial*, 154.

16 See Harold Perkin, 'Individualism versus Collectivism in Nineteenth Century Britain: A False Antithesis', in *The Structured Crowd. Essays in English Social History* (Brighton: Harvester Press, 1981), 57–69.

17 Williams, *Culture and Society*, 312–318.

18 Todd, 'Social Transformation'; Etzioni, 'Creating Good Communities'.

19 John Ruskin, *Munera Pulveris* (Orpington: George Allen, 1880), 115.

Select Bibliography

Abercrombie, Nick, Hill, Stephen, and Turner, Bryan S. *Penguin Dictionary of Sociology*. 4th ed. London: Penguin, 2000.

Addams, Jane. 'A Function of the Social Settlement'. *Annals of the American Academy of Political and Social Science* 13, (May, 1899): 33–55.

Aiken, W. Francis. *Canon Barnett, Warden of Toynbee Hall*. London: S.W. Partridge, 1902.

Alexander, Hartley Burr. 'The Fear of Machines'. *International Journal of Ethics* 28, no. 1 (1917): 80–93.

Alston, Richard. 'The Space of Politics: Classics, Utopia and the Defence of Order', in *Greek and Roman Classics in the British Struggle for Social Reform*, edited by Henry Stead and Edith Hall, 183–196. London: Bloomsbury, 2015.

Anheier, H.K. *Civil Society, Measurement, Evaluation, Policy*. London: Earthscan, 2004.

Anson, W.R. 'The Oxford House in Bethnal Green'. *Economic Review* (January 1893): 10–22.

Aristotle. 'The Politics', in *The Politics of Aristotle*, trans. Ernest Barker. Oxford: Clarendon Press 1946.

Aristotle. *The Nichomachean Ethics*. Oxford: Oxford University Press, 1980.

Arnold, F. 'Oxford House and Toynbee Hall'. *Leisure Hour* (April 1888): 274–279.

Arnold, Matthew. (1869) *Culture and Anarchy*. Cambridge: Cambridge University Press, 1960.

Ashby, A.W. *The Rural Problem. Social Reconstruction Pamphlets No. 1*. London: The Athenaeum, 1917.

Ashley, Percy. 'University Settlements in Great Britain'. *The Harvard Theological Review* 4, no. 2 (1911): 175–203.

Atherton, John. *Christianity and the Market. Christian Social Thought for our Times*. London: Society for the Promotion of Christian Knowledge, 1992.

Attlee, Clement. *The Social Worker*. London, G. Bell, 1920.

Babbington-Smith, H. 'Reconstruction in Britain Following the War'. *Scientific Monthly* 8, no. 4 (1919): 298–305.

Baden Powell, Robert. *Scouting for Boys*. 3rd ed. London: C. Arthur Pearson, c. 1910.

Baigent, Elizabeth. 'God's Earth will be Sacred': Religion, Theology, and the Open Space Movement in Victorian England'. *Rural History* 22, no.1 (2011): 31–58.

Bailey, Peter. *Leisure and Class in Victorian England: Rational Recreation and the Contest for Control, 1830–1885*. London: Methuen, 1987.

Bailward, William A. *The Slippery Slope*. London: John Murray, 1920.

Balderstone, Laura. 'Semi-detached Britain? Reviewing Suburban Engagement in Twentieth-century Society'. *Urban History* 41, no. 1 (2014): 141–160.

Balmforth, Owen. *The Huddersfield Industrial Society: History of Fifty years Progress 1870-1910*. Manchester: Co-operative Wholesale Society, n.d.

Barker, Ambrose G. *Seventy Years a Club, being a Brief History of the Formation and Events in the Life of the Walthamstow Working Men's Club and Institute.* (Privately Published, 1932).

Barker, Ernest. *The Political Thought of Plato and Aristotle*. London: Methuen, 1906.

Barker, Ernest. *Political Thought in England 1848-1914*. London: Oxford University Press, 1928.

Barker, Ernest. 'New Housing Estates – The Problem'. *Social Service Review* 12, no. 3, (1931): 47–50.

Barker, Ernest. *Reflections on Leisure*. London: National Council of Social Service, n.d.

Barker, Ernest. *The Uses of Leisure*. London: World Association for Adult Education, 1936.

Barker, Ernest. *Greek Political Theory: Plato and his Predecessors*. 1918. London: Methuen, 1960.

Barnett, Henrietta. *Canon Barnett: His Life, Work and Friends, Vol. One*. London: John Murray, 1918.

Barnett, Samuel Augustus and Barnett, Henrietta. *Practicable Socialism: Essays in Social Reform*. London: Longmans, Green, 1888.

Barnett, Samuel Augustus and Barnett, Henrietta. *Towards Social Reform*. London: T. Fisher Unwin, 1909.

Barnett, Samuel Augustus and Barnett, Henrietta. *Practicable Socialism: Essays in Social Reform*. New Series. London: Longmans, Green, 1915.

Barron, Hester. 'Changing Conceptions of the Poor Child: The Children's Country Holiday Fund 1918–1939'. *Journal of the History of Childhood and Youth* 9, no. 1 (2016): 29–47.

Bauman, Z. *Community. Seeking Safety in an Insecure World*. Cambridge: Polity Press, 2001.

Bayliss, Darrin. 'Revisiting the Cottage Council Estates: England, 1919–39'. *Planning Perspectives* 16 (2001): 169–200.

Bayliss, Darrin. 'Building Better Communities: Social Life on London's Cottage Council Estates 1919–1939'. *Journal of Historical Geography* 29, no. 3 (2003): 376–395.

Beach, Abigail and Tiratsoo, Nick. 'The Planners and the Public'. In *The Cambridge Urban History of Britain Volume Three, 1840-1950*, edited by Martin Daunton, 525–550. Cambridge: Cambridge University Press, 2000.

Beardmore, William. 'Welfare as a Business Asset'. *Journal of Industrial Welfare* 2, no. 1 (1920): 29–30.

Beaumont, Caitriona. *Housewives and Citizens. Domesticity and the Women's Movement in England, 1928-64*. Manchester: Manchester University Press, 2013.

Beaumont, Caitriona. 'Fighting for the "Privileges of Citizenship": The Young Women's Christian Association (YWCA), Feminism and the Women's Movement, 1928–1945'. *Women's History Review* 23, no. 3 (2014): 463–479.

Beaven, Brad. *Leisure, Citizenship and Working-class Men in Britain, 1850–1945.* Manchester: Manchester University Press, 2005.

Beaven, Brad. 'Going to the Cinema: Mass Commercial Leisure and Working-class Cultures in 1930s Britain'. In *Leisure and Cultural Conflict in Twentieth-century Britain*, edited by Brett Bebber, 63–83. Manchester: Manchester University Press, 2012.

Beaven, Brad and Griffiths, John. 'Creating the Exemplary Citizen: The Changing Notion of Citizenship in Britain 1870–1939'. *Contemporary British History* 22, no. 2 (2008): 203–225.

Bebbington, David W. *Evangelicalism in Modern Britain. A History from the 1730s to the 1980s.* London, Routledge, 1989.

Bell, Clive. *Civilization: An Essay.* London: Chatto and Windus, 1929.

Bell, Valentine. *Junior Instruction Centres and Their Future.* Edinburgh: Constable, 1934.

Besant, Walter. *All Sorts and Conditions of Men. An Impossible Story.* London: Chatto and Windus, 1882.

Beveridge, William. *Unemployment. A Problem of Industry.* 2nd ed. London: Longmans Green, 1930.

Beveridge, William. *Voluntary Action. A Report on Methods of Social Advance.* London: George Allen and Unwin, 1948.

Bevir, Mark. *The Making of British Socialism.* Oxford: Princeton University Press, 2011.

Biggs, Lindy. *The Rational Factory: Architecture, Technology, and Work in America's Age of Mass Production.* London: Johns Hopkins University Press, 1996.

Bingham, J.H. 'The Greeks Had a Word for It'. *Adult Education* 11, no. 1 (1938): 24–30.

Bishop, J. and Hoggett, P. *Organizing Around Enthusiasms: Patterns of Mutual Aid in Leisure.* London: Comedia, 1985.

Blatchford, Robert. *Merrie England.* London: Walter Scott, 1894.

Blocker, J.S., Fahey, D.M. and Tyrell, I.E. (eds). *Alcohol and Temperance in Modern History: An International Encyclopaedia, Volume One.* Oxford: ABC-Clio, 2003.

Blond, P. and Noyes, J. *Holistic Mission: Social Action and the Church of England.* Lincoln: ResPublica, 2013.

Boddice, Rob. 'In Loco Parentis? Public-School Authority, Cricket and Manly Character, 1855–62'. *Gender and Education* 21, no. 2 (2009): 159–172.

Booth, Charles. *Life and Labour of the People in London.* London: Williams and Norgate, 1891.

Bosanquet, Bernard. *Aspects of the Social Problem.* London: Macmillan, 1895.

Bosanquet, Bernard. 'The Duties of Citizenship'. In *Aspects of the Social Problem*, edited by Bernard. Bosanquet, 1–27. London: Macmillan, 1895.

Bosanquet, Bernard. 'The Meaning of Social Work'. *International Journal of Ethics* 11, no. 3 (1901): 291–306.

Bosanquet, Bernard. 'The Place of Leisure in Life'. *International Journal of Ethics* 21, no. 2 (1911): 153–165.

Bosanquet, Helen. *The Strength of the People: A Study in Social Economics*. 2nd ed. London: Macmillan, 1903.

Boucher, David and Vincent, Andrew. *British Idealism and Political Theory*. Edinburgh: Edinburgh University Press, 2000.

Bourdillon, A.F.C. (ed.). *Voluntary Social Services: Their Place in the Modern State*. London: Methuen, 1945.

Bourke, Joanna. *Working-Class Cultures in Britain 1890–1960. Gender, Class and Ethnicity*. London: Routledge, 1994.

Bowpitt, Graham. 'Evangelical Christianity, Secular Humanism and the Genesis of British Social Work'. *British Journal of Social Work* 28, no. 5 (1998): 675–693.

Bracey, H.E. *English Rural Life. Village Activities, Organisations and Institutions*. London: Routledge & Kegan Paul, 1959.

Bradford Council of Social Service. *The Texture of Welfare. A Survey of Social Service in Bradford*. London: P.S. King, 1923.

Bradley, Kate. 'Juvenile Delinquency, the Juvenile Courts and the Settlement Movement 1908–1950: Basil Henriques and Toynbee Hall'. *Twentieth Century British History* 19, no. 2, (2008): 133–155.

Bradley, Kate. *Poverty, Philanthropy and the State: Charities and the Working Classes in London, 1918–79*. Manchester: Manchester University Press, 2009.

Brake, Mike. *Comparative Youth Culture. The Sociology of Youth Cultures and Youth Sub-Cultures in America, Britain and Canada*. London: Routledge, 2003.

Branford, Sybil. 'Citizenship and the Civic Association'. *Sociological Review* 13, no. 4 (1921): 228–234.

Branford, Victor and Geddes, Patrick. *The Coming Polity. A Study in Reconstruction*. London: Williams and Norgate, 1917.

Branford, Victor and Geddes, Patrick. *The Making of the Future: Our Social Inheritance*. London: Williams and Norgate, 1919.

Brasnett, Margaret. *Voluntary Social Action: a History of the National Council of Social Service 1919–1969*. London: National Council of Social Service, 1969.

Brassley, P., Burchardt, J., and Thompson, P. (eds). *The English Countryside between the Wars: Regeneration or Decline?* Woodbridge: Boydell, 2006.

Bremner, C.S. 'Garden City, the Housing Experiment at Letchworth'. *Fortnightly Review* 88 (1910): 512–526.

Brewis, Georgina. 'From Working Parties to Social Work: Middle-Class Girls' Education and Social Service 1890–1914'. *History of Education* 38, no. 6 (2009): 761–777.

Brewis, Georgina. *A Social History of Student Volunteering: Britain and Beyond 1880–1980*. New York: Palgrave Macmillan, 2014.

Briggs, Asa. *Victorian Cities*. London: Pelican, 1968.

Bristol Juvenile Organizations Committee Handbook. Bristol: E.S.A. Robinson, 1920.

Brown, Callum G. *The Death of Christian Britain: Understanding Secularization 1800–2000*. London: Routledge, 2009.

Browne, Joan D. 'The Toynbee Travellers' Club'. *History of Education* 15, no. 1 (1986): 11–17. DOI: 10.1080/0046760860150102

Burchardt, Jeremy. 'Reconstructing the Rural Community: Village Halls and the National Council of Social Service 1919 to 1939'. *Rural History* 10, no. 2 (1999): 193–216. DOI: http://dx.doi.org/10.1017/S0956793300001783

Burchardt, Jeremy. *Paradise Lost. Rural Idyll and Social Change in England since 1800*. London: I.B. Tauris, 2002.

Burchardt, Jeremy. 'Agricultural History, Rural History or Countryside History?' *Historical Journal* 50, no. 2 (2007): 465–481.

Burchardt, Jeremy. 'Rethinking the Rural Idyll'. *Cultural and Social History* 8, no. 1 (2011): 73–94.

Burchardt, Jeremy. 'State and Society in the English Countryside: The Rural Community Movement 1918–39'. *Rural History* 23, no. 1 (2012): 81–106. DOI: 10.1017/S0956793311000161

Burnett, John. *A Social History of Housing 1815–1970*. London: Methuen, 1980.

Burnett, John. *Idle Hands. The Experience of Unemployment 1790–1990*. London: Routledge, 1994.

Burns, Cecil Delisle. 'The Moral Effects of War and Peace'. *International Journal of Ethics* 25, no. 3 (1915): 317–327.

Burns, Cecil Delisle. 'When Peace Breaks Out'. *International Journal of Ethics* 26, no. 1 (1915): 82–91.

Burns, Cecil Delisle. 'Ideals of Democracy in England'. *International Journal of Ethics* 27, no. 4 (July 1917): 432–445.

Burns, Cecil Delisle. 'Poverty and Reconstruction'. *International Journal of Ethics* 28, no. 3 (1918): 393–405.

Burns, Cecil Delisle. *Government and Industry*. London: George Allen and Unwin, 1921.

Burns, Cecil Delisle. *Industry and Civilization*. London: Allen and Unwin, 1925.

Burns, Cecil Delisle. *Democracy: its Defects and Advantages*. London: George Allen & Unwin, 1929.

Burns, Cecil Delisle. 'Art and Understanding'. *Social Service Review* 11, no. 8 (1930): 165–170.

Burns, Cecil Delisle. *Modern Civilization on Trial*. London: George Allen & Unwin, 1931.

Burns, Cecil Delisle. *Leisure in the Modern World*. London: Allen and Unwin, 1932.

Cadbury, Edward. *Experiments in Industrial Organization*. London: Longmans, Green, 1912.

Caird, Edward. *Lay Sermons and Addresses delivered in the Hall of Balliol College, Oxford*. Glasgow: James Maclehose, 1907.

Campbell, B.A. 'Boys' Clubs', in *Report on the National Conference on the Leisure of the People*. Manchester, 1919.

Carlyle, Thomas. 'Signs of the Times'. 1829, in *Critical and Miscellaneous Essays Volume One*, 472–492. London: Chapman and Hall, 1887.

Carnegie United Kingdom Trust. *The Film in National Life*. London: George Allen and Unwin, 1932.

Carnegie United Kingdom Trust. *Disinherited Youth: A Survey 1936–1939*. Edinburgh: Constable, 1943.

Carter, M. *T. H. Green and the Development of Ethical Socialism*. Exeter: Imprint Academic, 2003.

Carvell-Williams, J. 'Nonconformity in the Nineteenth Century'. In *Congregational Yearbook*, 34–39. London: Jackson and Walford, 1899.

Chase, Malcolm. *Chartism: A New History*. Manchester: Manchester University Press, 2007.

Cherrington, Ruth Louise. 'The Development of Working Men's Clubs: A Case Study of Implicit Cultural Policy'. *International Journal of Cultural Policy* 15, no. 2 (2009): 187–199.

Church of England. *The Church and Social Service*. London: Society for the Promotion of Christian Knowledge, 1920.

Clapson, Mark. *Invincible Green Suburbs, Brave New Towns: Social Change and Urban Dispersal in Post-war England*. Manchester: Manchester University Press, 1998.

Clapson, Mark. 'Working-Class Women's Experiences of Moving to New Housing Estates in England since 1919'. *Twentieth Century British History* 10, no. 3 (1999): 345–365.

Clark, Peter. *British Clubs and Societies 1580–1800*. Oxford: Clarendon Press, 2000.

Clift, C.E. 'The Leisure Occupation of Young People'. In *Reconstruction and Social Service: Report of a Conference called by the National Council of Social Service*, 127–137. London: P.S. King, 1920.

Coit, Stanton. *Neighbourhood Guilds: An Instrument of Social Reform*. London: Swan Sonnenschein, 1892.

Cole, G.D.H. 'Mutual Aid Movements in their Relation to Voluntary Social Service'. In *Voluntary Social Services. Their Place in the Modern State*, edited by A.F.C. Bourdillon, 118–134. London: Methuen, 1945.

Cole, G.D.H. 'A Retrospect of the History of Voluntary Social Service'. In *Voluntary Social Services. Their Place in the Modern State*, edited by A.F.C. Bourdillon, 11–30. London: Methuen, 1945.

Cole, G.D.H. *A Century of Co-operation*. London: George Allen and Unwin, 1947.

Collings, T.C. 'The Settlements of London'. *The Leisure Hour* (July 1895): 600–606.

Collini, Stefan. 'Hobhouse, Bosanquet and the State: Philosophical Idealism and Political Argument in England 1880–1918'. *Past and Present* 72 (1976): 86–111.

Collini, Stefan. *Public Moralists. Political Thought and Intellectual Life in Britain*. Oxford: Oxford University Press, 1991.

Collins, Arthur. 'The Organization of Voluntary Social Service in Relation to the Work of Statutory Authorities'. In *Reconstruction and Social Service: Report of a Conference Called by the National Council of Social Service*, 151–165. London: P.S. King, 1920.

Collins, Tony. *Sport in Capitalist Society: A Short History*. London: Routledge, 2013.

Collis, Edgar L. 'Efficiency and Fatigue'. *Journal of Industrial Welfare* 2, no. 8 (1920).

Collis, Edgar L. 'Industrial Efficiency and Fatigue'. *Journal of the Royal Society for the Promotion of Health* 41, (1920): 235–241.

Colls, Robert. *Identity of England*. Oxford: Oxford University Press, 2002.

Conference on Christian Politics, Economics and Citizenship. *The Social Function of the Church*. London: Longmans Green, 1924.

Conference on Christian Politics, Economics and Citizenship. *Report on Leisure*. London: Longmans Green, 1924.

Conference on Christian Politics, Economics and Citizenship. *Report on Politics and Citizenship*. London: Longmans Green, 1924.

Conway, Rebecca. 'Making the Mill Girl Modern? Beauty, Industry, and the Popular Newspaper in 1930s' England'. *Twentieth Century British History* 24, no. 4 (2013): 518–541.

Cooke, Maeve. *Re-presenting the Good Society*. London: MIT Press, 2006.

Cooke Taylor, William. *Notes of a Tour in the Manufacturing Districts of Lancashire*. London: Duncan and Malcolm, 1842.

Cordery, S. *British Friendly Societies, 1750–1914*. Basingstoke: Palgrave Macmillan, 2003.

Couling, S. *A History of the Temperance Movement in Great Britain and Ireland*. London: William Tweedie, 1862.

Crawford, William H. *The Church and the Slum. A Study of English Wesleyan Mission Halls*. New York: Eaton and Mains, 1908.

Croll, Andy and Johnes, Martin. 'A Heart of Darkness? Leisure, Respectability and the Aesthetics of Vice in Victorian Wales'. In *Disreputable Pleasures. Less Virtuous Victorians at Play*, edited by Mike Huggins and J.A. Mangan, 153–171. London: Frank Cass, 2004.

Cross, G. *A Quest for Time. The Reduction of Work in Britain and France, 1840–1940*. London: University of California Press, 1989.

Crow, G. and Allan, G. *Community Life. An Introduction to Local Social Relations*. London: Harvester Wheatsheaf, 1994.

Cummings, Edward. 'University Settlements'. *Quarterly Journal of Economics* 6, no. 3 (1892): 257–279.

Cunningham, Hugh. *Leisure in the Industrial Revolution, c.1780–c.1880*. London: Croom Helm, 1980.

Cunningham, Hugh. 'Leisure and Culture'. In *The Cambridge Social History of Britain, Volume 2. People and their Environment*, edited by F.M.L. Thompson, 279–340. Cambridge: Cambridge University Press, 1990.

Cunningham, Hugh. *Time, Work and Leisure. Life Changes in England since 1700*. Manchester: Manchester University Press, 2014.

Davies, A. *To Build a New Jerusalem: The British Labour Movement from the 1880s to the 1990s*. London: Michael Joseph, 1992.

Davis, J. *A History of Britain 1885–1939*. Basingstoke: Macmillan, 1999.

Davis, Mary. *Fashioning a New World: A History of the Woodcraft Folk.* Loughborough: Holyoake Books, 2000.

Davis, Mary. *Comrade or Brother? A History of the British Labour Movement.* 2nd ed. London: Pluto Press, 2009.

Davis, Robert Gunn. 'Slum Environment and Social Causation'. *Westminster Review* 166, no. 3 (1906): 249–257.

Davis, Robert Gunn. 'The Social Question: A Plea for More Scientific Methods'. *Westminster Review* 165, no. 3 (1906): 265–268.

Dawson, Sandra. 'Working Class Consumers and the Campaign for Holidays with Pay'. *Twentieth Century British History* 18, no. 3 (2007): 277–305.

Deakin, Derrick (ed.). *Wythenshawe: The Story of a Garden City.* Chichester: Phillimore, 1989.

Dearmer, Percy. *Christian Socialism. Practical Christianity.* London: Clarion Newspaper Company, 1897.

Delanty, Gerard. *Social Theory in a Changing World: Conceptions of Modernity.* Cambridge: Polity Press, 1999.

Delanty, Gerard. *Community.* London: Routledge, 2010.

Demos. *The Meaning of Reconstruction.* London: The Atheneaum Literature Department, 1918.

Dendy, Helen. 'The Industrial Residuum'. In *Aspects of the Social Problem*, edited by Bernard Bosanquet, 82–102. London: Macmillan, 1895.

Dendy, Helen. 'Marriage in East London', in *Slum Travellers. Ladies and London Poverty 1860–1920* edited by Ellen Ross, 64–71. London: University of California Press, 2007.

Dentith, Simon. *Society and Cultural Forms in Nineteenth Century England.* Basingstoke: Macmillan, 1998.

de Tocqueville, Alexis. *Journeys to England and Ireland.* 1835; New York: Doubleday, 1968.

Dewar, Katharine C. *The Girl.* London: G. Bell, 1921.

Dickens, C. 1854. *Hard Times.* Harmondsworth: Penguin, 1969.

Doyle, Barry. 'The Structure of Elite Power in the Early Twentieth Century City: Norwich 1900–35'. *Urban History* 24 (1997): 179–199.

Drever, J. 'The Human Factor in Industrial Relations'. In *Industrial Psychology*, edited by C.S. Myers, 18–88. London: Thornton Butterworth, 1929.

Duckerschoff, E. *How the English Workman Lives.* London: P.S. King, 1899.

Duffy, Eamon. *The Stripping of the Altars: Traditional Religion in England 1400–1580.* London, Yale University Press, 1992.

Duppa, F. Baldwin. *A Manual for Mechanics' Institutes.* London: Society for the Diffusion of Useful Knowledge, 1839.

Durant, Henry. *The Problem of Leisure.* London: Routledge, 1938.

Durant, Ruth. 'Watling': A Survey of Social life on a New Housing Estate.* London: P.S. King, 1939.

Eardley, Francis. 'A Workman's Club in the East End'. *Good Words* (1895): 227–229.

Edwards, Michael. *Civil Society*. Cambridge: Polity Press, 2004.

Ellwood, Charles A. 'The Social Problem and the Present'. *Sociological Review* 8, no. 1 (1915): 1–14.

Engels, Frederick. *The Condition of the Working Class in England*. London: Panther, 1969.

Erdozain, Dominic. *The Problem of Pleasure: Sport, Recreation and the Crisis of Victorian Religion*. Woodbridge: Boydell Press, 2010.

Etzioni, Amitai. 'Creating Good Communities and Good Societies'. *Contemporary Sociology* 29, no. 1 (2000): 188–195.

Fabes, R. and Skinner, A. 'The Girls' Friendly Society and the Development of Rural Youth Work', in *Essays in the History of Community and Youth Work*, edited by R. Gilchrist, T. Jeffs and J. Spence, 185–90. Leicester: Youth Work Press, 2001.

Faucher, Leon. *Manchester in 1844: Its Present Condition and Future Prospects*. London, 1844.

Finlayson, G. 'A Moving Frontier: Voluntarism and the State in British Social Welfare 1911–1949'. *Twentieth Century British History* 1, no. 2 (1990): 183–206.

Fisher, H.A.L. *The Common Weal*. Oxford: Clarendon Press, 1924.

Flanders, Judith. *Consuming Passions: Leisure and Pleasure in Victorian Britain*. London: Harper Press, 2006.

Foley, Alice. *A Bolton Childhood*. Manchester: Manchester University Extra-Mural Department, 1973.

Forster, E.M. 'The Machine Stops', in *Collected Short Stories of E.M. Forster*, 115–158. London: Sidgwick and Jackson, 1965.

Foster, Michael J. *The History of the British Boy Scouts 1909–1987: An Early Breakaway Movement*. Aylesbury: Brotherhood of British Scouts, 1987.

Fowler, David. *The First Teenagers. The Lifestyle of Young Wage-earners in Interwar Britain*. London: Woburn Press, 1995.

Fowler, David. *Youth Culture in Modern Britain, c. 1920–c. 1970*. Basingstoke: Palgrave Macmillan, 2008.

Frankl, Paul T. *Machine-made Leisure*. London: Harper, 1932.

Fraser, Derek. *The Evolution of the British Welfare State: A History of British Social Policy since the Industrial Revolution*. 4th ed. Basingstoke: Palgrave Macmillan, 2009.

Freeden, Michael. *The New Liberalism: An Ideology of Social Reform*. Oxford: Clarendon Press, 1978.

Freeden, Michael. *Liberalism Divided. A Study in British Political Thought 1914–1939*. Oxford: Clarendon Press, 1986.

Freeden, Michael. 'Civil Society and the Good Citizen: Competing Conceptions of Citizenship in Twentieth-century Britain'. In *Civil Society in British History. Ideas, Identities, Institutions*, edited by Jose Harris, 275–291. Oxford: Oxford University Press, 2003.

Freeden, Michael (ed.). *Minutes of the Rainbow Circle, 1894–1924*. London: Offices of the Royal Historical Society, 1989.

Freeman, Mark. 'No Finer School than a Settlement: The Development of the Educational Settlement Movement'. *History of Education* 31, no. 3 (2002): 245–262.

Fried, A. and Elman, R.M. (eds). *Charles Booth's London*. London: Pelican, 1971.

Frow, Ruth and Edmund. 'The Workers' Theatre Movement in Manchester and Salford, 1931–1940'. *North West Labour History* 17, (1992–93): 66–71.

Fusetti, Cristina. 'Social Capital and Sport Governance in France'. In *Social Capital and Sport Governance in Europe* edited by Margaret Groeneveld and Barrie Houlihan, 108–129. Abingdon: Routledge, 2011.

Gardiner, Juliet. *The Thirties: An Intimate History*. London: Harper Press, 2010.

Garrard, John. *Democratisation in Britain. Elites, Civil Society and Reform since 1800*. Basingstoke: Palgrave, 2002.

Gaskell, Elizabeth. *Mary Barton: A Tale of Manchester Life*. 1848. Reprinted with notes and introduction. London, J.M. Dent, 1996.

Gaskell, P. *Artisans and Machinery: The Moral and Physical Condition of the Manufacturing Population*. 1836. Reprinted with notes and introduction. London: Frank Cass, 1968.

George, Walter L. *Labour and Housing at Port Sunlight*. London: Alston Rivers, 1900.

Goldman, Lawrence. *The Life of R.H. Tawney. Socialism and History*. London: Bloomsbury, 2014.

Good, Kenneth. 'The Drive for Participatory Democracy in Nineteenth Century Britain'. *Commonwealth & Comparative Politics* 47, no. 3 (2009): 231–247.

Gorsky, Martin. 'Mutual Aid and Civil Society: Friendly Societies in Nineteenth Century Bristol', *Urban History*, 25, no. 3 (1998): 302–322.

Gorsky, Martin. 'The Growth and Distribution of English Friendly Societies in the Early Nineteenth Century'. *Economic History Review* New Series 51, no. 3 (1998): 489–511.

Gorst, John. 'Settlements in England and America'. In *The Universities and the Social Problem*, edited by John Knapp, 1–30. London: Rivington, Percival, 1895.

Goss, Mary Lathrop. *Welfare Work in Corporations*. Philadelphia: American Baptist Publication Society, 1911.

Grant, Peter. 'Voluntarism and the Impact of the First World War'. In *The Ages of Voluntarism: How We Got to the Big Society*, edited by M. Hilton and J. McKay, 27–46. Oxford: British Academy, 2011.

Graves, Robert and Hodge, Alan. *The Long Weekend: A Social History of Great Britain 1918–1939*. 1940. London: Sphere Books, 1991.

Great Britain. Board of Education. *The Service of Youth*. Circular to Local Education Authorities for Higher Education. 27 November, 1939.

Great Britain. Committee on Adult Education. *Industrial and Social Conditions in Relation to Adult Education*. London: HMSO, 1918.

Great Britain Committee on Industry and Trade. *Survey of Industrial Relations*. London: HMSO, 1926.

Great Britain. Home Office. *Welfare and Welfare Supervision in Factories and Workshops*. London: HMSO, 1919.

Great Britain. Juvenile Organisations Committee. *Notes on Work and Progress of Local Committees*. London: Board of Education, 1920.

Great Britain, Ministry of Munitions Health of Munitions Workers Committee. *Final Report: Industrial Health and Effici*ency. London: HMSO, 1918.

Green, Thomas Hill. *Lectures on the Principles of Political Obligation*. 1882. Reprinted with notes and introduction. London: Longmans, Green, 1941.

Greenhalgh, Paul. 'Education, Entertainment and Politics: Lessons from the Great International Exhibitions'. In *The New Museology*, edited by Peter Vero. London: Reaktion Books, 1989.

Greenwood, Arthur. *The Education of the Citizen*. London: National Adult School Union, 1920.

Greenwood, Walter. *How the Other Man Lives*. London: Labour Book Service. n.d.

Griffin, Emma. *England's Revelry. A History of Popular Sports and Pastimes, 1600–1830*. Oxford: Oxford University Press, 2005.

Griffiths, Trevor. *The Lancashire Working Classes c.1880–1930*. Oxford: Clarendon Press, 2001.

Groom, Tom. *The Fifty-year Story of the Club. Jubilee Souvenir*. Halifax: Alex Taylor/ National Clarion Cycling Club, 1944.

Gunn, Simon. 'Translating Bourdieu: Cultural Capital and the English Middle Class in Historical Perspective'. *British Journal of Sociology* 56, no. 1 (2005): 49–64.

Hadow, William Henry. *A Report upon the History and Prospects of Music in the United Kingdo*m. Dunfermline: Carnegie United Kingdom Trust, 1921.

Hall, A.D. 'The Revival of Country Life'. *Social Service Bulletin* 8, no. 5 (1927): 67–69.

Hall, B.T. *Our Sixty Years: The Story of the Working Men's Club and Institute Union*. London: Working Men's Club and Institute Union, 1922.

Hall, G. Stanley. *Adolescence, Volume One*. London: Appleton, 1914.

Hannam, June and Hunt, Karen. *Socialist Women. Britain, 1880s to 1920s*. London: Routledge, 2002.

Hannington, Walter. *The Problem of the Distressed Areas*. London: Gollancz, 1937.

Hardy, Dennis. *Utopian England: Community Experiments 1900–1945*. London: Routledge, 2000.

Harford, Charles F. *The Keswick Convention. Its Message, Its Method and Its Men*. London: Marshall Brothers, 1907.

Harford, M.L. 'The Contribution of Settlements to Community Centres'. *Adult Education* 11, no. 1 (1938): 17–24.

Hargrave, John. *The Confession of the Kibbo Kift. A Declaration and General Exposition of the Work of the Kindred*. London: Duckworth, 1927.

Harris, Alexandra. *Romantic Moderns: English Writers, Artists and the Imagination from Virginia Woolf to John Piper*. London: Thames Hudson, 2010.

Harris, Bernard. *The Origins of the British Welfare State. Society, State and Social Welfare in England and Wales, 1800–1945*. Basingstoke: Palgrave Macmillan, 2004.

Harris, Constance. *The Use of Leisure in Bethnal Green: A Survey of Social Conditions in the Borough 1925 to 1926*. London: The Lindsey Press, 1927.

Harris, John. 'State Social Work: Constructing the Present from Moments in the Past'. *British Journal of Social Work* 38 (2008): 662–679. DOI:10.1093/bjsw/bcn024

Harris, Jose. 'Political Thought and the Welfare State 1870–1940: An Intellectual Framework for British Social Policy'. *Past and Present* 35, no. 1 (1992): 116–141.

Harris, Jose. *Private Lives, Public Spirit: Britain 1870–1914*. London: Penguin, 1994.

Harris, Jose. *Community and Civil Society/Ferdinand Tonnies*. Cambridge: Cambridge University Press, 2001.

Harris, Jose. 'From Richard Hooker to Harold Laski: Changing Perceptions of Civil Society in British Political Thought, Late Sixteenth to Early Twentieth Centuries'. In *Civil Society in British History: Ideas, Identities, Institutions*, edited by Jose Harris, 13–37. Oxford: Oxford University Press, 2003.

Harris, Jose (ed.). *Civil Society in British History: Ideas, Identities, Institutions*. Oxford: Oxford University Press, 2003.

Harris, Trevor. 'Anti-social City: Science and Crime in Late Victorian Britain'. In *Anti-Social Behaviour in Britain. Victorian and Contemporary Perspectives*, edited by Sarah Pickard, 18–29. Basingstoke: Palgrave Macmillan, 2014.

Harrison, Brian. 'For Church, Queen and Family: The Girls' Friendly Society 1874–1920'. *Past & Present* no. 61 (1973): 107–138.

Hayes, Nick. 'Counting Civil Society: Deconstructing Elite Participation in the English Provincial City 1900–1950'. *Urban History* 40, no. 22 (2013): 287–314.

Heighton, J.M. *The Place of the Voluntary Worker in Civic Life and Social Work*. London: Simpkin Marshall, 1918.

Heller, Michael M. 'Sport, Bureaucracies and London Clerks 1880–1939'. *International Journal of the History of Sport* 25, no. 5 (2008): 579–614. DOI: 10.1080/09523360701875541

Hemingway, J.L. 'Leisure, Social Capital and Democratic Citizenship'. *Journal of Leisure Research* 31, no. 2 (1999): 150–65.

Hennock, E.P. *Fit and Proper Persons. Ideal and Reality in Nineteenth Century Urban Government*. London: Edward Arnold, 1973.

Hennock, E.P. *The Origin of the Welfare State in England and Germany 1850–1914: Social Policies Compared*. Cambridge: Cambridge University Press, 2007.

Hewitt, Lucy. 'Associational Culture and the Shaping of Urban Space: Civic Societies in Britain before 1960'. *Urban History* 39, no. 4 (2012): 590–606.

Hewitt, Lucy. *A Brief History of the Civic Society Movement*. Canterbury: Civic Voice, 2014.

Hill, Jeffrey. *Nelson: Politics, Economy, Community*. Edinburgh: Keele University Press, 1997.

Hill, Jeffrey. *Sport, Leisure and Culture in Twentieth-Century Britain*. Basingstoke: Palgrave, 2002.

Hilliard, Chris. 'Producers by Hand and Brain: Working-Class Writers and Left-Wing Publishers in 1930s Britain'. *Journal of Modern History* 78, no. 1 (2006): 37–64.

Hobhouse, L.T. *The Labour Movement*. London: Fisher Unwin, 1906.

Hobhouse, L.T. *Liberalism*. Oxford: Oxford University Press, 1911.

Hobsbawm, Eric. 'The Making of the Working Class, 1870–1914'. In *Uncommon People. Resistance, Rebellion and Jazz*, 76–99. London: Abacus, 1999.

Hobson, John A. *The Social Problem, Life and Work*. 2nd ed. London: James Nisbet, 1902.

Hobson, John A. *John Ruskin Social Reformer*. 3rd ed. London: James Nisbet, 1904.

Hobson John A. *Work and Wealth: A Human Valuation*. London: Macmillan, 1914.

Hobson, John A. *Democracy after the War*. 2nd ed. London: George Allen and Unwin, 1918.

Hobson, John A. *Problems of a New World*. London: George Allen and Unwin, 1921.

Hobson, John A. *Wealth and Life. A Study in Values*. London: Macmillan, 1929.

Hole, J. *An Essay on the History and Management of Literary, Scientific and Mechanics' Institutions*. London: Longman, 1853.

Hollins, Dorothea (ed.). *Utopian Papers*. London: Masters & Co., 1908.

Holt, A. *A Ministry to the Poor: Being the History of the Liverpool Domestic Mission Society 1836–1936*. Liverpool: Henry Young, 1936.

Hope, Douglas. 'The Democratisation of Tourism in the English Lake District: The Role of the Co-operative Holidays Association and the Holiday Fellowship'. *Journal of Tourism History* 8, no. 2 (2016): 105–126.

Hopkinson, Alfred. *Rebuilding Britain: A Survey of Problems of Reconstruction after the War*. London: Cassell, 1918.

Hosgood, Christopher P. 'Negotiating Lower-Middle-Class Masculinity in Britain: The Leicester Young Men's Christian Association, 1870–1914'. *Canadian Journal of History* 37, no. 2 (2002): 253–273.

Howard, Ebenezer. *Garden Cities of Tomorrow. (Being the Second Edition of 'Tomorrow: A Peaceful Path to Real Reform')*. London: Swan Sonnenschein, 1902.

Hughes, W.R. *New Town. A Proposal in Agricultural, Industrial, Educational, Civic and Social Reconstruction*. London: Dent, 1919.

Hulme, Tom. 'Putting the City Back into Citizenship: Civics Education and Local Government in Britain, 1918–45'. *Twentieth Century British History* 26, no. 1 (2015): 26–51.

Hunnicutt, Benjamin Kline. 'Plato on Leisure, Play, and Learning'. *Leisure Sciences* 12, no. 2 (1990): 211–227.

Hunt, C.J. 'Sex versus Class in Two British Trade Unions in the Early Twentieth Century'. *Journal of Women's History*, 24 no. 1 (2012): 86–110.

Huta, Veronica. 'Eudaimonia'. In The *Oxford Handbook of Happiness*, edited by Susan A. David, Ilona Bonniwell and Amanda Conley Ayers, 201–213. Oxford: Oxford University Press, 2013.

Hyde, Robert R. 'Organisation of Welfare Schemes'. *Journal of the Royal Society for the Promotion of Health* 42 (1921): 175–179.

Hyndman, Henry. *Further Reminiscences*. London: Macmillan, 1912.

Industrial Council Plan in Great Britain. *Report of the Whitley Committee on Relations between Employers and Employed of the Ministry of Reconstruction.* Washington: Bureau of Industrial Research, 1919.

Iveson, Stan and Brown, Roger. *A Monument to a Movement.* Preston: Independent Labour Party Publications, 1987.

Jacks, Lawrence Pearsall. *Constructive Citizenship.* London: Hodder and Stoughton, c. 1927.

Jacks, Lawrence Pearsall. *The Education of the Whole Man: A Plea for a New Spirit in Education.* London: London University Press, 1931.

Jacks, Lawrence Pearsall. *Education through Recreation.* London: University of London Press, 1932.

James, Robert. '"A Very Profitable Enterprise": South Wales Miners' Institute Cinemas in the 1930s'. *Historical Journal of Film, Radio and Television* 27, no. 1 (2007): 27–61.

Jameson, Storm. *The Soul of Man in the Age of Leisure.* London: Stanley Nott, 1935. Pamphlets on the New Economics no. 17.

Janoski, T. *Citizenship and Civil Society.* Cambridge: Cambridge University Press, 1998.

Jennings, Hilda. 'Voluntary Social Services in Urban Areas'. In *Voluntary Social Services since 1918*, edited by Henry Mess, 28–39. London: Kegan Paul, Trench, Trubner, 1947.

Jephcott, Pearl. 'Work Among Boys and Girls'. In *Voluntary Services since 1918*, edited by Henry A. Mess, 129–145. London: Kegan Paul, Trench, Trubner, 1947.

Jeremy, David J. 'The Enlightened Paternalist in Action: William Hesketh Lever at Port Sunlight before 1914'. *Business History* 33, no. 1 (1991): 58–81.

Joad, C.E.M. *Diogenes, or the Future of Leisure.* London: Kegan Paul, 1928.

Johnson, A.G. *Leisure for Workmen and National Wealth.* London: P.S. King, 1908.

Johnston, James. 'The Work of an Educational Department in a Co-operative Society'. *Manchester and Salford Equitable Co-operative Society's Monthly Herald* no. 86 (1896): 8–10.

Jolly, W. P. *Lord Leverhulme: A Biography.* London: Constable, 1976.

Jones, D. Caradog. *The Social Survey of Merseyside Vol. 2.* London: Hodder and Stoughton, 1934.

Jones, D. Caradog. *The Social Survey of Merseyside Vol. 3.* London: Hodder and Stoughton, 1934.

Jones, D. Caradog. 'Mental Deficiency on Merseyside. Its Connection with the Social Problem Group'. *Eugenics Review* 24, no. 2 (1932): 97–105.

Jones, G. Stedman. 'Class Expression Versus Social Control? A Critique of Recent Trends in the Social History of Leisure'. *History Workshop Journal* 4, no. 1 (1997): 62–70.

Jones, Helen. 'Employers' Welfare Schemes and Industrial Relations in Inter-War Britain'. *Business History* 25, no. 1 (1983): 61–75. DOI: 10.1080/00076798300000005

Jones, Helen. 'Darning, Doylies and Dancing: The Work of the Leeds Association of Girls' Clubs (1904–1913)'. *Women's History Review* 20, no. 3 (2011): 369–388.

Jones, Rhys, Merriman, Peter and Mills, Sarah. 'Youth Organizations and the Reproduction of Nationalism in Britain: The Role of Urdd Gobaith Cymru'. *Social and Cultural Geography* 17, no. 5 (2016): 714–34.

Jones, Stephen G. 'Work, Leisure and the Political Economy of the Cotton Districts between the Wars'. *Textile History* 18, no. 1 (1987): 33–58.

Jones, Stephen G. *Sport, Politics and the Working Class. Organised Labour and Sport in Interwar Britain.* Manchester: Manchester University Press, 1988.

Joyce, Patrick. *Work, Society and Politics: The Culture of the Factory in Later Victorian England.* London: Methuen, 1982.

Judge, T. *Gardens of Eden. British Socialists in the Open Air 1890*–1939. London: Alpha House, 2014.

Kay, Joyce. '"Maintaining the Traditions of British Sport?" The Private Sports Club in the Twentieth Century'. *The International Journal of the History of Sport* 30, no. 4 (2013): 1655–166.

Keeble, Samuel E. 'The Future of Social Service'. In *The Social Outlook. Report of the Oxford Conference, Easter 1910,* edited by the Wesley Methodist Union for Social Service, 195–215. London: Robert Culley, 1910.

Kelly, Eleanor T. 'The Relation of Industry to the Welfare of the Community'. *Welfare Work* 4, no. 43 (1923): 123–124.

Kelly, Eleanor T. *Welfare Work in Industry.* London: Pitman, 1925.

Kelly, Thomas. *A History of Public Libraries in Great Britain 1845–1975.* London: The Library Association, 1977.

Kelly, Thomas. *A History of Adult Education in Great Britain.* Liverpool: Liverpool University Press, 1992.

Kennedy, Douglas. 'The Folk Dance Revival in England'. *Folk Dance: The Journal of the English Folk Dance and Song Society* 2, no. 1 (1935): 72–83.

Keskinen, Lauri. 'Working-class Sports Clubs as Agents of Political Socialisation in Finland, 1903–1923'. *International Journal of the History of Sport* 28, no. 6 (2011): 853–875.

Khilnani, S. 'The Development of Civil Society', in *Civil Society: History and Possibilities,* edited by S. Kaviraj and S. Khilnani, 11–32. Cambridge: Cambridge University Press, 2001.

Kidson, Frank and Neal, Mary. *English Folk-Song and Dance.* Cambridge: Cambridge University Press, 1915.

King, Carole. 'The Rise and Decline of Village Reading Rooms'. *Rural History* 20, no. 2 (2009): 163–186. DOI: 10.1017/S0956793309990033

Kinna, Ruth. *William Morris: The Art of Socialism.* Cardiff: University of Wales Press, 2000.

Kinnaird, E. *Reminiscences.* London: J. Murray, 1925.

Klugmann, James. 'The Crisis of the Thirties: A View from the Left'. In *Culture and Crisis in Britain in the Thirties,* edited by Jon Clark, Margot Heinemann, David Margolies and Carole Snee, 13–36. London: Lawrence and Wishart, 1979.

Kohler-Koch, B. and Quittkat, C. 'What is "Civil" Society and Who Represents It? In *The New Politics of European Civil Society* edited by B. Kohler-Koch and Hans-Jorg Trenz, 19–39. Abingdon: Routledge, 2011.

Koshar, Rudy. 'Seeing, Traveling and Consuming: An Introduction'. In *Histories of Leisure*, edited by R. Koshar, 1–26. Oxford: Berg, 2007.

Kracht, G.V. 'Social Ideals and Social Progress'. *International Journal of Ethics* 27, no. 4 (1917): 472–484.

Kruger, Arnd and Riordan, James. *The Story of Worker Sport*. Champaign: Human Kinetics, 1996.

Kumar, Krishan. *The Making of English National Identity*. Cambridge: Cambridge University Press, 2003.

Labour Party. *Labour and the New Social Order: A Report on Reconstruction*. London: Labour Party, 1918.

Lane, Melissa. *Greek and Roman Political Ideas*. London: Penguin, 2014.

Laski, Harold. 'The Pluralistic State'. *Philosophical Review* 28, no. 6 (1919): 562–575.

Lawson, R.B., Graham, J.E. and Baker, K.M. *A History of Psychology: Globalization, Ideas and Applications*. Hove: Routledge, 2016.

Lawson, Zoe. 'Wheels within Wheels – the Lancashire Cycling Clubs of the 1880s and 90s'. In *Lancashire Local Studies in Honour of Diana Winterbotham*, edited by Alan G. Crosby, 123–145. Preston: Carnegie, 1993.

Laybourn, Keith. 'The Guild of Help and the Changing Face of Edwardian Philanthropy'. *Urban History* 20, no. 1 (1993): 43–60.

Leavis, F.R. *Mass Civilization and Minority Culture*. Cambridge: Gordon Fraser, 1930.

Leavis, F.R. and Thompson, Denys. *Culture and Environment: the Training of Critical Awareness*. 1933; London: Chatto and Windus, 1959.

Leavis, Q. D. *Fiction and the Reading Public*. London: Chatto and Windus, 1932.

Leeworthy, Daryl. 'A Diversion from the New Leisure: Greyhound Racing, Working-Class Culture, and the Politics of Unemployment in Inter-war South Wales'. *Sport in History* 32, no. 1 (2012), 53–73.

Leeworthy, Daryl. 'Partisan Players: Sport, Working-Class Culture, and the Labour Movement in South Wales 1920–1939'. *Labor History* 55, no. 5 (2014): 580–593.

Legge, Hugh. 'The Repton Club'. In *The Universities and the Social Problem. An Account of the University Settlements in East London*, edited by J. M. Knapp, 131–147. London: Rivington Percival, 1895.

Le Mahieu, D.L. *A Culture for Democracy: Mass Communication and the Cultivated Mind in Britain between the Wars*. Oxford: Oxford University Press, 1998.

Lever, William. *The Buildings Erected at Port Sunlight and Thornton Hough*. Paper presented to Meeting of the Architectural Association, March 1st 1902.

Lever, William. *The Six Hour Day and other Industrial Questions*. 2nd ed. London: George Allen and Unwin, 1919.

Lewis, Jane. *Women and Social Action in Victorian and Edwardian England*. Aldershot: Edward Elgar, 1991.

Liberal Party. *Liberal Policy in the Task of Political and Social Reconstruction*. London: Liberal Party, 1918.

Little, C. Deane. *The History and Romance of our Mother Sunday School: 150 Years of Methodism in Bolton*. London: Epworth Press, 1935.

Liverpool Council of Voluntary Aid. *Report on the Uses of Leisure in Liverpool*. Liverpool, 1923.

Liverpool University Settlement. *Booklet No. 5 Character*. Liverpool c. 1930.

Lockhart, Leonard L.P. 'Industrial Problems from the Standpoint of General Practice'. *British Medical Journal* 2, no. 3682 (1931): 179–182.

London School of Economics. *New Survey of London Life and Labour Volume One. 'Forty Years of Change'*. London: P.S. King, 1935.

London School of Economics. *New Survey of London Life and labour, Volume Nine. Life and Leisure*. London, P.S. King, 1935.

Low, Eugenia. 'The Concept of Citizenship in Twentieth Century Britain: Analysing Contexts of Development'. In *Reforming the Constitution. Debates in Twentieth-century Britain*, edited by P. Catterall, W. Kaiser and U. Walton-Jordan, 179–200. London: Frank Cass, 2000.

Luckin, Bill. 'Revisiting the Slums in Manchester and Salford in the 1930s'. In *Urban Politics and Space in the Nineteenth and Twentieth Centuries*, edited by Barry M. Doyle, 134–147. Newcastle: Cambridge Scholars Publishing, 2007.

Luckin, Bill. *Death and Survival in Urban Britain: Disease, Pollution and Environment 1800–1950*. London: I.B. Tauris, 2015.

Lundberg, G.A., Komarovsky, M. and McInerny, M.A. *Leisure: A Suburban Study*. New York: Columbia University Press, 1934.

Lynd, R.S. and Lynd, H.M. *Middletown: A Study in American Culture*. New York: Harcourt Brace, 1929.

McAllister, Annemarie. 'Picturing the Demon Drink: How Children were Shown Temperance Principles in the Band of Hope'. *Visual Resources* 28, no. 4 (2012): 309–323.

McArthur, Euan. *Scotland, CEMA and the Arts Council 1919–1967*. Abingdon: Routledge, 2016.

McCarthy, Helen. 'Parties, Voluntary Associations and Democratic Politics in Inter-War Britain'. *Historical Journal* 50, no. 4 (2007): 891–912.

McCarthy, Helen. 'Service Clubs, Citizenship and Equality: Gender Relations and Middle-Class Associations in Britain between the Wars'. *Historical Research* 81, no. 213 (2008): 531–552.

McCarthy, Helen. 'Associational Voluntarism in Interwar Britain'. In *The Ages of Voluntarism: How We Got to the Big Society*, edited by Matthew Hilton and James McKay, 47–68. Oxford: Oxford University Press, 2011.

McCarthy, Helen. *The British People and the League of Nations. Democracy, Citizenship and Internationalism c.1914–48*. Manchester: Manchester University Press, 2011.

McCarthy, Helen. 'Whose Democracy? Histories of British Political Culture between the Wars'. *Historical Journal* 33, no. 1 (2012): 221–238.

McDougall, William. *The Group Mind*. Cambridge: Cambridge University Press, 1927.

MacIver, R.M. *Community: A Sociological Study*. 2nd ed. London: Macmillan, 1920.

McKibbin, Ross. *Classes and Cultures, England 1918–1951*. Oxford: Oxford University Press, 1998.

McKibbin, Ross. *Parties and People. England 1914–1951*. Oxford: Oxford University Press, 2011.

Mabane, W. 'The Present Condition of University and Social Settlements in Great Britain'. *Sociological Review* 15, no. 1 (1923): 29–34.

Mander, W.J. *British Idealism: a History*. Oxford: Oxford University Press, 2011.

Mangan, J.A. 'Games Field and Battlefield: A Romantic Alliance in Verse and the Creation of Militaristic Masculinity'. *International Journal of the History of Sport* 27, nos. 1 & 2 (2010): 190–204.

Manners, John. 'Speech on Field-Garden Allotments, Bingley, 11th October 1844'. In J. Morrow, *Young England: The New Generation*, 67–68. London: Leicester University Press, 1999.

Mansfield, Nick. 'Paternalistic Consumer Co-operatives in Rural England, 1870–1930'. *Rural History*, 23, no. 2 (2012): 205–211.

Marquis, Fred. 'The Settlement's Problem'. Reprint from *The Optimist*, October 1913, Liverpool University Settlement Archive, D7/5/5/1.

Marquis, F.J. and Ogden, S.E.F. *Palaces for the People: A Suggestion for the Recreation of the Poorest People*. Liverpool: Liverpool University Settlement, 1912.

Marwick, Arthur. *The Deluge. British Society and the First World War*. 2nd ed. Basingstoke: Macmillan, 1991.

Mass Observation. *The Pub and the People*. London: The Cresset Library, 1987.

Masterman, C.F.G. *The Condition of England*. 3rd ed. London: Methuen, 1909.

Matless, David. *Landscape and Englishness*. 2nd ed. London: Reaktion Books, 2016.

Matthews-Jones, Lucinda. '"I Still Remain One of the Old Settlement Boys": Cross-class Friendship in the First World War Letters of Cardiff University Settlement Lads' Club'. *Cultural and Social History* 13, no. 2 (2016), 195–211.

May, Trevor. *An Economic and Social History of Britain 1760–1990*. Harlow: Longman, 1996.

Mayne, Alan. *The Imagined Slum: Newspaper Representation in Three Cities, 1870–1914*. Leicester: Leicester University Press, 1993.

Meakin, Budgett. *Model Factories and Villages: Ideal Conditions of Labour and Housing*. London: Fisher Unwin, 1905.

Mearns, A. and Preston, W.C. *The Bitter Cry of Outcast London*. London: James Clarke & Co., 1883.

Meller, Helen. *Leisure and the Changing City 1870–1914*. London: Routledge & Kegan Paul, 1976.

Merritt, J. F. 'Religion and the English Parish'. In *The Oxford History of Anglicanism, Volume One*, edited by Anthony Milton, 122–147. Oxford: Oxford University Press, 2017.

Mess, Henry A. *Voluntary Social Services since 1918*. London: Kegan Paul, Trench, Trubner, 1947.

Mess, Henry A. 'Social Service with the Unemployed'. In H. Mess, *Voluntary Social Services since 1918*, edited by Gertrude Williams, 40–54. London: Kegan Paul, Trench, Trubner, 1947.

Mess, Henry A. and Braithwaite, Constance. 'The Great Philanthropic Trusts'. In H. Mess, *Voluntary Social Services since 1918*, 172–187.

Mess, Henry A. and King, Harold. 'Community Centres and Community Associations'. In H. Mess, *Voluntary Social Services since 1918*, 69–98.

Mill, John Stuart. *The Subjection of Women*. London: Longmans, Green, Reader and Dyer, 1869.

Mill, John Stuart. 'Utilitarianism'. In *Utilitarianism and Other Essays*, edited by Alan Ryan, 272–338. Harmondsworth: Penguin, 1987.

Mills, Sarah. 'Geographies of Education, Volunteering and the Lifecourse: The Woodcraft Folk in Britain (1925–75)'. *Cultural Geographies* 23, no. 1 (2016): 103–119.

More, Hannah. *Thoughts on the Importance of the Manners of the Great to Society*. London: T. Cadell, 1818.

More, Thomas. *Utopia*. London: Penguin, 2012.

Morgan, Simon. *A Victorian Woman's Place: Public Culture in the Nineteenth Century*. London: I.B. Tauris, 2007.

Morlais Jones, J. 'Wanting is What', in *Congregational Yearbook*, 16–35. London: Jackson and Walford, 1897.

Morris, Bob and Smyth, Jim. 'Paternalism as an Employer Strategy, 1800–1960'. In *Employer Strategy in the Labour Market*, edited by Jill Rubery and Frank Wilkinson, 195–225. Oxford: Oxford University Press, 1994.

Morris, Jeremy. 'The Strange Death of Christian Britain: Another Look at the Secularization Debate'. *Historical Journal* 46, 4 (2003): 963–976.

Morris, R.J. 'Clubs, Societies and Associations'. In *The Cambridge Social History of Britain 1750–1950 Volume Three Social Agencies and Institutions*, edited by F.M.L. Thompson, 395–443. Cambridge: Cambridge University Press, 1993.

Morris, R.J. 'Civil Society and the Nature of Urbanism: Britain, 1750–1850'. *Urban History* 25, no. 3 (1998): 289–301. DOI: 10.1017/S096392680001292X

Morris, R.J. 'Structure, Culture and Society in British Towns'. In *The Cambridge Urban History of Britain Volume Three, 1840–1950*, edited by Martin Daunton, 395–426. Cambridge: Cambridge University Press, 2000.

Morris, William. 'How I Became a Socialist', in *Collected Works of William Morris, Vol. 23*. London: Longman, 1915.

Morris, William. *News from Nowhere and Selected Writings and Designs*. Harmondsworth: Penguin, 1962.

Morris, William. 'How We Live and How We Might Live'. In *News from Nowhere and Selected Writings and Designs*, edited by Asa Briggs, 158–178. 1888. Harmondsworth: Penguin, 1962.

Morris, William. 'Useful Work versus Useless Toil'. In *News from Nowhere and Selected Writings and Designs*, edited by Asa Briggs, 117–135. 1888. Harmondsworth: Penguin, 1962.

Morrow, J. *Young England: The New Generation*. London: Leicester University Press, 1999.

Mowat, C.L. *Britain between the Wars 1918–1940*. London: Methuen, 1956.

Mumford, Lewis. *Technics and Civilization*. 1934. London: Routledge and Kegan Paul, 1955.

National Council of Social Service. *Report on the National Conference on the Leisure of the People*. Manchester, 1919.

National Council of Social Service. 'A Rural Community Council'. In *The Reconstruction of Country Life, Being Notes on a Conference of Rural Community Councils held at Oxford in 1925*, 39–43. London: National Council of Social Service, 1925.

National Council of Social Service. *Village Halls. Their Construction and Management*. London: National Council of Social Service, n.d.

National Council of Social Service. *Unemployment and Community Service*. London: NCSS, 1936.

National Council of Social Service. Community Centres and Associations Committee of the National Council of Social Service. *New Housing Estates and their Social Problems*. 4th ed. London: NCSS, 1937.

National Institute of Industrial Psychology. *Leisure Pursuits Outside the Factory. An Account of an Investigation into the Leisure Pursuits Outside the Family Circle in a County Town, a Rural District and in a Holiday Camp*. London: National Institute of Industrial Psychology, 1939.

Nauright, John and Parrish, Charles (eds). *Sports around the World: History, Culture, and Practice, Volume Two*. Santa Barbara: ABC-CLIO, 2012.

Neal, Mary. *The Esperance Morris Book. A Manual of Morris Dances, Folk-Songs and Singing Games*. London: J. Curwen, 1910.

Neumeyer, M. and E. Neumeyer. *Leisure and Recreation: A Study of Leisure and Recreation in their Sociological Aspects*. New York: Barnes & Co., 1936.

Neville, Edith. 'Warden's Report'. *Mary Ward Settlement Annual Report*, 1923.

Norris, Arthur H. *Report on the National Conference on the Leisure of the People*. Manchester, 1919.

Nott, James. *Music for the People. Popular Music and Dance in Interwar Britain*. Oxford: Oxford University Press, 2002.

Nunn, Thomas Hancock. 'The Universities' Settlement in Whitechapel'. *Economic Review* 2, no. 4 (1892): 478–495.

O'Leary, Paul. 'Networking Respectability: Class, Gender and Ethnicity among the Irish in South Wales, 1845–1914'. *Immigrants & Minorities* 23, nos. 2–3 (2005): 255–275.

Olechnowicz, Andrzej. *Working-class Housing in England between the Wars: The Becontree Estate*. Oxford: Clarendon Press, 1997.

Olechnowicz, Andrzej. 'Unemployed Workers, "Enforced Leisure" and Education for "the Right use of Leisure" in Britain in the 1930s'. *Labour History Review* 70, (2005): 27–52.

Oliver, L. '"No Hard-Brimmed Hats Please" Bolton Women Cotton-Workers and the Game of Rounders 1911–39'. *Oral History* 25 (1995): 40–45.

Olsen, S. *Juvenile Nation. Youth, Emotions and the Making of the Modern British Citizen.* London: Bloomsbury, 2014.

Orchard, S. 'The Free Churches and their Nation', in *Free Churches and Society. The Nonconformist Contribution to Social Welfare 1800–2010* edited by Lesley Husselbee and Paul Ballard, 5–21. London: Continuum, 2012.

Ormrod, Margaret A. '"For as Many as Will"; Some Notes on Folk Dancing'. *The Mark* 1, no. 3 (August 1922), 37–38.

Orwell, George. *Essays.* London: Everyman, 2002.

Otter, Sandra Den. *British Idealism and Social Explanation: A Study in Late Victorian Thought.* Oxford: Clarendon Press, 1996.

Overy, Richard. *The Morbid Age. Britain and the Crisis of Civilization, 1919–1939.* London: Penguin, 2010.

Owen, Robert. *A New View of Society.* London: Penguin, 1991.

Palisi, J. and Jacobson, P.E. 'Dominant Statuses and Involvement in Types Of Instrumental and Expressive Voluntary Associations'. *Journal of Voluntary Action Research* 6, no. 1 (1977): 80–88.

Parsons, G. *Religion in Victorian Britain Volume One, Traditions.* Manchester: Manchester University Press, 1988.

Parsons, G. 'From Dissenters to Free Churchmen: The Transitions of Victorian Non-Conformity'. In *Religion in Victorian Britain, Volume One, Traditions,* edited by G. Parsons, 67–116. Manchester: Manchester University Press, 1988.

Paterson, J.G. 'Industry and Leisure. Fitness'. *Industrial Welfare and Personnel Management,* 16 (1934): 18–25.

Paton, John Brown. *A Plea for Recreative Evening Schools and for the Secondary Education of our Industrial Classes.* London: James Clarke, c. 1885.

Paton, John Brown. *Evening Schools under Healthy Conditions.* London: Isbister, 1886.

Paton, John Brown. *Recreative Instruction of Young People.* London: James Clarke, 1886.

Paton, John Brown. *The Inner Mission: Four Addresses.* London: Isbister, 1888.

Paton, John Brown. 'A Social Institute in Every Board School'. *The Review of Reviews,* (March, 1898): 299.

Paton, John Brown. *Applied Christianity: A Civic League – Social and Educational – for Our Cities and Towns.* London: James Clarke, 1905.

Paton, John Brown. *The Social Institutes Union. Inner Mission Leaflets to Promote Christian Union in Social Service.* London: J. Clarke, n.d.

Paton, John Lewis. *John Brown Paton. A Biography.* London: Hodder and Stoughton, 1914.

Paul, Leslie. *Angry Young Man.* London: Faber & Faber, 1951.

Penlington, Neil. 'Masculinity and Domesticity in 1930s South Wales: Did Unemployment Change the Domestic Division of Labour?' *Twentieth Century British History* 21, no. 3 (2010): 281–299.

Peretz, Elizabeth. 'The Forgotten Survey: Social Services in the Oxford District: 1935–40'. *Twentieth Century British History* 22, no. 1 (2011): 103–113.

Perkin, Harold. 'Individualism versus Collectivism in Nineteenth Century Britain: A False Antithesis'. In *The Structured Crowd. Essays in English Social History*, 57–69. Brighton: Harvester Press, 1981.

Perkin, Harold. *The Rise of Professional Society: England since 1880*. London: Routledge, 1989.

Phillips, Simon. '"Fellowship in Recreation, Fellowship in Ideals": Sport, Leisure and Culture at Boots Pure Drug Company, Nottingham c. 1883–1945'. *Midland History* 29, no. 1 (2004): 107–123.

Pilgrim Trust. *Men without Work*. Cambridge: Cambridge University Press, 1938.

Pilkington, R.M.S. 'Boys 'Clubs'. *Boy's Welfare Journal* 1, no. 5 (1919): 69–70.

Pimlott, John A.R. *Toynbee Hall: Fifty Years of Social Progress 1884–1934*. London: Dent, 1935.

Pollen, Annebella. *The Kindred of the Kibbo Kift: Intellectual Barbarians*. London: Donlan Books, 2015.

Poole, Robert. *Popular Leisure and the Music Hall in Nineteenth-Century Bolton*. Lancaster: Centre for North-West Regional Studies, University of Lancaster, 1982.

Priestley, J.B. *English Journey*. London: Heinemann, 1934.

Prochaska, F. *Schools of Citizenship: Charity and Civic Virtue*. London: Civitas, 2002.

Prochaska, Frank. *Christianity and Social Service in Modern Britain: The Disinherited Spirit*. Oxford: Oxford University Press, 2006.

Proud, Dorothea E. *Welfare Work. Employers' Experiments for Improving Working Conditions in Factories*. London: G. Bell, 1916.

Prynn, David. 'The Clarion Clubs, Rambling and the Holiday Associations in Britain since the 1890s'. *Journal of Contemporary History* 11, nos. 2/3 (1976): 65–77.

Prynn, David. 'The Woodcraft Folk and the Labour Movement 1925–70'. *Journal of Contemporary History* 1, no. 18 (1983): 79–95.

Pugh, Martin. *'We Danced All Night'. A Social History of Britain between the Wars*. London: Bodley Head, 2008.

Pugh, Martin. *State and Society. A Social and Political History of Britain since 1870*. 5th ed. London: Bloomsbury, 2017.

Putnam, Robert. *Bowling Alone. The Collapse and Revival of American Community*. London: Simon and Schuster, 2001.

Pye, Denis. *Fellowship is Life. The National Clarion Cycling Club 1895–1995*. Bolton: Clarion Publishing, 1995.

Pye, Denis. 'Bolton Socialist Party and Club: 100 Years at Wood Street, 1905–2005'. *North West Labour History* 30 (2005): 8–11.

Rappaport, E. 'Sacred and Useful Pleasures: The Temperance Tea Party and the Creation of a Sober Consumer Culture in Early Industrial Britain'. *Journal of British Studies* 52, no. 4 (2013): 990–1016.

Ravetz, Alison. *Council Housing and Culture. The History of a Social Experiment.* London: Routledge, 2001.

Reason, Will. *University and Social Settlements.* London: Methuen, 1898.

Rees, Rosemary. *Britain 1890–1939.* London: Heinemann, 2003.

Reid, D.A. 'Playing and Praying'. In *The Cambridge Urban History of Britain, Volume Three 1849–1950,* edited by Martin Daunton, 745–807. Cambridge: Cambridge University Press, 2000.

Richter, Melvin. *The Politics of Conscience. T.H. Green and His Age.* London: Weidenfeld and Nicolson, 1964.

Riordan, James. 'The Worker Sport Movement'. In *The International Politics of Sport in the Twentieth Century,* edited by James Riordan and Arnd Kruger, 105–20. London: Routledge, 1999.

Roberts, Elizabeth. *A Woman's Place. An Oral History of Working-Class Women 1890–1940.* Oxford: Blackwell, 1995.

Roberts, Ken. 'Social Class and Leisure during Recent Recessions in Britain'. *Leisure Studies* 34, no. 2 (2015): 131–149.

Roberts, M.J.D. *Making English Morals. Voluntary Association and Moral Reform in England, 1787–1886.* Cambridge: Cambridge University Press, 2004.

Robertson, E., Korczynski, E. and Pickering, M. 'Harmonious Relations? Music at Work in the Rowntree and Cadbury Factories'. *Business History* 49, no. 2 (2007): 211–234. DOI: 10.1080/00076790601170355

Robinson, Jane. *A Force to be Reckoned With: A History of the Women's Institute.* London: Virago, 2011.

Rochester, Colin. *Rediscovering Voluntary Action: The Beat of a Different Drum.* Basingstoke: Palgrave Macmillan, 2013.

Rodger, R. and Colls, R. 'Civil Society and British Cities'. In *Cities of Ideas: Civil Society and Urban Governance in Britain, 1800–2000,* edited by R. Colls and R. Rodger, 1–20. Aldershot: Ashgate, 2004.

Rodgers, John. *Mary Ward Settlement. A History 1891–1931.* Passmore Edwards Research Series no.1 (London: Mary Ward Settlement, 1931).

Rojek, Chris. '"Leisure" in the writings of Walter Benjamin'. *Leisure Studies* 16, no. 3 (1997): 155–171.

Rojek, Chris. *Leisure Theory: Principles and Practices.* Basingstoke: Palgrave Macmillan, 2005.

Romanes, G.J. 'Recreation'. *Nineteenth Century* 6, no. 31 (1879): 401–424.

Rooff, Madeline. *Youth and Leisure: A Survey of Girls Organisations in England and Wales.* Edinburgh: Carnegie United Kingdom Trust, 1935.

Rose, Jonathan. *The Intellectual Life of the British Working Classes.* London: Yale University Press, 2001.

Rosman, Doreen. The *Evolution of the English Churches 1500–2000.* Cambridge: Cambridge University Press, 2003.

Rowntree, B. Seebohm. 'The Aims and Principles of Welfare Work'. *Welfare Work* 1, no. 1 (1920): 5.

Rowntree, B. Seebohm. *The Human Factor in Business*. London: Longmans Green, 1921.

Rowntree, B. Seebohm. Paper given to meeting of Industrial Welfare Society 21 November 1929. Borthwick Institute Rowntree Papers, ART/17/15.

Rowntree, B. Seebohm. *Poverty and Progress: A Second Social Survey of York*. London: Longmans, Green & Co. 1941.

Rowntree, B. Seebohm and Lavers, G.R. *English Life and Leisure: A Social Study*. London: Longmans, Green, 1951.

Rubinstein, W.D. 'Britain's Elites in the Inter-War Period 1918–1939'. *Contemporary British History* 12, no. 1 (1998): 1–18.

Ruskin, John. 'The Moral of Landscape'. *Modern Painters* 3, 286–331. London: Smith, Elder & Co. 1856.

Ruskin, John. *Time and Tide*. London: Smith Elder, 1872.

Ruskin, John. 'Co-operation'. In *Time and Tide,* 1–5. London: Smith Elder, 1872.

Ruskin, John. *Munera Pulveris*. Orpington: George Allen, 1880.

Ruskin, John. 'Unto this Last'. In *Unto this Last and Other Essays*, 107–193. London: Dent, 1907.

Ruskin, John. 'Essays on Political Economy'. In *Unto this Last and Other Essays*, 197–307. London: Dent, 1907.

Russell, Bertrand. *Principles of Social Reconstruction*. London: George Allen & Unwin. 1916.

Russell, Bertrand. *In Praise of Idleness*. 1935. London: Routledge, 2004.

Russell, Charles E.B. and Russell, Lilian M. *Lads' Clubs: Their History, Organisation and Management*. Rev. Ed. London: Black, 1932.

Russell, John. *Man and the Machine*. London: Lindsey Press, 1931.

Rutherford, Sarah. *Garden Cities*. Oxford: Shire Publications, 2014.

Sabine, George. 'The Social Origin of Absolute Idealism'. *Journal of Philosophy, Psychology and Scientific Methods* 12, no. 7 (1915): 169–177.

St. Philip's Settlement. *The Equipment of the Workers: An Enquiry by the St. Philip's Settlement [YMCA Sheffield] Education and Research Society into the Adequacy of the Adult Manual Workers for the Discharge of their Responsibilities as Heads of Households, Producers and Citizens*. London: George Allen and Unwin, 1919.

Salvemini, Gaetano. *Under the Axe of Fascism*. London: Victor Gollancz, 1936.

Salveson, Paul. *Socialism with a Northern Accent. Radical Traditions for Modern Times*. London: Lawrence and Wishart, 2012.

Savage, Jon. *Teenage. The Creation of Youth Culture*. London: Pimlico, 2008.

Schulze, Hagen. *Germany: A New History*. Trans. Deborah Lucas Schneider. London: Harvard University Press, 1998.

Scotland, Nigel. *Squires in the Slums. Settlements and Missions in Late-Victorian London*. London: I.B. Tauris, 2007.

Self, P.J.O. 'Voluntary Organizations in Bethnal Green'. In *Voluntary Social Services: Their Place in the Modern State* edited by A.F.C. Bourdillon, 235–262. London: Methuen, 1945.

Shadwell, Arthur. *Industrial Efficiency. A Comparative Study of Industrial Life in England, Germany and America.* London: Longmans, Green, 1906.

Sharp, Cecil. *The Dance: An Historical Survey of Dancing in Europe.* London: Halton and Truscott Smith, 1924.

Sharp, Cecil. *The Country Dance Book, Part 1.* 1911. London: Novello, 1927.

A Short History of the Working Men's Club and Institute Union. London: WMCIU, 1927.

Simey, Margaret. *Charity Re-discovered: A Study of Philanthropic Effort in Nineteenth Century Liverpool.* Liverpool: Liverpool University Press, 1992.

Simey, Margaret. *From Rhetoric to Reality. A Study of the Work of F.G. D'Aeth, Social Administrator.* Liverpool: Liverpool University Press, 2005.

Sinfield, George W. 'The Worker's Sport Movement'. *Labour Monthly* 12, no. 2 (March 1930): 167–171.

Skillen, Fiona. 'Woman and the Sport Fetish: Modernity, Consumerism and Sports Participation in Interwar Britain'. *International Journal of the History of Sport* 29, no. 15 (2012): 750–765.

Skinner, Neil and Taylor, Matthew. '"It's Nice to Belong", Boxing, Heritage and Community in London'. In *Sport, History and Heritage. Studies in Public Representation*, edited by Jeffrey Hill, Kevin Moore and Jason Wood, 59–76. Woodbridge: Boydell Press, 2012.

Slaney, R.A. *Essay on the Beneficial Direction of Rural Expenditure.* London, 1824.

Smith, A. 'Cars, Cricket, and Alf Smith: The Place of Works based Sports and Social Clubs in the Life of Mid-Twentieth-Century Coventry'. *International Journal of the History of Sport* 19, no. 1 (2002): 137–150. DOI: 10.1080/714001702

Snape, Robert. *Leisure and the Rise of the Public Library.* London: Library Association Publishing, 1995.

Snape, Robert. 'The National Home Reading Union'. *Journal of Victorian Culture* 7, no. 1 (2002): 86–110.

Snape, Robert. 'The Co-operative Holidays Association and the Cultural Formation of Countryside Leisure Practice'. *Leisure Studies* 23, no. 2 (2004): 143–158.

Snape, Robert. 'Continuity, Change and Performativity in Leisure: English Folk Dance and Modernity 1900-1939'. *Leisure Studies* 28, no. 3 (2009): 297–311. DOI: 10.1080/0261436090304623

Snape, Robert. 'An English Chautauqua: The National Home Reading Union and the Development of Rational Holidays in late Victorian Britain'. *Journal of Tourism History* 2, no. 3 (2010): 213–234.

Snape, Robert. 'The National Home Reading Union Abroad'. In *Reading Communities from Salons to Cyberspace*, edited by DeNel Rheberg Sedo, 60–80. Basingstoke: Palgrave Macmillan, 2011.

Snape, Robert. 'All-in Wrestling in Inter-War Britain: Science and Spectacle in Mass Observation's "Worktown"'. *International Journal of the History of Sport* 30, no. 2 (2013): 1418–1435. DOI: 10.1080/09523367.2013.804812

Snape, Robert. 'The New Leisure, Voluntarism and Social Reconstruction in Inter-War Britain', *Contemporary British History* 29, no. 1 (2014): 51–83. DOI: 10.1080/13619462.2014.963060

Snape, Robert. 'Voluntary Action and Leisure: An Historical Perspective'. *Voluntary Sector Review* 6, no. 2 (2015): 153–171.

Snape, Robert. 'Everyday Leisure and Northernness in Mass Observation's Worktown 1937–1939'. *Journal for Cultural Research* 20, no. 1 (2016): 31–44.

Snape, Robert. 'Industrial Welfare, Sport and Leisure in Post-First World War Social Reconstruction'. In *Sport and Leisure on the Eve of the First World War*, edited by D. Day, 1–21. Crewe: Manchester Metropolitan University, 2016.

Sohn, Kitae. 'Did Unemployed Workers Choose not to Work in Interwar Britain? Evidence from the Voices of Unemployed Workers'. *Labor History* 54, no. 4 (2013): 377–392.

Solly, Henry. *Working Men's Social Clubs and Educational Institutes*. London: Working Men's Club and Institute Union, 1867.

Solly, Henry. *Working Men's Clubs and Alcoholic Drinks: Is the Prohibitory Policy Necessary or Expedient?* London: Palmer, 1872.

Spender, Stephen. *Forward from Liberalism*. London: Gollancz, 1937.

Spracklen, Karl. *The Meaning and Purpose of Leisure: Habermas and Leisure at the end of Modernity*. Basingstoke: Palgrave Macmillan, 2009.

Spracklen, Karl, Lashua, Brett, Sharpe, Erin and Swain, Spencer (eds). *The Palgrave Handbook of Leisure Theory*. London: Palgrave Macmillan, 2017.

Springhall, John. *Youth, Empire and Society: British Youth Movements 1883–1940*. London: Croom Helm, 1977.

Spurr, Geoff. 'Lower-Middle-Class Masculinity and the Young Men's Christian Association 1844–1880'. *Social History* 47, no. 5 (2014): 547–576.

Stanley, Maude. *Clubs for Working Girls*. London: Macmillan, 1890.

Stanton, Coit. *Neighbourhood Guilds*. 2nd edn. London: Swan Sonnenschein, 1892.

The Star of Temperance, A Weekly Publication for the Diffusion of Temperance Information. Edited by Rev. F. Beardsall (Manchester) and Rev. J. Baker (Chester), 8 (1836).

Stead, Henry and Edith Hall (eds). *Greek and Roman Classics in the British Struggle for Social Reform*. London: Bloomsbury, 2015.

Stearn, Roger T. 'Vane, Sir Francis Patrick Fletcher, Fifth Caronet (1861–1934)'. *Oxford Dictionary of National Biography*, Oxford University Press, 2004; online edn, May 2006 [http://www.oxforddnb.com/view/article/77196, accessed 27 Sept 2016].

Stears, Marc. *Progressives, Pluralists and the Problems of the State. Ideologies of Reform in the United States and Britain 1906–1926*. Oxford: Oxford University Press, 2002.

Stevenson, John. *British Society 1914–45*. London: Allen Lane, 1984.

Stevenson, John. 'The Countryside, Planning, and Civil Society in Britain, 1926–1947'. In *Civil Society in British History*, edited by Jose Harris, 191–211. Oxford: Oxford University Press, 2003.

Stevenson, Nick. 'Cultural Citizenship, Education and Democracy: Redefining the Good Society'. *Citizenship Studies* 14, no. 3 (2010): 275–291.

Sutherland, John. *Mrs Humphry Ward: Eminent Victorian and Pre-Eminent Edwardian.* Oxford: Oxford University Press, 1991.

Swain, Peter. '"Bolton against All England for a Cool Hundred": Crown Green Bowls in South Lancashire, 1787–1914'. *Sport in History* 33, no. 2 (2013): 146–168.

Tawney, R.H. *The Acquisitive Society.* 1920. New York: Dover, 2004.

Tawney, R.H. *Equality.* 1931; London: George Allen & Unwin, 1952.

Taylor, A.J.P. *English History 1914–1945.* Oxford: Oxford University Press, 1992.

Taylor, Carolyn. 'Humanitarian Narrative: Bodies and Detail in Late-Victorian Social Work'. *British Journal of Social Work* 38 (2008): 680–696.

Taylor, Harvey. *A Claim on the Countryside: A History of the British Outdoor Movement.* Edinburgh: Keele University Press, 1997.

Taylor, M. *Public Policy in the Community.* Basingstoke: Palgrave, 2003.

Taylor, P. *Popular Politics in Early Industrial Britain: Bolton 1825–1850.* Keele University: Ryburn Publishing, 1995.

Taylor, W.C. *Notes of a Tour in the Manufacturing Districts of Lancashire*, 3rd ed. 1842. London: Frank Cass, 1968.

Tebbutt, Melanie. 'Rambling and Manly Identity in Derbyshire's Dark Peak, 1880s–1920s'. *Historical Journal* 49, no. 4 (2006): 1125–1153.

Tebbutt, Melanie. *Being Boys. Youth, Leisure and Identity in the Inter-War Years.* Manchester: Manchester University Press, 2012.

Thanassis, Samaras. 'Leisure in Classical Greek Society'. In *The Palgrave Handbook of Leisure Theory*, edited by Karl Spracklen, Brett Lashua, Erin Sharpe and Spencer Swain, 229–247. London: Palgrave Macmillan, 2017.

Thane, P. *Foundations of the Welfare State.* 2nd ed. London: Longman, 1996.

The Oxford House in Bethnal Green. London: T. Brakell, 1948.

Thomas, Keith. 'Work and Leisure'. *Past & Present* no. 29 (1964): 50–66.

Thomas, Keith. 'Work and Leisure in Industrial Society'. *Past & Present* no. 30 (1965): 96–103.

Thompson, E.P. 'Time, Work Discipline and Industrial Capitalism'. *Past and Present*, no. 38 (1967): 56–97.

Thompson, E.P. *The Making of the English Working Class.* London: Pelican, 1968.

Thompson, F.M.L. *The Rise of Respectable Society. A Social History of Victorian Britain 1830–1900.* London: Fontana, 1988.

Thompson, Paul and McHugh, David. *Work Organisations: A Critical Approach.* Basingstoke: Palgrave Macmillan, 2009.

Thorpe, Andrew. 'The Membership of the Communist Party of Great Britain'. *Historical Journal* 43, no. 3 (2000): 777–800.

Tinkler, Penny. 'Feminine Modernity in Interwar Britain and North America: Corsets, Cars and Cigarettes'. *Journal of Women's History* 20, no. 3 (2008): 113–143.

Todd, Jennifer. 'Social Transformation, Collective Categories, and Identity Change'. *Theory and Society* 34, no. 4 (2005): 429–463.

Todd, Selina. *Young Women, Work and Family in England 1918–1950*. Oxford: Oxford University Press, 2005.

Todd, Selina. 'Young Women, Work and Leisure in Inter-war England'. *Historical Journal* 48, no. 3 (2005): 789–809.

Todd, Selina. *The People. The Rise and Fall of the Working Class 1910–2010*. London: John Murray, 2014.

Tombs, Robert. *The English and their History*. London: Penguin, 2015.

Toynbee, Arnold. *Lectures on the Industrial Revolution of the Eighteenth Century in England*. London: Longmans, Green, 1913.

Twells, Alison. *The Civilising Mission and the English Middle-Class, 1792–1850*. Basingstoke: Palgrave Macmillan, 2009.

Vamplew, Wray. 'Sport, Industry and Industrial Sport in Britain before 1914: Review and Revision'. *International Journal of the History of Sport* 19, no. 3 (2015): 340–355.

Veblen, Thorstein. *The Theory of the Leisure Class: An Economic Study in the Evolution of Institutions*. New York: Macmillan, 1899. New York: Dover, 1994.

Verdon, Nicola. 'The Modern Countrywoman: Farm Women, Domesticity and Social Change in Interwar Britain'. *History Workshop Journal* 70 (2010): 86–107.

Walter, Henriette R. *Munition Workers in England and France*. New York: Division of Industrial Studies, Russell Sage Foundation, 1917.

Waters, Chris. 'Beyond "Americanization": Re-thinking Anglo-American Cultural Exchange between the Wars'. *Cultural and Social History* 4, no. 4 (2007): 451–459. DOI 10.2752/147800407X243451

Waters, Chris. *British Socialists and the Politics of Popular Culture*. Manchester: Manchester University Press, 1990.

Weaver, Lawrence. *Village Clubs and Halls*. London: George Newnes, 1920.

Webb, S. and Cox, H. *The Eight Hours Day*. London: Walter Scott, 1891.

Webb, Stephen A. 'The Comfort of Strangers: Social Work, Modernity and Late Victorian England – Part I'. *European Journal of Social Work* 10, no. 1 (2007): 39–54.

Webb, Stephen A. 'The Comfort of Strangers: Social work, Modernity and Late Victorian England – Part II'. *European Journal of Social Work* 10, no. 2 (2007): 193–207.

Welshman, John. 'The Concept of the Unemployable'. *Economic History Review* 59, no. 3 (2006): 578–606.

Wild, Martin T. *Village England: A Social History of the Countryside*. London: I.B. Tauris, 2004.

Wildman, Charlotte. 'Religious Selfhoods and the City in Inter-war Manchester'. *Urban History* 38, no. 1 (2011): 103–123.

Wilkinson, Ellen. *The Town that was Murdered: the Life-Story of Jarrow*. London: Gollancz Left Book Club, 1939.

Williams, C. *Accrington Mechanics' Institution 1845–1895: A Story of Fifty Years Jubilee Booklet*. Accrington: Broadley, 1895.

Williams, Gertrude. 'The Training and Recruitment of Social Workers', in Henry Mess, *Voluntary Social Services since 1918*, edited by Gertrude Williams, 214–246. London: Kegan Paul, Trench, Trubner, 1947.

Williams, Jack. 'Recreational Cricket in the Bolton Area between the Wars'. In *Sport and the Working Class in Modern Britain*, edited by Richard Holt, 101–20. Manchester: Manchester University Press, 1990.

Williams, Raymond. *The Long Revolution*. London: Pelican, 1965.

Williams, Raymond. *Culture and Society 1780-1950*. Harmondsworth, Penguin, 1961.

Williams, Rosalind. *Notes on the Underground. An Essay on Technology, Society and the Imagination*. London: MIT Press, 1990.

Williams, W.E. 'Adult Education'. In Henry Mess *Voluntary Social Services since 1918*, edited by Gertrude Williams, 146–171. London: Kegan Paul, Trench, Trubner, 1947.

Williamson, P. 'The Monarchy and Public Values, 1900-1953'. In *The Monarchy and the British Nation, 1780 to the Present*, edited by Andrzej Olechnowicz, 223–257. Cambridge: Cambridge University Press, 2007.

Winnington Ingram, A.F. 'Working Men's Clubs'. In *The Universities and the Social Problem: An account of the University Settlements in East London*, edited by John M. Knapp, 33–50. London: Rivington Percival & Co., 1895.

Wolff, Henry W. *Rural Reconstruction*. London: Selwyn and Blount, 1921.

Wollenberg, B. *Christian Social Thought in Great Britain between the Wars*. London: University Press of America, 1997.

Womack, Peter. 'Dialogue and Leisure at the Fin de Siecle'. *Cambridge Quarterly* 24, no. 1 (2013): 134–156.

Woodhead, E.W. 'Community Centres and the Local Authority'. *Adult Education* 11, no. 1 (1938): 11–17.

Woods, R. Archey. *English Social Movements*, 2nd ed. London: Swann Sonnenschein, 1895.

Woolton, Lord. *Memoirs*. London: Cassell, 1959.

Wright, T. 'On a Possible Popular Culture'. *Contemporary Review* 40, (1881): 25–44.

Young, Terence. *Becontree and Dagenham. A Report made for the Pilgrim Trust*. London: Sidders & Son, 1934.

Zimmern, E. 'The Control of Industry after the War'. In *The Re-organization of Industry* Oxford: Ruskin College, 1916.

Index

Bourdieu, Pierre 19
Bournville 51, 136–8
Bournville Women Workers' Social Service
    League 137
boxing 43–4, 143
Boy Scouts 5, 29, 93, 106, 112, 115, 118–19,
    131, 151
Boys' Brigades 118, 131
Bradford 21
    Bradford Unemployed Association 125
    Civic Theatre 90
    Federation of Young People's Societies
        113
    Guild of Help 33
Branford, Sybella 90, 183
Branford, Victor 51–2, 94, 107, 183
Bright Young Things 78
Brighton Boys' Club 30
Bristol 3, 29
    Clifton College 32
    Co-operative Wholesale Society 121
    Juvenile Organizations Committee
        113
    Recreation Council 113
    YMCA and YWCA 29
British and Foreign Temperance Society
    21
British Association of Residential
    Settlements 104
British Boy Scouts 118
British Broadcasting Corporation 32, 65,
    67, 87, 197
British Drama League 99, 140
British Institute of Social Service 12, 34,
    92, 199
British Workers' Sports Federation 68, 143
Brooke, Stopford 44
Browning Hall 37
Brynmawr 124
Burnley 21
    Burnley Wheelers 59
    unemployment 115–16, 126
Burns, Cecil Delisle 11, 13, 58, 93, 106, 133,
    136, 141–2, 144–5, 149–51
    mass culture 85–7
    New Estates Community Committee
        104
    new leisure 80–1, 85, 104
    women's institutes 81

Cadbury Brothers 34, 51, 118, 134, 136–8
Caird, Edward 37, 72
Camp Fire Girls 120
Carlyle, Thomas 32, 34, 78, 82
Carnegie, Andrew 59, 97
Carnegie United Kingdom Trust 10, 14,
    96–8, 152
    Becontree 107
    English Folk Dance Society 100
    unemployment 127, 129, 132
    village halls 97–102
Carpenter, Edward 58, 121
Catholic Boys' Brigade 118
Chaplin, Charlie 82
character 19, 38, 41, 43–8, 81, 111–14,
    116–17
    unemployment 125–6, 130
Charity Organisation Society 8, 35–6, 38,
    49, 73, 149
Chartism 10, 53
Chautauqua Literary and Scientific Circle
    32
Cheltenham Ladies College 45
children 53, 65, 68, 83, 86, 105–6, 120,
    125
Children's Country Holiday Fund 38
Christian Social Union 33–4, 164
Christian Socialism 5, 12, 27–31, 58, 61, 63,
    71, 91
Christian Socialist League 33, 162
Church Lads' Brigade 30, 93, 106, 118
cinema 13, 65–8, 80–6, 96–7, 108, 118, 127,
    150
    juveniles 94, 118
citizenship 4, 7, 13–14, 23–4, 34–8, 41–3,
    53–5, 102–4, 119, 137, 148
    civil society 10–11
    education 107, 111, 114, 116, 131–2
    philosophy 8, 51, 47, 72, 75–7
    planning 52
    reconstruction 79–84, 90–7, 108–9
    Stevenson Lecturer in Citizenship,
        Glasgow 74
    unemployment 132
civic gospel 12, 28, 31, 34, 66, 148
Civic Leagues 33, 90, 113
Civic Societies 90
civic spirit 72
civil society 9–11, 17, 28, 61, 71, 132, 153

Lightning Source UK Ltd.
Milton Keynes UK
UKHW021150270120
357677UK00003B/228